The JETAGE

The JET AGE

Forty Years of Jet Aviation

Edited by

WALTER J. BOYNE
Executive Officer, National Air and Space Museum

and

DONALD S. LOPEZ
Assistant Director for Aeronautics, National Air and Space Museum .

with contributions by

ANSELM FRANZ

NAJEEB E. HALABY

GERHARD NEUMANN

DOMINICK A. PISANO

JOHN E. STEINER

HANS VON OHAIN

FRANK WHITTLE

CHARLES E. YEAGER

Published by the

NATIONAL AIR AND SPACE MUSEUM
SMITHSONIAN INSTITUTION

Distributed by

SMITHSONIAN INSTITUTION PRESS

Washington City

1979

Library of Congress Cataloging in Publication Data

The Jet age.

  Lectures presented at a symposium held Oct. 26, 1979
and sponsored by the National Air and Space Museum.
  Bibliography: p.
  1. Airplanes—Jet propulsion—History—Congresses.
I. Boyne, Walter J., 1929-   II. Lopez, Donald S., 1923-
    III. Franz, Anselm. IV. National Air and Space
Museum.
TL709.J46 629.133'349 79-20216

ISBN 0-87474-247-1 paper
ISBN 0-87474-248-x cloth

Designed by Gerard A. Valerio, Bookmark Studio

Composed in Eras and Palatino by
General Typographers, Inc., Washington, D. C.

Printed on Sterling Matte by
The John D. Lucas Printing Company, Baltimore, Maryland

Table of Contents

v

Acknowledgments

The editors wish to express their thanks to the following individuals who assisted in the preparation of this volume. Ms. Claudia Oakes, assistant curator in the Aeronautics Department, very ably coordinated and collated the many individual manuscripts and photographs. Mr. Jay Spenser, research assistant in the Aeronautics Department, located and assisted in the selection of the photographs. Peter Rohrbach edited the manuscript, and Gerard Valerio designed the volume.

Foreword

This compilation of the proceedings of the forty years of jet aviation is unique in that the primary contributors to the book were also seminal contributors to the fascinating forty years of progress.

The brief biographical sketches which precede each chapter give but an inkling of the fundamental importance of the contribution of the authors. The articles themselves, however, convey the essence of the often revolutionary changes they imposed upon our life and times.

We will see how great ideas are arrived at independently when perceived need and technology coincide; we will see that once the jet engine was invented how quickly other men of genius were able to develop it from a rather delicate, low power laboratory instrument to a dependable roaring power source with a thousand applications.

The pilot's viewpoint of jet aviation is reflected in a chapter by the test pilot who first exceeded the speed of sound, while some of the social and economic impacts are related by an individual who had key roles in both government and private industry.

The growth of jet aviation would not have been possible without the entrepreneurial daring of many great commercial companies; the final chapter shows just how some of the most crucial decisions in the history of jet aviation were made by a commercial giant.

Finally, interwoven into the book are photo histories of jet fighters, bomber and transport aircraft, which are, after all, the ultimate tribute to the men who made them.

WALTER J. BOYNE

DONALD S. LOPEZ

The JETAGE

The Birth of the Jet Engine in Britain

Sir Frank Whittle

After three years as an aircraft apprentice in the Royal Air Force at Cranwell, I was fortunate enough to be selected for officer and pilot training at the Royal Air Force College (also at Cranwell) in 1926, from which I graduated as a Pilot Officer in 1928. One of our tasks as Flight Cadets was to write a thesis on a technical subject of our own choice each term. For my first three terms, I wrote a three-part thesis entitled "Chemistry in the Service of the R.A.F.," but in my fourth and last term I became more venturesome and chose the ambitious subject "Future Developments in Aircraft Design." In the course of it, I derived a formula for the still air range of an airplane (which I later found was the well-known "Breguet Range Equation") which intrigued me greatly because it meant that for it to be possible to fly fast and far it would be necessary to fly at very great heights—far higher than was possible with the

AIR COMMODORE SIR FRANK WHITTLE was a 22-year-old R.A.F. officer at Whittering, England, in 1929 when he conceived the idea of using a gas turbine to produce a propelling jet. His patent for the turbojet was granted in 1932 and published widely, but he received little encouragement from the Air Ministry or from private enterprise. Finally, in 1936 Power Jets was founded with support from a firm of investment bankers, and Whittle was assigned to the company on special duty to work on the design and development of his concept. Test flights of the engine in the Gloster E.28/39 began in 1941, leading to the Meteor jet that became operational in 1944. Recipient of many honors world-wide for his singular contributions to jet aviation, he was knighted by King George VI in 1948. Now retired from the R.A.F., he is presently a part-time research professor at the U. S. Naval Academy.

then conventional piston engine and propeller. Even with a supercharged piston engine the power dropped with height faster than aircraft drag, so much so that the ceiling of an average fighter was not much above 20,000 feet.

In those days (the 1920's) the top speed of a fighter was about 150 mph and the world speed record was something over 200 mph. High speeds also meant problems with the propeller because the resultant of the blade speed at and near the tips and the aircraft forward speed meant compressibility troubles and much reduced propeller efficiency. (Near, at, and above the speed of sound, shock waves are formed and these cause a large rise in drag.) Nevertheless, in my youthful optimism (I was then 21) I thought that there had to be some more suitable alternative power plant for very high altitude flight.

In my thesis I discussed rocket propulsion and gas turbines driving propellers, but at that time it did not occur to me to combine the two ideas. The very low efficiency of rockets ruled them out for long range aircraft, and the gas turbine propeller combination did not look promising for the order of speed I was thinking about, namely 500 mph. So my thesis did not provide the answer I was looking for. Nevertheless, it marked the beginning of my quest for an alternative to the piston engine propeller combination.

On graduating from Cranwell, I was commissioned as a pilot officer and posted to 111 Fighter Squadron. My quest continued. I ex-

3

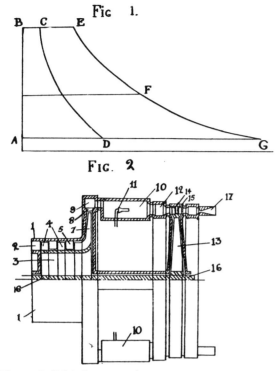

Figure 1. Whittle patent drawing.

amined at some length the possibility of using a piston engine driving a low pressure ratio compressor within a hollow fuselage. In this scheme, a propelling jet would be produced, but I found that, for adequate thrust, the heating effect of the engine cooling and exhaust would have to be supplemented by the burning of extra fuel before final expansion through the jet nozzle. I was eventually forced to abandon this scheme (later tried by the Italians) because rough calculations indicated that there was little or no saving of power plant weight as compared with the piston engine propeller combination and that the fuel consumption would be much higher.

At the end of 1929, I was sent to a flying instructors course at the Central Flying School and while there the "penny dropped." I suddenly thought, "Why not increase the compressor compression ratio and substitute a turbine for the piston engine?" This was the birth of the turbojet.

I discussed the proposal with one of the C.F.S. instructors—W. E. P. Johnson—with whom I

had become friendly. Before joining the R.A.F., he had qualified as a patent agent. He was so favorably impressed that he insisted that I should describe my proposals to the Commandant of the C.F.S., then Group Captain "Jack" Baldwin (later Air Marshal Sir John Baldwin). The Commandant was distinctly impressed and arranged for me to discuss my scheme with officials at the Air Ministry. In due course I had an interview with W. L. Tweedie of the Department of Engine Development. In turn, he sent me to talk with Dr. A. A. Griffith at the Ministry's Kensington Laboratory, who—Tweedie told me—was interested in gas turbine possibilities. The result was extremely disappointing. Griffith rightly pointed out that there was a serious error in my calculations and he was generally skeptical about the feasibility of the project. The net outcome was a letter from the Ministry to the effect that it was considered that any form of gas turbine was impracticable in the light of the long history of failure and lack of materials capable of withstanding the high combination of temperature and stress in turbine blading. So the Ministry was not interested.

I was well aware of the many prior failures in the gas turbine field early in the century, but was convinced that the causes of these—low compressor efficiency, low turbine efficiency, and lack of suitable materials—could be overcome in due course, especially in the case of aircraft where, at height, low air temperatures substantially offset the adverse factors. Moreover, I discovered another error in my calculations which virtually cancelled out the error pointed out by Griffith.

W. E. P. Johnson urged me not to give up and advised that I apply for a patent which he volunteered to handle. So a Provisional Patent Application was duly filed on January 16th, 1930, and a Patent was granted about 18 months later. Figure 1. Because of Ministry disinterest, it was not put on the secret list, and so, in mid-1932 it was published and became available worldwide.

During 1931, I was a flying instructor at No. 2 Flying Training School, Digby. In that year, Johnson and I made several attempts to interest a number of industrial firms, but with no success. A fact, worthy of record, is that one of the firms which turned it down was the British Thomson-Houston Company (B.T.H.) in Rugby, which later became closely involved with the development.

In 1932, I was posted to the Marine Aircraft Experimental Establishment (M.A.E.E.) at Felixstowe, as a floatplane test pilot. There, I continued with efforts to enlist the interest of manufacturers (without result) and the civilian technical staff of the M.A.E.E., from whom I received some encouragement. My brother officers regarded the scheme as something of a joke and called it "Whittle's Flaming Touchhole."

By this time, I was beginning to lose hope and felt that I was years before my time. Also, my attention had turned to other ideas: an improved gun turret for bombers, a pilot operated catapult (part of my test flying duties included the testing of new catapults), a bomb loading device, etc. At Felixstowe, however, on temporary assignment, was Flying Officer R. D. Williams (now Sir Rolf Dudley-Williams) who had been a fellow cadet at Cranwell. He had sufficient faith in me to attempt to obtain money from relatives for foreign patent applications. He was unsuccessful at the time, but ultimately became a key figure in the course of jet engine history.

In those days it was a rule that officers with permanent commissions must take a specialist course of their own choosing after four years of General Duties. The alternatives were Armament, Navigation, Signals (i.e., radio), Physical Training, and Engineering. I would probably have chosen armament, having served as Armament Officer for six months at Felixstowe in the absence (through illness) of the regular Armament Officer, but I was given no choice. I was bluntly told that my record plainly showed that I should specialize in Engineering—and no argument. So, in July 1932, I was posted to the Officers' School of Engineering at R.A.F. Henlow for a two year course. There was an entrance examination in which my "score" was so high (98% average) that the authorities felt it would be a waste of time for me to take the first year lectures, and so I was attached to the senior year for lectures. The net result was that I passed out top of the senior year finals with

distinction in every subject except mechanical drawing. I completed my workshop course in the following six months.

In preceding years it had been the practice of the Air Ministry to send outstanding individuals to Cambridge University to take the Mechanical Sciences Tripos—an honors degree course. But this had been discontinued shortly before I graduated from the Officers' School of Engineering. However, my C.O. succeeded in persuading the Air Ministry that an exception should be made in my case.

In the six months interim, I was promoted to Flight Lieutenant and placed in charge of the engine test bench section. (The main function of R.A.F. Henlow was repair and maintenance.)

In due course, I was sent to Cambridge University as an undergraduate of Peterhouse College to take the Mechanical Sciences course in two years instead of the usual three. I was attached to the Cambridge University Air Squadron for administrative purposes and flying practice. After one year, I was made a Senior Scholar of Peterhouse, and finally graduated with First Class Honors in June 1936.

Before graduation, however, the jet engine had, like the Phoenix, risen from its ashes. My tutor, Roy Lubbock, became convinced that I was on the right track. I also received much encouragement from the late Sir Melvill Jones, then Professor of Aerodynamics, but the key event in all that followed was a letter handed to me in May 1935 by the C.O. of the Cambridge University Air Squadron. It was from R. D. Williams who had then been invalided out of the R.A.F. and was in business with another ex-R.A.F. officer, J.C.B. Tinling, who also featured prominently in later events.

Williams wrote that if the jet engine schemes had not yet been taken up he thought that he and Tinling could get something started.

By then the original patent was void because I had failed to pay the renewal fee. However, when Williams and Tingling visited me at my home near Cambridge a week or two later, I assured them that I had a number of fresh ideas to rebuild a strong patent position.

I cautioned them about making any approaches to the aircraft industry because of the

Figure 2. Whittle compressor/turbine assembly.

weak patent position, and I was therefore much alarmed when I learned that Tingling's father had discussed the proposal with a friend who, in turn, had talked to his nephew, M. L. Bramson, a consulting engineer, who was a very able pilot and had many connections with the aircraft industry.

However, my fears proved to be ill grounded. Bramson enlisted the interest of O. T. Falk and Partners—a small commercial banking firm—one of the directors was L. L. Whyte, a physicist turned banker. He became very excited by the idea, though when I met him I warned him that anyone putting up money should do so on the basis that the chances of success were 30:1 against. This did not deter him and Falk and Partners commissioned Bramson to write a formal report on my project. This was wholly favorable.

The outcome was that a small company named Power Jets Ltd. was formed in March 1936 with a nominal capital of £10,000, and £2,000 subscribed in cash by Falk and Partners.

At that time the Tripos finals were drawing near. I was desperately keen to obtain first class honors; nevertheless, before Power Jets was actually formed (towards the end of 1935, in fact) I started work on the design of a bench test engine subsequently known as the W.U. (Whittle Unit). Also, before the incorporation of Power Jets, Falk and Partners placed a contract with the B.T.H. for design drawings to my requirements. Shortly after the formation of the company, a further contract to build the test engine was accepted by the B.T.H. on a "cost plus" basis.

It was originally intended to do component testing before building a complete engine, but the B.T.H. quotation for a compressor test set was £28,000 which was far beyond our means, so we were obliged to take a major gamble and go for a complete engine.

Until five weeks before the Tripos finals, I was devoting most of my time to the engine and making frequent journeys between Cambridge and the Rugby factory of the B.T.H., and between Cambridge and London for consultations with my colleagues.

When Power Jets was formed, the Air Ministry required that it be a party to the "Four Party Agreement" and required that a substantial proportion of my shares be assigned to the Ministry. The Agreement also allowed me to act as Honorary Chief Engineer to Power Jets but also stipulated that I must not spend more than six hours a week on the project. This proviso I ignored.

The fact that the Air Ministry had a stake in Power Jets did not mean that the official disbelief in my schemes had altered. On the contrary, all Whyte's attempts to get the Air Ministry to put money into the venture failed and, indeed, an atmosphere of hostility towards Whyte became manifest on the part of the Director of Scientific Research (D.S.R.) D. R. Pye and his deputy, W. S. Farren. They apparently regarded Whyte as a "city slicker" aiming to get rich fast when, in fact, I knew that he was sincerely concerned with the national interest. So we had to rely on a dribble of money from private sources.

In 1936 I graduated with first class honors. In the normal course of events, I would have been posted to an R.A.F. station as an engineer officer which would have seriously prejudiced

Figure 3. Combustion chamber test assembly.

my ability to continue work on the jet engine, especially if it had been an overseas appointment for which I was due. Fortunately, my tutor at Peterhouse succeeded in pursuading the Director of Education of the Air Ministry that means should be found to allow me to continue "research" under cover of the fact that I was assisting Professor Melvill Jones. In this he was supported by "Bones." The D of E in turn succeeded in convincing the Air Member for Personnel, Air Marshal Sir Frederick Bowhill, that I should be granted a postgraduate year for research. Both the D of E and Sir Frederick were well aware that this was a "cover" to enable me to continue with the engine, so I was able to devote an increasing amount of my time to supervising the design and manufacture of the W.U. In fact, the B.T.H. were good enough to provide me with an office in the turbine factory and I was able to "stand over" the designers and draughtsmen engaged on the project; to cut corners by direct contact with the fitters, machinists, sheet metal workers, etc., working on the job. Also to check the cost accounting.

The W.U. was designed for a very high flying 500 mph mail plane with 2,000 lb weight. This meant a sea level static thrust of about 1200 lbs at 17,750 r.p.m. It had a single stage double

sided centrifugal compressor of 19 inches diameter driven by a single stage axial flow turbine of 16.4 inches diameter. Figure 2. The compressed air from the compressor passed to the nozzle volute of the turbine via a single large combustion chamber of helical form. The exhaust from the turbine finally expanded through a jet nozzle.

I was confident (too confident) that I would have no difficulty in obtaining the compressor and turbine efficiencies on which the design was based but was far from certain about the combustion problem because we were aiming for combustion intensities of the order of 24 times anything previously achieved. So, at the end of 1936, with the aid of a Scottish combustion engineering firm (Laidlaw, Drew and Company) we conducted a series of combustion experiments on a site immediately outside the B.T.H. turbine factory. Figure 3. After many experiments we succeeded in achieving the desired combustion intensity—or so we thought.

The W.U. was completed and apparently ready for testing in March 1937. Unfortunately, the torque fluctuations from the starter motor—

Figure 4a. The original version of Whittle's first experimental engine.

a horizontally opposed two cylinder piston engine designed for light aircraft and called the "Sprite"—were too violent and the connecting shaft was severely distorted. Additionally, the compressor impeller fouled the casing. This was an inauspicious start. We could not afford new parts, so we had to be satisfied with cleaning up the damage and using a 20K watt electric motor for starting. This made the whole assembly too heavy for the four wheeled platform on which the engine was mounted, so the wheels had to be removed. This made it impossible to measure thrust by the spring balance interposed between the platform and an anchor support on the factory wall.

For these tests, the engine was positioned on a gallery of the B.T.H. turbine factory with its jet pipe protruding through a window. The only protection against a disastrous rotor failure was a "shield" of three sheets of 1½ inch steel plating—two vertical on each side, the third bridging them from above the engine.

The first real run of the engine under its own power was on April 12, 1937. The experience was frightening. The starting procedure went as planned. By a system of hand signals from me the engine was accelerated to 2,000 r.p.m. by the electric motor. I turned on a pilot fuel jet and ignited it with a hand turned magneto connected to a spark plug with extended elec-

trodes; then I received a "thumbs up" signal from a test fitter looking into the combustion chamber through a small quartz "window." When I started to open the fuel supply valve to the main burner (the fuel was diesel oil), immediately, with a rising scream, the engine began to accelerate out of control. I promptly shut the control valve, but the uncontrolled acceleration continued. Everyone around took to their heels except me. I was paralyzed with fright and remained rooted to the spot. I should have realized, of course, that acceleration to a dangerous speed was most unlikely unless the engine was more efficient than design, and, in fact, it began to slow down after reaching about half design full speed. The explanation was simple. The independently driven fuel pump had been tested a number of times, and, unknown to us, because of air in the fuel lines, the burner nozzle valve had opened for a short time with each pump test so that a pool of fuel had accumulated in the main part of the combustion chamber. The ignition of this was the cause of the "runaway." A drain was quickly fitted to ensure that this could not happen again.

Nevertheless, the following day, there was another uncontrolled acceleration. This time because the valve spring in the fuel injector was weakened by overheating. This experience was more frightening than the first because local overheating had caused combustion chamber joints to leak and the escaping fuel vapor took fire above the engine. Altogether a petrifying situation—except for those who once more disappeared with record breaking speed. This was by no means the last of the uncontrolled accelerations and I began to wonder whether we had a fundamentally uncontrollable device.

The next occasion (in the same week) was after I had a hastily constructed vaporizer fitted into the exhaust pipe and switched to kerosene as fuel on the "primus" principle. At first all seemed well and the initial acceleration was fully under control, but at about 4,000 r.p.m. it went out of control again. This time because the vaporizer had insufficient surface and "primed," i.e., it started to inject liquid kerosene instead of vapor. Fortunately, the engine responded to cutting off the fuel. But once again I found myself alone with the monster I had created.

There were other occasions of uncontrolled acceleration but, in general, changes in the fuel injection system resulted in a controllable engine—but a very inefficient one. Though we achieved a speed of 13,600 r.p.m. under full control, it was becoming obvious that compressor and turbine efficiencies were below design expectations. This was manifested in dangerously high exhaust temperatures. Moreover, the engine had suffered damage from a series of mishaps—including an occasion when the compressor impeller fouled its casing at 12,000 r.p.m. and the engine came to a screaming halt in about 1½ seconds.

July of 1937 was a critical month. The Chief of the B.T.H. decided that running it in the open factory was too dangerous, and that we must find some other place for continued testing. The engine was little more than a heap of scrap because of overheating, casing distortion, etc. My postgraduate year was at an end and my fate was in the balance; and we were out of money. Things looked pretty black from every point of view. Further, I was worried about my own prospects for promotion.

This very complex situation was resolved in a number of ways. Perhaps the most important factor was that I had a very encouraging interview with Sir Henry Tizard, the then Chairman of the Aeronautical Research Council. He subsequently recorded his opinion that I was on the right track and had the necessary ability for the work but warned that ultimate success was by no means certain and that we must face up to the fact that much work lay ahead before our goals could be achieved. Despite this opinion, Falk and Partners refused to exercise their option to finance the project to the amount stipulated in the Agreement but undertook to find a further £3,000 if Williams, Tinling, and I would not exercise our full rights under the Agreement. Eventually a compromise was reached, but control of Power Jets passed to the "A" shareholders (Williams, Tinling and myself). We agreed, however, to allow L. L. Whyte to continue as Chairman and Managing Director. This may have been a mistake in the light of the fact that he was "persona non grata" with the Air Ministry but we respected his ability and his integrity.

To this day, I do not know what lay behind Falk and Partners decision, made in spite of a further favorable report by M. L. Bramson and Sir Henry Tizard's encouraging opinion.

The financial situation was further saved by a very slim margin through a number of factors. The B.T.H. (much to my surprise) and Laidlaw Drew and Co. agreed to accept shares in lieu of payment for part of their work.

The opinions of Sir Henry Tizard, though he had no executive authority at the Air Ministry, undoubtedly influenced the latter because the D.S.R. began to regard our work as "long term research" and possibly of use to gas turbine work then in progress at the Royal Aircraft Establishment (see below) with whom we had begun to exchange ideas. Accordingly, at long last, the Air Ministry gave us modest contracts —£200 an hour for test running up to 20 hours and £1,000 for a detailed report on the testing of the first edition of W.U. The acceptance of this contract had severe disadvantages which we did not foresee at the time. The work went on the Official Secrets List which made it virtually impossible to raise private money except from a few who were willing to take a "blind chance."

My personal position was resolved when Sir Frederick Bowhill had me appointed to the Special Duty List, attached to No. 6 Group for administrative purposes. (The A.O.C. of 6 Group

Figure 4b. The first experimental engine, after the second reconstruction in 1938.

had me exempted from the promotion exam and I received my very welcome promotion to Squadron Leader which meant, inter alia, that I became entitled to marriage allowances.)

Out test site problem was resolved when the B.T.H. agreed to let us use a part of their disused foundry at Lutterworth—about seven miles from Rugby. The core store became our test cell and we converted the core ovens to combustion test cells.

When we were "expelled" from the B.T.H. turbine factory for testing we had already decided that a reconstruction of the engine was necessary. It was for the cost of this reconstruction that the B.T.H. accepted shares in lieu of cash.

The reconstructed engine did not last long. There was a major turbine blade failure in May 1938. So a second reconstruction was designed —still using the more expensive components of the original W.U. because we could not afford to do otherwise.

This second reconstruction was carried out by the B.T.H. at a cost of £2,400. This was paid for by an Air Ministry contract which included further payments for running time. Figure 4.

This second reconstruction was a major advance in the development. I had decided to use ten combustion chambers in parallel, having found that the primary difficulty I formerly feared, namely, virtual simultaneous ignition in all combustion chambers, could be ensured by interconnecting tubes.

The ten combustion chambers were of "counter flow" tube. I have often been asked why I chose this arrangement. The answer is that it was the only way that the sheet metal work could be adapted to the rotor and other more expensive parts of the engine. Nevertheless, the counter flow arrangement had important advantages. It was largely free from thermal expansion problems and it was possible to make very rapid changes in the combustion chamber "innards."

The reconstruction was completed in October 1938. It was now virtually the prototype of a number of later engines. For starting purposes

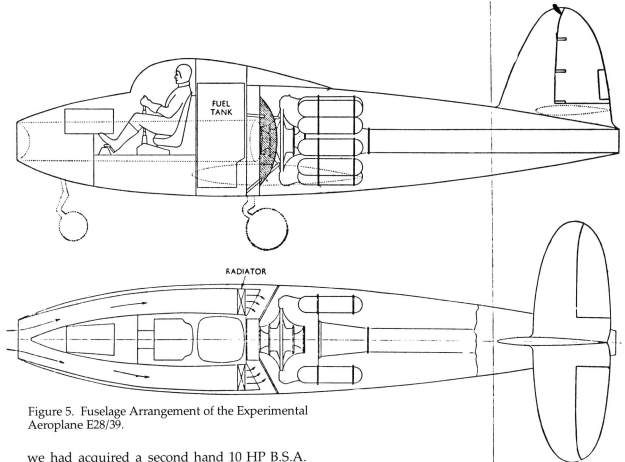

Figure 5. Fuselage Arrangement of the Experimental Aeroplane E28/39.

we had acquired a second hand 10 HP B.S.A. car engine. (I have to confess that it took us a year to find out that the starter of the B.S.A. engine proved adequate for starting the W.U.)

In the interim between May and October 1938, I concentrated on combustion chamber testing — again outside the B.T.H. turbine factory. I was planning to use kerosene vaporizers once more, one in each chamber. I apparently got excellent results, and so I was able to specify the details of the ten engine combustion chambers. However, when engine testing was resumed in October, we ran into a seemingly endless series of combustion troubles and so we intensified the combustion chamber experiments. But every scheme which worked well when tested separately gave trouble in the engine.

There was surging of fuel supply as between the ten vaporizers; the latter coked up or primed or burnt out. Equalization of the fuel supply was obtained by a set of equalizing valves controlled by a master valve, but the other troubles persisted. However, we did succeed in getting runs up to half an hour for speeds up to 16,500 r.p.m., but this took over a

year during which we were plagued by other troubles—bearing failures, compressor impeller tip failure, damage to turbine blades when burnt away pieces of metal from the combus-chambers and other foreign bodies passed throught. Vaporizer after vaporizer was tried— over 30 all told, combined with numerous other alterations in the internal components of the combustion chambers. Success always appeared to be just around the corner. The basic reason why successful combustion chamber tests could not be repeated in the engine was the difference in the distribution of the air flow at combustion chamber entry. For some time this seemed unlikely as the point of air admission was quite remote from the primary combustion zone with the counterflow arrangement. But we were eventually forced to realize that combustion was as much an aerodynamic problem as anything else.

Matters weren't helped by the fact that after

being used as a foundry for many years the Ladywood Works roofing had become loaded with foundry sand, so that when the engine was running there was a fine rain of sand. This almost certainly caused the bearing failures.

On June 30th 1939, the D.S.R. visited Ladywood and witnessed a 20 minute run at 16,500 r.p.m. He became a convert at last. He decided that we were to receive a contract for a flight engine and that the Air Ministry would place a contract for a flight engine and an experimental aeroplane. He also assured Whyte, that in the event of war (now imminent) I would not be taken off the job. A short time later the contract for W.1 was received and the Gloster Aircraft Company were selected to build the airplane— the E28/39. Power Jets was enabled to build up a sheet metal shop and acquire a few machine tools so that it ceased to be necessary to make numerous journeys to and from the B.T.H. for repairs and modifications. Figure 5. We also began to build up a drawing office.

Meanwhile, Power Jets was building up a highly qualified team of engineers, and a few skilled fitters and other skilled labor. The engineers were mostly younger than I. In 1938, apart from the Board, Power Jets numbered six, my secretary, an assistant engineer, two night watchmen, an office boy and myself (and a timid watch dog named "Sandy"). We grew partly by direct recruiting, but also by loans of personnel by the Air Ministry, the R.A.E. and the B.T.H. Wing Commander George Lees (one of my former instructors at Cranwell and Henlow) was attached to us and became my deputy. Later W. E. P. Johnson, who had been called up as a Flight Lieutenant on the R.A.F. Reserve, was posted to Power Jets with a wide range of duties. W. R. Hawthorne (now Sir William Hawthorne) and Squadron Leader G. W. Bone were sent on loan from the R.A.E. (all this over a period of several months). A very able turbine designer, L. J. Chashire, was loaned to us by the B.T.H., which was rather surprising in the light of the fact that relations between Power Jets and the B.T.H. had become somewhat soured by our dissatisfaction with the (as it seemed to us) unduly long delivery times, and the degree of accuracy of parts (a turbine factory unequipped for uniform temperatures was basically unsuited to obtaining the fine limits we demanded). Also, there had been some rather acrimonious technical controversies between myself and the B.T.H. turbine designers.

It would take far too long to describe the building of the Power Jets team and the high standard of its quality, but I have to say that the success of the jet engine was largely based on a team which, in proportion to its size, was unequalled in ability and enthusiasm.

The contract for the W.1 flight engine was subcontracted to the B.T.H. The E28/39 was primarily designed by George Carter, but there was close collaboration between the Gloster design staff, the R.A.E. and Power Jets.

Meanwhile, after Britain declared war on Germany on September 3, 1939, we continued to be plagued by combustion problems. Fortunately for us a helpful observer was Isaac Lubbock, head of the Shell Fulham Laboratory. Initially (unknown to us) he was having experiments done at the Shell Laboratory with the object of extracting us from the mire in which we were floundering. He and his team succeeded. Using the same basic "scenery" of our combustion system, he substituted an atomizing fuel injector for our vaporizers. This marked a turning point in the problem which had bedevilled the development for three years.

Prior to this, in the bitter weather of January 1940 we were independently visited by Sir Henry Tizard and Air Vice Marshal Sir Arthur Tedder, then Director General of Reseach and Development (D.G.R.D.), and later Marshal of the Royal Air Force Lord Tedder. Both witnessed demonstration runs of the W.U. (still fitted with vaporizers) and were duly impressed. I later heard that the jet engine was classed as a "potential war winner."

Another consequence was that the Air Ministry decided that production planning should be put in hand for a twin engined jet fighter plane and for the production of a 1,600 lb static thrust version of the W.1., known as the W.2 initially, and later as the W.2B. All this before the flight testing of the W.1.

Unfortunately (in my opinion) their enthusiasm clouded their judgment.

Figure 6. The W.1 engine less tail pipe and propelling nozzle (1941).

Being dissatisfied with the quality of B.T.H. work, we had negotiated with the Rover Company to act as subcontractors. Rover had a high reputation as automobile manufacturers and also as managers of "shadow factories" building Bristol aero engines. But they were not satisfied with the mere role of subcontractors to Power Jets and went behind our backs to the Director of Engine Development and persuaded him that they were more competent to deal with the jet engine than "a bunch of gifted amateurs," despite the fact that they had no engineers with experience in turbine design. They succeeded in being selected for the production planning of the W.2B, and Power Jets were instructed to supply the Rover Company with complete sets of drawings and to provide all necessary information. Meanwhile, Sir Henry Tizard brought Vauxhall Motors into the picture, and later, the De Havilland Engine Company. Again, Power Jets were called upon to provide all necessary assistance. Further, the B.T.H. received independent contracts for jet

engine development. All this threw a heavy burden on the Power Jets small staff. Worse still was the competition for scarce materials and parts. All this very severely hindered our ability to concentrate on development. To add insult to injury, we were constantly being accused of failing to cooperate, particularly by the Rover Company. I tried to put an end to this latter by inviting Rover to send a design draughtsman on attachment to Power Jets who would be free to see everything we were doing. This they did, but it did not stop the accusations.

The W.1 engine was nearing completion at the end of 1940. Figure 6. In the course of its manufacture a number of parts had to be rejected. With these, and a spare rotor which had been intended for the W.U. we built a "lash-up" version of the W.1. It was known as the W.1X. Both the W.1 and W.1X closely resembled the W.U. but were little more than half the weight.

Figure 7. Damaged turbine wheel of W.1X.

The W.1 was designed to produce a static thrust of 1,240 lbs at 17,750 r.p.m.

The W.1X first ran in December 1940 and gave a performance greatly superior to the W.U. which by this time was little more than a heap of junk and clearly on its last legs, so we just used it for a series of endurance runs of up to ten hours at a time at moderate speeds until it finally gave up the ghost in February 1941 when several turbine blade roots failed. Figure 7. This did not bother us because we had switched the blade root design from the de Laval type to what was known as the "fir tree" type for the W.1 and all future engines. Moreover, the strength-temperature properties of the blade material had been greatly improved by Firth-Vickers.

With the W.1X we were able to finalize the design of the W.1 combustion chambers.

The E28/39 was completed by Gloster at the end of March 1941 but its W.1 engine was not yet complete so we sent along the unairworthy W.1X to check the installation and do taxiing trials at Gloster's airfield at Brockworth near Cheltenham. Figure 8. The engine was duly assembled into the aircraft without problems on April 5, and the first taxiing run was made by Gloster's chief test pilot, P. E. G. Sayer, at dusk on the 6th. Brockworth was a grass airfield and the grass was soggy with rain. Also we had set a throttle stop to limit engine r.p.m. to 12,000. Under this combination of conditions the aircraft could not do more than 20 mph. "Jerry" Sayer looked very crestfallen after this run. We were not worried. I told Jerry that the thrust increased very rapidly with r.p.m., but he did not seem to be convinced though he had witnessed this fact during a visit to Lutterworth. There was a distinct cloud of gloom hanging over the heads of the Gloster personnel present.

The following day we increased the engine speed in stages and, as we had foretold, Jerry experienced a sharp rise in taxiing speed. When we increased the throttle stop to a setting of 16,000 r.p.m. I did a taxiing run. I taxied slowly to the far end of the rather small airfield, turned and opened up to 16,000 r.p.m. The aircraft quickly gathered speed until at about 60 mph I could scarcely feel the wheel rumble and realized that the slightest pull back on the control column would lift me off, but the airfield was becoming uncomfortably close and I did not feel too sure of the brakes, so I snatched the throttle back and braked to slow taxiing speed until I stopped by the group of Power Jets and Gloster spectators.

The experience was a very thrilling one. I was most impressed with the forward visibility and was more than satisfied with the general feel of the aircraft. Jerry Sayer then took over and, selecting the longest available stretch of the field, made two fast runs, lifting off for two or three hundred yards each time. He was naturally much happier than on the previous evening. (Incidentally, some of the spectators were prepared to swear that I lifted off during my run, but if so it was no more than a long gentle bounce. Possibly this gave rise to the often repeated but false story that I made the first test flight.)

A few days later we received the W.1 in parts as requested, assembled it with the combustion chamber components we had made for it, and

Figure 8. The Gloster E28/39.

put it through the "special category test" specified by the Ministry. The special category tests were for a total of 25 hours with maximum speed restricted to 16,500 at which the static thrust was 860 lbs. The test was completed without a hitch and the engine officially cleared for flight. It was duly installed in the E28 early in May 1941.

Cranwell had been selected for the flight trials. These began on the evening of May 15th, 1941, weather having prevented an earlier moment. The takeoff run was about 600 yards and Jerry climbed steadily until he was hidden by the clouds. We saw little of him until 17 minutes later when he made his landing approach. The manner in which he did this—far from cautious —showed that he felt completely at ease with his new toy.

The specified test program, frequently hampered by weather, of ten hours was completed in two weeks. My engineers never felt it necessary to check the engine (a fact which astounded the Gloster technicians) because they knew from experience that if it sounded right it *was* right. This was probably the first time in aviation history that a prototype airplane *and* a prototype engine had ever completed ten hours without other than superficial inspection of the airframe.

For one flight only the Ministry gave permission for engine r.p.m. to be increased to 17,000. At this power setting, the E28 clearly demonstrated that it out-performed the Spitfire. This fact was driven home about one year later when the E28 was flown the short distance from an airfield near Cheltenham to Hatfield for a demonstration performance before Winston Churchill. Being unarmed and since random enemy missions were frequent, it was provided with an escort of two Spitfires and a Tempest. It left its escorts far behind and had landed and taxied to the apron before the "escorts" arrived in a screaming dive.

Figure 9. W2B in tail of Wellington test bed.

The initial flight of the E28 was ignored by senior Ministry officials. W.E.P. Johnson's request for an official filming of the event was ignored. However, a few days later, the Secretary of State for Air, Sir Archibald Sinclair, and many other VIPs from the Ministry and the aircraft industry, witnessed a demonstration flight and were duly impressed. In a way, this had unfortunate consequences for Power Jets. The pressure increased, the visitors multiplied, indeed it seemed to us that everyone was trying "to get in on the act."

The success of the E28 had become of secondary interest to me. The all important goal was to get F9/40 (later named the "Meteor") into production with its W2B engines.

The W2B was a variant of the W2 series. Fig-

ure 9. In designing the W2, I set my sights a little too high and we ran into a sea of troubles. The performance of the first of the series (built mainly by the Rover Co.) was a terrible disappointment. For the first time we ran into the compressor surging problem which was to bedevil development for the next two years.

In the years '41, '42 and '43 so much happened that it is very difficult to present a satisfactory chronological record without confusing the reader, so the main facts will be briefly set out in order of importance rather than in chronological sequence.

Though the Battle of Britain killed the German plans for invasion by September 1940, the U.K. was subjected to sporadic daylight raids and intensive night time "blitzes." A few bombs fell near the Ladywood Works and we naturally assumed that we were the target, but I think we were mistaken because it is extremely doubtful that the Germans knew what was going on at Ladywood.

We were, however, affected by air raids. A daylight raider dropped a stick of bombs very near the B.T.H. The direct material damage was negligible but it happened that a fitter was carrying an urgently needed compressor impeller to a buffing machine and, startled by the explosions, he dropped it and it had to be scrapped. It took three months to replace it. Again, the foundry of High Duty Alloys at Slough who were supplying compressor casing castings to the B.T.H., Rover and Power Jets, was wrecked by a direct hit in a night raid. This caused several months delay. The night attacks in particular were becoming a serious threat to the U.K. production effort in general. So it was decided between Sir Henry Tizard and USAAF General "Hap" Arnold that our jet engine production should be backed up by production in the U.S.A. Accordingly, we were visited by USAAF officers and representatives of General Electric. The outcome was that General Electric, because of their experience with turbo-superchargers, were selected for production in the U.S.A.

Accordingly, on October 1st 1941, the disassembled W.1X and a team from Power Jets were flown to the U.S.A. in the bomb bay of a Liberator. A set of drawings of the W2B was also sent to G.E. The Power Jets team was one of our senior engineers (D. N. Walker) and two technicians (Warrant Officer King, on loan from the R.A.F., and our very able fitter G. B. Buzzoni).

This was the starting point of jet development in the U.S.A., though Pearl Harbor was still some nine weeks in the future (December 7, 1941).

The G.E. Co. worked so fast that they had their version of the W2B (the I-14) on the test bench by April 1942, and the Bell Aircraft Co. was rapidly building the XP-59A—a twin engined fighter to be powered by two I-14's.

I visited the U.S.A. myself in June-September 1942, (the first time I had been out of the U.K.), to assist and advise the G.E., the USAAF, the Bell Aircraft Co., Inc.

Not long after my return to the U.K. the Bell XP-59A started its test flights at Muroc Lake (now Edwards AFB) on October 2, 1942, almost exactly one year after sending over the W.1X, etc. An astonishing achievement!

Thereafter, there was a continuous interchange of information between the U.K. and U.S.A.

From 1936 onwards there had been a growing collaboration between the Engine Section of the R.A.E. at Farnborough and Power Jets. The former was working initially on a turbo-prop with an axial flow compressor, but on seeing the way the wind was blowing at Power Jets, the R.A.E. team, headed by Hayne Constant converted their turbo-prop into a turbo-jet known as the F.2, and subcontracted the manufacture to Metropolitan-Vickers. The relationship between Constant's team and "Metro-Vick" was very similar to that between Power Jets and the B.T.H. but, while there was a very full interchange of information between P.J. and the R.A.E.—though both the B.T.H. and Metro-Vick were subsidiaries of Associated Electrical Industries (A.E.I.)—there was no corresponding collaboration. Indeed they behaved as though they were deadly commercial rivals until some degree of cooperation was forced upon them by the formation of the Gas Turbine Collaboration Committee in November 1941. In contrast to this, the R.A.E. invited P.J. (in 1940) to take part in their F2 project, which we agreed to do, but were forced to back down later through sheer pressure of work.

P.J.'s happy relationship with the R.A.E. was fortunate for the former. When we were wrongly accused of being uncooperative by Rover and others the R.A.E. sprang to our defense.

Meanwhile in Germany turbo-jet development, unknown to either side, was following a course of astonishing similarity. A young engineer, Hans von Ohain, was working on a centrifugal type turbo-jet, and others were thinking in terms of turbo-props with axial flow compressors which later, like the R.A.E., became converted to turbo-jets. Von Ohain, however, was not hampered by lack of financial support because he soon obtained the backing of the well known aircraft firm of Heinkel. Von Ohain has told me that Herr Heinkel was most anxious to break into the aero engine field and hoped that von Ohain's engine would enable him to get his "foot in the door." Consequently, Heinkel pressured von Ohain into developing a flight engine at the earliest possible date while at the same time building the He 178 to be powered by it. The net result was that Heinkel, unhampered by very cautious bureaucrats, was able to get the He 178 into the air in August 1939. Heinkel, however, was not very popular with the Luftministerium, the officials of which preferred to put their weight behind the axial flow Junkers 004 and the Messerschmitt twin engined fighter, the Me 262. Here again the development of the Me 262 ran closely parallel with that of the Gloster Meteor (the production version of the F9/40); the Me 262 led by a short head, mainly because the reliability requirements of the Luftministerium (if they had any) were far less stringent than those of the Ministry who stipulated that the W2B must pass a 125 hour type test before going into production as the "Welland."

In 1941 a "cross" between the W1 and the W2 was built jointly by P.J. and the B.T.H. It was known as the W1A. Its purpose was to test special features of the compressor intake of the W2 though, in fact, a Rover built W2 was completed a few days earlier. The first runs of the W1A were most unpromising, mainly because I had designed for far too high an exhaust velocity from the turbine and had also used an "aerofoil profile" for the turbine blades in accordance with R.A.E. advice. But when we rebladed the turbine in accordance with my previous practice of designing the blade profiles to conform with the inter-blade channels plus another small turbine modification the W1A gave its designed thrust of 1340 lbs. Shortly after the W1 gave its designed thrust of 1240 lbs. The W1A also had a significantly lower specific fuel consumption than the W1.

At Power Jets there followed a W2 Mark IV, four W2Bs built by Rover and handed over to P.J. on Ministry instructions, and the W2/500.

The W2 Mark IV was built jointly by P.J. and the B.T.H. It was initially a W2 but was progressively modified. Unhappily this engine (on which we had high hopes) was totally wrecked on its first run. The compressor impeller burst into two parts at 9,000 r.p.m. By a miracle, of the four individuals who were inside the test chamber at the time, only two received very minor injuries. The reason for the failure was plain. There had been an undetected crack in the forging almost in a diametrical plane. In effect, the impeller had been held together by its attachments to its shafting.

We struggled along with the W2B's but could not get near the target performance of 1,600 lbs. I was convinced that a 5° twist of the turbine blades would do the trick and advised the Rover Co. accordingly. They ignored it.

We had come to regard the W2B as a "dead duck" owing to Rover's grip on it. So, on March 2, 1942 we started a complete redesign. This was the W2/500. It was designed, built (mainly by Power Jets), and placed on test in exactly six calendar months. On September 2, 1942 it was run up to full speed and the results plotted so exactly on the design curves that I was foolish enough to declare that "jet engine design has become an exact science."

Much of the success of the W2/500 and later engines was due to a steady improvement in materials for turbine blades, particularly the dramatic increase in temperature-strength properties achieved by the Mond Nickel Company with a nickel-chromium alloy known as "Nimonic 80."

Our development work on the W2B now began to take a back seat. The W1 had been relegated for training new personnel, but the W1A was putting in considerable running time, both in the E28 and on the bench. With it we suddenly encountered a series of turbine blade failures (not that this was a new thing) of a mystifying kind. When failure is due to resonance it usually occurs at the same place. With the W1A this was far from the case. There was no consistent pattern; sometimes it would be near the tip, sometimes about midway, and sometimes at the root. It suddenly occurred to me, improbable though it seemed, that a movable thermocouple about three feet downstream from the turbine might be "throwing its shadow before" and causing fluctuations in blade loading. I instructed its removal. This did the trick. A 100 hour run was completed without any sign of blade failure. This event and the performance of the W2/500 had a dramatic effect on the Ministry. We had been allowed to grow at a modest rate wholly financed by the Ministry. We had been allowed to build two test houses. Part of an old country house (Brownsover Hall) three miles from Rugby and four from Lutterworth had been requisitioned for the design and project engineers and the main drawing office. The magnificent dining room became my office. The directors and administrative staff had a house located about midway between Brownsover and Ladywood which was now the seat of manufacture and engine development. The M.A.P. further authorized the planning of an 80,000 sq. ft. pre-production factory and shortly after gave us the go-ahead for its construction complete with a high altitude compressor test house, four engine test houses, etc. This factory was located at Whetstone, four miles on the Lutterworth side of Leicester.

But 1942 was mainly a year of setbacks. At Power Jets, after some 150 hours running with the W2/500, largely trouble free, a "disease" of compressor impeller blade failures started, usually with extensive damage to the engine. The similarity of the failures indicated resonant fatigue. This puzzled me greatly in the light of the engine's earlier record. I started an inquiry and learned that at 14,000 r.p.m. the engine produced a howling noise which the test personnel quickly avoided by accelerating through the "howling speed." I instructed that an engine be run for one hour at howling speed and then shut down for inspection. As I suspected, every compressor blade was found to be cracked over a length of its junction with the impeller disc. What had been evidently happening was that resonant fatigue was causing the cracks at the howling speed and led to major failures at higher speeds. The necessary stiffening of the impeller reduced engine performance from its design static thrust of 1,860 lbs to a little above 1,600 lbs.

Meanwhile, the Rover Company was struggling along with its work on the W2B, trying many alterations which, with the connivance of the Director of Engine Development (DED),

they were keeping secret from Power Jets. They were averaging some 40 hours a month with about six engines, and repeatedly failed to get the 1,400 lb thrust which was the minimum the Ministry would tolerate for flight trials of the F9/40.

A second E28/39 had been built with thin wings to make higher speeds possible, and it was used exclusively for flight tests of the Rover W2B. Unfortunately, this aircraft was lost when, through temperature differential contraction, the aileron controls seized up, and the pilot had to bail out. The first E28/39 continued flight testing throughout the war powered by a sequence of Power Jets engines. Flight testing was further supplemented by the conversion of a Wellington MkV (a twin engined bomber) into a flight test bed by replacing its tail gun turret with a jet engine test bay. Additionally, for flight testing the RAE-Metro Vick F2 engine, a Lancaster bomber was allotted and fitted with a test nacelle suspended below its fuselage.

Though much was happening in 1942 — both good and bad — the Allied need for a jet fighter had greatly weakened. The primary purpose of the development had been to counter the high altitude bombers which it was supposed the Germans intended to use. But, by the end of 1942, the Allies had gained air superiority and the menace the jet fighters were designed to meet never materialized. This virtual disappearance of the threat the Meteor was designed to counter, added to the development troubles of 1942, led to a drastic cutback in the program of production of both airframes and engines.

The situation was largely saved by Rolls Royce, the story of whose role in the development must now be briefly told.

In 1940 I had asked Sir Henry Tizard to involve Rolls Royce rather than Rover, Vauxhall (who withdrew from the picture after only six months), etc. Sir Henry replied that R-R had a scheme of their own in hand and would not be be interested.

However, one Sunday afternoon in 1940, the Chief Executive of R-R, E. W. Hives (later Lord Hives), and Dr. Stanley G. Hooker (now Sir Stanley Hooker) visited P.J. and saw a demonstration engine run. At first Hives was not impressed, but he changed his attitude when Hooker pointed out that the engine was at least as powerful as the Merlin for a fraction of the weight. From then on, there was increasing co-operation between P.J. and R-R. At first the latter volunteered to assist us in making parts and running compressor tests. Later, they started to design and build a larger and more powerful Whittle type engine, the W.R1.

There were discussions about a much closer relationship between R-R and P.J. These came to nothing because of a most unfortunate misunderstanding. Following a very friendly meet- at R-R's Derby factory in 1942, at which there seemed likely to be a fruitful outcome, I left believing that the next move was for R-R to make a formal proposal. R-R, on the other hand, was apparently expecting P.J. to make the next move, so each party, unwilling to seem too eager, sat waiting for the other to make a move. So, though cooperation continued at the engineering level, nothing happened at the management level, causing each side to think that the other side did not wish to pursue the matter further. Meanwhile, both the W.R1 and their own project, the C.R1—an extremely complicated device having a series of contrarotating rotors—were virtual failures.

Near the end of 1942, I was summoned to the M.A.P. by the Controller of Supplies, Air Chief Marshall Sir William Freeman. In a very difficult interview at which I was feeling most unwell, Sir William made a series of proposals wrapped up in a good deal of circumlocution. He did, however, make it clear that the Ministry was very disappointed with progress and had decided to slash production plans very severely. What was not so clear were his intentions concerning P.J. The gist was that P.J. and perhaps Rover were to be handed over to R-R. I repeatedly said I did not follow him, and pleaded for time on the grounds that I was unwell. At last I was allowed to leave and think it over.

The situation was revolutionized when R-R made a deal with Rover whereby Rover "traded" their jet engine factories at Barnoldswick and Clitheroe for R-R's marine engine division, R-R to become responsible for technical manage-

ment on January 1, 1943 and to take over completely at the end of March. The result was almost miraculous. In January, testing time on the Rover-built W2Bs jumped tenfold, and within about 12 weeks I received a jubilant phone call telling me that a 100 hour type test at the design rating of 1600 lbs thrust had been completed mainly as a result of twisting the turbine blades through the 5° I had advised two years earlier. This had the effect of reinstating the production program, and shortly after the Welland, the production version of the W2B, was in modest production.

One F9/40, the Meteor prototype was modified to take the de Havilland Engine Company's H-1 (later the Goblin) and, indeed, this was the first F9/40 to fly in March 1943. (This engine was also the first to power the Lockheed P-80. It was later replaced by the General Electric's I-40 of 4,000 lb static thrust, c.f., the 3,000 lb thrust of the H-1.

The H-1 was noteworthy in being the first of the centrifugal type jet engines to use "straight through" combustion chambers, in the design of which Power Jets had helped. (P.J. had a contract for a straight through engine—the W3—but it never got off the drawing board through pressure of other work and our reluctance to face the inevitable long period of combustion development.) the H-1 did not reach a production standard during the war, but it became the very successful Goblin which powered the D.H. Vampire.

The Meteor I powered by two Wellands was operational in July—a few months later than the Me 262. The Meteor's first operational use was most unexpected. It was used against the German V.1 flying bomb, being the only fighter with level speed enough for the purpose.

The Me 262, meanwhile, was proving a serious menace to the U. S. B-17 day bombers, so much so, that the Meteor was temporarily withdrawn from combat operations, for tactical exercises with the B-17's to see if a method of countering the Me 262 could be found. It could not. Thereafter, the Meteors joined with other Allied fighters in ground strafing during the drive through Northern France shortly before the end of the war in Europe.

Figure 10. The Whittle W2/700 Turbine Engine.

In 1943 and 1944, P.J.'s activities had greatly intensified. The W2/500 had flown in the F9/40 and the E28. It was being followed by more powerful engines culminating in the W2/700—a 2000-2500 lb thrust engine which went into pre-production at our Whetstone factory. Figures 10 and 11. The W2/700 was the last of the centrifugal engines for which I was responsible. It was in competition with R-R's Derwent 1, also a 2000 lb thrust engine, which differed from the W2/700 in having straight through combustion chambers, but was otherwise very similar. It was selected for production in preference to the W2/700 and, eventually, developed as the Derwent III which powered the Meteor III.

From the earliest days, I had been seeking a means of improving the propulsive efficiency of jet engines. I had always realized that it was desirable to "gear down" the jet, i.e., to generate a high mass low velocity jet rather than low mass high velocity jet of the "straight" jet

Figure 11. The Rotor of the Whittle W2/700 Engine.

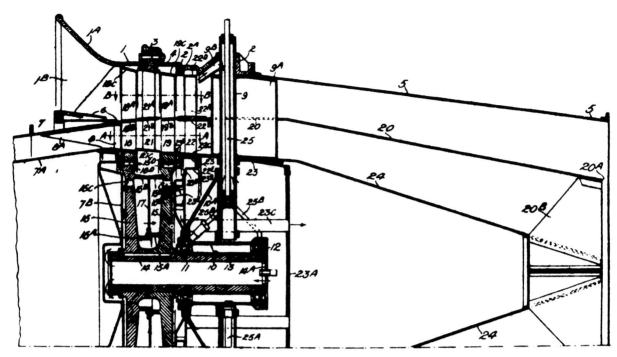

Figure 12. Whittle patent drawing.

engine. To this end, I filed a patent application in 1936 for what we then called a "bypass engine" but later came to be known as the "turbofan." Figure 12. We did not, however, have the manpower and resources for such a major re-routing of development, so I sought an interim solution which could be merely "tacked on" to a jet engine. Thus began a series of "thrust augmentor" schemes—later known as "aft fans." The first of these, the No. 1 Thrust Augmentor having a pair of contra-rotating rotors, with fan blades mounted as extensions of the turbine blades, was abandoned in the project phase when it was found that the required blade angles and relative velocities were quite impracticable.

The No. 2 Thrust Augmentor which had a more conventional two stage arrangement, again with fan blades external to, and extensions of, the turbine blades did not get past the design stage. But the drawings were sent to G.E. in 1942 and, much later, became the basis of the series of G.E. aft fans used in such aircraft as the Convair 990 and Phantom fanjet.

Our next attempt was the No. 3 Thrust Aug-mentor in which a single stage rotor had the turbine blades mounted external to the fan. This was designed and built. Figure 13. Unfortunately, this "tip turbine" arrangement required that the ducts leading the exhaust from the main turbine of the jet engine had to pass through the entry flow to the fan causing considerable disturbance to the latter. This was in 1943. A substantial increase of thrust was obtained but far below expectations. No doubt it could have been cleared up a lot, but, again, pressure of other work precluded further development.

Later, in 1944, we returned to a form of the No. 2 Thrust Augmentor. This, plus afterburning, was designed to be mounted behind the W2/700. It was designed to power the Miles M.52 supersonic airplane. Figure 14. This was "halted in its tracks" for reasons stated below.

In 1943 I took the three months War Course at the R.A.F. Staff College. While there I arranged a debate to determine the specification of a long range bomber for operations in the Pacific. As a result, when I returned to Power Jets we embarked on the design of the LR1. This was intended to be an all purpose engine. It was designed to be usable as a straight jet, or turbo-prop or turbo-fan. Its "core" engine comprised

Figure 14. The Miles M.52.

a nine stage axial flow compressor with a final centrifugal stage driven by a two stage turbine via straight through combustion chambers. As a turbo-jet the core engine only would be used. As a turbo-fan or turbo-prop the fan or propeller was to be driven via a reduction gear assembly—one suited to a propeller and another suited to a two stage fan.

This scheme was also "halted in its tracks" when half built.

In 1944, Power Jets was nationalized as Power Jets (R&D) on the grounds that it had almost entirely been supported by government funds. (This was equally true of all the other engine firms in the jet engine business.) For a time this did not greatly affect our activities, but these became increasingly affected by the rulings of a committee established by the Ministry and which included senior executives from aero engine firms who could hardly be expected to encourage the activities of an "upstart" competitor. The directives laid down by this committee became increasingly restrictive of P.J. activities.

The final blow came in 1946 when the Minis-

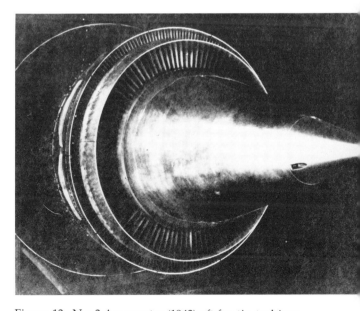

Figure 13. No. 3 Augmentor (1943) aft fan tip turbines.

try (now the Ministry of Supply) decided to merge all except a small rump of P.J. (R&D) and the recently formed gas turbine division of the R.A.E. into the National Gas Turbine Establishment. This was the last straw for me and several of the leading members of the team, because the Terms of Reference of the N.G.T.E. proscribed the right to design and build engines. It was to be essentially a research establishment like the R.A.E. It was to become the servant of the aircraft engine industry and carry out such research and development as the industry deemed necessary. In short, those who had originated and developed the jet engine and its derivatives were stripped of their right to continue such work. I resigned, and so did many of the leading members of my team, who became scattered through industry.

As a consequence of these events, the contracts for the LR1, the Miles M.52 aircraft and the No. 4 Thrust Augmentor, all about 50% complete, were cancelled. In my opinion this set back turbo-fan development and supersonic aircraft for many years.

Not wishing to end on this sad note, it would be appropriate to mention some of the highlights of that time. These may be summarized as follows:

1. In 1945 R-R built the Nene, originally of 4,000 lb thrust and quickly developed to 5,000 lb.

2. Also in 1945 a scaled down version of the Nene to fit into the Meteor—the Derwent V—was designed and built in six months and powered the Meteor IV which captured the world speed record in November 1945 (606 mph). Subsequently, the Derwent V was built in thousands, and Fighter Command of the R.A.F. was largely equipped with Meteor IVs and Goblin engined Vampires. Piston-propeller engined fighter aircraft had become completely obsolete in the U.K., and U.S.A. and elsewhere.

3. The axial flow engine, fathered by the R.A.E., lagged somewhat behind the centrifugals initially, but as higher speeds demanded smaller frontal area for the power plant, "axials" began to overtake, and eventually superseded the centrifugals. In the U.K. the R-R Avon, the R.A.E.-Metro Vick Beryl, and the Armstrong Siddeley Sapphire and their U.S. counterparts,

though much more complicated and expensive, rendered the centrifugal type obsolescent except, perhaps, for the two stage centrifugal turbo-prop—the R-R Dart which powered the highly successful Vickers Viscount medium range civil airliner for more than 30 years (and is still in service in many parts of the world)—and except for certain small gas turbines for auxiliary power plant, etc. There are still a number of comparatively low power engines which have compound compressors, like the LR1, with a centrifugal final compression stage preceded by a multi-stage axial flow compressor.

Perhaps the highlight of the whole development for me personally was piloting a jet airplane myself. I had repeatedly tried to get my hand on the E28, but the Ministry refused permission, not wishing to risk the aircraft and the engine designer together. In 1943, the Ministry relented and gave permission for me to fly the E28 if I got in some practice in the Miles Master, the Hurricane, Spitfire and Mustang.

I never flew the Mustang (none available), but after flying the Master, Hurricane, and Spitfire, I was cleared to fly the E28. But, just as I was climbing into the cockpit, I was informed that it was unserviceable. I was told that the previous pilot had reported engine overheating. So I never got to fly the E28.

But I managed to fly one of the Meteor prototypes powered by W2/700 engines, by "cheating." During 1944, Power Jets had been allotted its own test flight and an airfield at Bruntingthorpe near Leicester. On a visit there, I said I wished to taxi the Meteor prototype engined by two W2/700s. There being no one senior enough to deny me, I climbed in, gave myself a quick cockpit check and started off to the main runway, still uncertain of my own intentions, but the plane felt so pleasant and easy that when I quickly reached flying speed I eased back the control column and took off, did a very gentle circuit and landed. I had over forty types in my log book and the Meteor was pleasanter to fly than any of them.

An even bigger thrill was when (officially this time) I flew a Meteor III flat out along the high speed course at Herne Bay at a height of 50 feet.

The Evolution and Future of Aeropropulsion Systems

Hans von Ohain

In this discussion about the evolution and future of aeropropulsion systems, I will address four main topics:

1. I will give a very condensed overview of the entire evolution of aeropropulsion systems.

2. Then I will highlight the beginning of jet propulsion, including my activities in the early phases of jet engine development.

3. I will show how the evolution progressed from first generation simple, fixed geometry turbojets to the highly complex, giant jet and fanjet engines of today.

4. Finally, I will discuss future potentialities of aeropropulsion systems.

1. Since the beginning of powered flight, the evolutions of both the aero-vehicle and aeropropulsion systems are strongly interrelated, and

DR. HANS VON OHAIN received his doctorate in physics in 1935 at the University of Goettingen, Germany, and remained at the University for the next two years while he privately developed a theory of turbojet engines and then built a working model. In 1936 he became associated with the Heinkel Company in Stuttgart for the development of his turbojet ideas. He directed a research and development program that resulted in the HeS-3B engine that powered the He-178 which made the world's first turbojet powered flight on August 27, 1939, at Marienehe Airfield in Germany. He remained with the Heinkel-Hirth firm during World War II, but in 1947 he came to America under contract to the U. S. Air Force to do theoretical work on advanced air-breathing propulsion systems. Subsequently he became associated with the Aerospace Research Laboratories at Wright-Patterson Air Force Base in Ohio where he became Chief Scientist. He is now retired but extremely active as a consultant.

are governed by a few major thrusts, namely: demands for improving reliability, endurance and lifetime; improvements in flight performance, such as speed, range, altitude maneuverability; and in more recent time, strongest emphasis on overall economy. Under these thrusts the technologies of aero-vehicle and propulsion system advanced continuously.

To gain a better insight in the evolution of aeropropulsion systems it is necessary to be aware of the problems and advancements in aero-vehicle technology: We can observe a continuous trend towards lighter and stronger airframe structures and materials; from wood and fabric to all metal structures to lighter and more heat resistant materials, and finally to composite materials. At the same time, the aerodynamic quality of the vehicle, characterized by the ratio of "Lift to Drag" (L/D) increased over the years and extended to higher flight speeds. This is illustrated in Fig 1, which I would like to discuss briefly. In order not to lose proper historical perspective, let us recall that at the turn of our century the science of aerodynamics was in its infancy; specifically, the phenomenon of aerodynamic lift was not understood. Therefore, the early pioneers could not benefit from scientific knowledge; they had to conduct their own fundamental investigations. The world's first successful glider vehicle by Lilienthal in the early 1890s had an L/D of about 5; by comparison, birds have an L/D ranging from 5 to 20. The world's first man-controlled powered aircraft, by the Wright brothers in 1903, had an L/D of about 7.5. As the L/D values increased over the

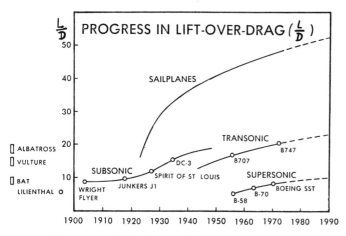

Figure 1. Lift to drag ratio.

years, soar planes advanced most rapidly and are currently attaining the enormously high values of about 50. This was achieved by employing ultra high wing aspect ratios and profiles especially tailored to the low Reynolds and Mach numbers of these airplanes. Powered aircraft advanced to L/D values of about 20 in the late 40s by continuously improving aerodynamic shapes employing advanced profiles, extremely smooth and accurate surfaces, engine cowls, and retractable landing gears. In the 1940s, this high aerodynamic quality was extended from the subsonic to the transonic flight speed regime by employing the swept wing principle, and later in 1952, the area rule of Whitcomb. In the late 60s, the Boeing 747 attained in transonic flight an L/D of about 20. In the supersonic flight speed regime L/D improved from 5 in the mid 50s to the currently considered L/D values of about 10. This progress can be attributed to the application of artificial stability and also to area rule, and advanced supersonic profile shapes which are made possible by advanced structures. The hypersonic speed regime is not fully explored. Current emphasis is place on winged reentry vehicles and lifting bodies where a high L/D is not of greatest importance. Fundamental investigations have shown that much greater values of L/D than those currently employed are attainable.

To appreciate the technological advancements in propulsion technology, let us again look back at the beginning of our century. Steam and in-

ternal combustion engines were then in existence, but were far too heavy for flight application. The Wright brothers recognized the great future potential of the internal combustion engine and developed both a relatively lightweight engine suitable for flight application and an efficient propeller. Let us now look at the progress of propulsion systems over the years (Fig 2): The Wright brothers' first aeropropulsion system had a shaft power of 12 horsepower, and its ratio of power output to total propulsion system weight including propeller and transmission was about 0.04. Through the subsequent four decades the horsepower weight ratio improved by more than an order of magnitude, to about 0.7 Hp/lb. The power output of the largest engine amounted to about 4000 hp and the *overall* efficiency (engine and propeller) reached about 25%. In the mid 30s, the turbojet came into being. This new propulsion system was immediately superior over the reciprocating engine with respect to power-to-weight ratio; however, its overall efficiency was initially lower than that of the reciprocating engine. As can be seen, progress was rapid. In less than four decades the power-to-weight ratio increased more than tenfold and the overall efficiency exceeded that of a diesel propulsion system. The power output of today's largest gasturbine engines reaches nearly 100,000 horsepower.

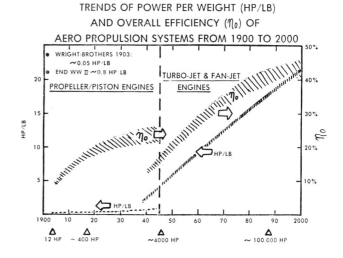

Figure 2. Progress in propulsion systems.

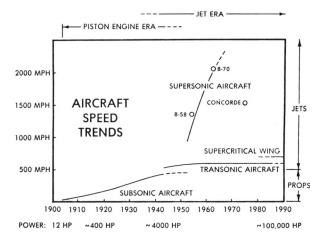

Figure 3. Increase in flight speeds.

These truly gigantic technological advancements had an enormous impact on flight performance. The improvements in aerodynamic quality and overall engine efficiency tremendously increased the flight range and total aircraft economy. The lighter vehicle structures and greater engine power/weight ratios had a crucial impact on aircraft maneuverability and flight speed.

The increase in flight speed over the years (Fig. 3) may be best suited as a basis for discussing the evolutions of aero-vehicle and aeropropulsion systems: In December 1903, the Wright brothers succeeded with the first man-controlled powered flight in the world. While the flight speed was only 30 mph, the consequences of the first flights were enormous:

- Worldwide interest in powered flight was stimulated.
- The science of aerodynamics received a strong motivation.
- The US Government became interested in powered flight for potential defense applications.

In 1909 the Wright brothers built the first military aircraft under Government contract. During World War I, aircraft technology progressed rapidly. The flight speed reached about 150 mph, and the engine power output 400 horsepower. After the war military interest dropped, but aircraft technology had reached such a degree of maturity that two nonmilitary application fields could emerge, namely:

a. Commercial Aviation—Mail and passenger transport. (First all metal monoplane for passenger and mail transport: Junkers F13, 1919).

b. Stunt Flying leading to General Aviation. (Sport and private transportation).

In the period from 1920-1940, the speed increased to about 350 mph through evolutionary improvements in vehicle aerodynamics and engine technology; such as supercharger; variable pitch propeller; and improvements in engine design, structures, and materials.

At the end of World War II, the flight speed of propeller aircraft reached about 400 to 450 mph and the power output of the largest reciprocating engines was 4000 horsepower. This constituted about the performance limit of the propeller/reciprocating engine propulsion system. Today, the propeller/reciprocating engine survives only in smaller, lower speed aircraft used in general aviation.

During the 1930s, jet propulsion emerged which promised far greater flight speeds than attainable with the propeller/piston engine.

The first jet propelled experimental aircraft flew in Summer 1939, and in early 1941 the first prototype jet fighter began flight tests.

In 1944, mass produced jet fighters reached a speed of 620 mph.

In the early 50s, jet aircraft transgressed the sonic speed. In the mid 50s, the first supersonic jet bomber (Hustler) appeared, and later the B-70 which reached Mach 3.

Also during the 50s, through more than 15 years of military development, gas turbine technology had reached such a maturity that commercial applications became attractive:

a. Commercial Aircraft, e.g. Comet, Caravelle and Boeing 707.

b. Surface Transportation (land; sea).

c. Stationary Gas Turbines.

In the early 60s, the high bypass engine appeared which revolutionized military transportation.

In the end 60s, based on the military experience with high bypass engines, the second generation of commercial jet aircraft, the "Wide Body Aircraft" with large passenger capacity, such as the Boeing 747, and later the "Tri-Stars," came into being. By that time the entire commercial fleet exclusively used gas turbine engines.

Advantages for the Airlines were:
- Overall fan jet efficiency equivalent to diesel.
- Overhaul between about 5 million miles.
- Short turn-around time.
- Passengers enjoy the very quiet and vibration-free flight, the short travel time, and the comfort of smooth stratospheric flight.

By the end of the 60s essentially the entire business of passenger transportation was diverted from ships and railroads to aircraft.

In the mid 1970s, the third generation of commercial transport, the supersonic Concorde, 1500 mph, appeared with an equivalent power output of about 100,000 horsepower.

In summary, the evolution of aero-vehicle and areopropulsion systems looks, in hindsight, like a masterplan. The evolution began with piston engine and propeller which constituted the best propulsion system for the initially low flight speeds, and had an outstanding growth potential up to about 450 mph.

In the late 30s, when flight vehicle technology reached the ability to enter into the transonic flight speed regime (in excess of 500 mph) which was beyond the capability of the propeller/ piston engine, the jet engine had just demonstrated its suitability for this flight speed regime. A vigorous jet engine development program could be launched. Soon the jet engine proved to be not only an excellent transonic but also a supersonic propulsion system. This resulted in the truly exploding growth in flight speed.

It is interesting to note that military development preceded commercial applications by about fifteen to twenty years of both the propeller engine and the gas turbine engine. The rea-son is that too many generations of improved propulsion systems were required before a commercial utility could be envisioned.

Today, after 75 years of powered flight, the aircraft has outranked all other modes of passenger transportation and also has become one of America's greatest single export articles.

The evolutions of both aero-vehicle and aero-propulsion systems have in no way reached a technological level which is close to the ultimate potential! The evolution will go on for many decades toward capabilities way beyond current feasibility and, perhaps, imagination, which I will discuss later.

2. Let us now bring the beginning of jet propulsion in focus.

In the time period around the early 30s, aircraft performance was in a state of continuous advancement. The flight speed was around 250 mph, sufficiently away from any critical speed limit for airplane or propeller/piston engine; and therefore no immediate need for a radically new propulsion system seemed to exist. However, this situation changed in 1935 when the theoretical possibility of flight speeds near and above the speed of sound was envisioned by a swept-back wing. This historical event is described in Dr. T. von Karman's Memoirs, "The Wind and Beyond." Let me quote:

"The fifth Volta Congress in Rome 1935 was the first serious international scientific congress devoted to the possibilities of supersonic flight. I was one of those who had received a formal invitation to give a paper at the conference from Italy's great Guglielmo Marconi, inventor of the wireless telegraph. All of the world's leading aerodynamicists were invited.

"This meeting was historic because it marked the beginning of the supersonic age. It was the beginning in the sense that the conference opened the door to supersonics as a meaningful study in connection with supersonic flight, and secondly because most developments in supersonics occurred rapidly from then on, culminating in 1946—a mere eleven years later—in Captain Charles Yeager's piercing the sound barrier with the X-1 plane in level flight. . . . In terms of future aircraft development, the most significant paper at the conference proved to be one given by a young man Dr. Adolf Busemann of Germany . . . by first publicly suggesting the swept-back wing and showing how its properties might solve many aerodynamic problems at speeds just below and above the speed of sound."

The prospects of the propeller/piston engine as a propulsion system for flight speeds above subsonic speed were by far not as good as those of the aero-vehicle for a number of reasons. One of the major reasons is that the propeller becomes inefficient and very noisy at high subsonic flight speeds; another reason is that the power-to-weight ratio of the reciprocating engine is too small for high subsonic and supersonic flight speeds.

In hindsight, this situation was ideal for launching the development of a radically new propulsion system that promised the capability of flying much faster than the propeller piston engine. At that time time, however, the aircraft engine industry had no understanding of the need for future high speed propulsion systems. As a matter of fact in 1938, when the German Air Ministry tried to sponsor the development of turbojets, the aircraft engine industry was completely negative to such a project.

I cannot claim that I had a clear picture of the imminent need for jet propulsion, nor was I aware of the various turbojet propulsion patents already in existence such as the patent of Guillaume (1921) and the farsighted patent of F. Whittle (1930). My enthusiasm in jet propulsion was based more on the intuition that a continuous aerothermodynamic propulsion process could be inherently more powerful, smoother, lighter, and more compatible with the aero-vehicle than a propeller-piston engine.

In the Fall of 1933, my thoughts began to focus on a steady aerodynamic flow process in which the energy for compressing the fresh air would be extracted from the expanding exhaust gas. Such a steady flow process promised a far greater air volume handling capability than that of a reciprocating engine and consequently a much greater power concentration and power-to-weight ratio. Also, the air ducted into such a system could be decelerated prior to reaching

any Mach number-sensitive engine component. Both of these characteristics are of greatest significance for a high speed propulsion system.

First, I intended to accomplish this process without employing moving machinery by bringing the inflowing fresh air in direct contact with the expanding combustion gas (a kind of ejector process). But after studying specific processes and configurations, it became apparent that such types of processes would have enormous problems with respect to internal losses and adverse heat transfer effects caused by mixing between fresh air and combustor gas. I put this idea aside for future considerations and began to investigate a propulsion process in which compression and expansion were separated, and carried out by a turbo compressor and turbine respectively. Searching for an extremely lightweight, compact and simple configuration having a minimum development rise, I chose a radial outflow compressor rotor back-to-back with a radial inflow turbine rotor. This configuration also promised correct matching simply by providing equal outer diameters for the straight radial outflow compressor rotor and the straight radial inflow turbine rotor. I was aware of the possibility of employing axial flow compressors and turbines, and I considered an axial flow configuration as very desirable for future developments from a standpoint of small frontal area, but as too complex and expensive for the beginning. In particular, stage matching of a multistage axial flow compressor and matching of axial flow compressor and turbine without component test facilities appeared to me too risky.

During 1934, I conducted rudimentary design and weight studies and made some performance calculations based on a pressure ratio of 3:1 which appeared attainable with a single stage compressor and a turbine inlet temperature of about 1200 to 1400°F. It appeared that at a high flight speed of about 500 miles per hour, an overall efficiency could be obtained which was around 60% of that of an equivalent propeller piston engine. The corresponding high fuel consumption was somewhat discouraging. However, the weight of such a propulsion system promised to be only a fraction (quarter or

Figure 4. Back-to-back compressor-turbine rotor.

less) of that of an equivalent propeller-piston engine system. At that time the propulsion system of a fighter aircraft constituted a much greater weight portion than the fuel, and consequently the above trade between fuel weight and propulsion system weight seemed to be a very favorable one.

All in all, I was encouraged and began patent procedures. My greatest concern was what approach to choose for selling the idea of turbojet propulsion. I felt that in any case a working model would be most important, and so I decided at the end of 1934 to have a model built at my own expense at the auto repair shop and garage "Bartels & Becker" in Goettingen.

I was well acquainted with this repair shop and with the head mechanic and machinist, Max Hahn, long before I thought of jet engines. I had a small car which I parked there, and in this way I had frequent conversations with Hahn about automobiles and other technical subjects, and I had gained the impression that Max Hahn had an outstanding natural engineering talent and was specifically knowledgeable in manufacturing methods.

So it came that I discussed with Max Hahn

the cost and possibilities of building my demonstration model. I showed Max Hahn my sketches; he made many suggestions for simplification and changes to enable manufacturing the model with the machine tools of the auto repair shop. Hahn's ingenuity and practical mind brought the construction of my model within the realm of my financial means. Including combustor the total price estimate was slightly greater than 1000 marks! The actual price was somewhat greater, mainly due to some changes. It is difficult to convert in a meaningful manner 1000 marks' worth of machine-man hours of 1935 into dollars of today. If I would build the same model today, it probably would cost more than $10,000.

The photos show:

a. The back-to-back compressor-turbine rotor (one shroud being removed). (Fig. 4)

b. Primitive balancing on a lathe of Bartels & Becker's repair shop. (Fig. 5)

c. Max Hahn with the complete model engine. (Fig. 6).

In this time period I worked at my PhD thesis in the Institute of Physics, G. A. University, Goettingen, under Prof. R. W. Pohl. I showed Prof. Pohl my theoretical investigations, the results, conclusions and a program for my working model. Although this was quite an extracurricular activity, completely unrelated to my thesis and to the work of the Institute, Prof. Pohl was open-minded and reacted very positively. Generously, he gave permission for the use of instruments and equipment of the Institute and for conducting experiments in the back of his Institute. I made essential measurements of temperature and pressure distribution and gained valuable experience. Unfortunately, the gasoline combustors were not functioning. It appeared that the combustion did not take place within the combustor, but rather inside the radial turbine rotor extending into the exhaust jet; long yellow flames leaked out of the turbine, and the apparatus resembled more a flamethrower than a turbine. The malfunctioning of the combustors was substantiated by temperature indications on the metal surfaces and the

Figure 5. Bartels and Becker's repair shop.

formation of lampblack depositions. Self-sustained operation could not be achieved, however, the starter engine was greatly unloaded. While the experimental outcome was very disappointing for me, I cannot forget an amusing instance. Max Hahn, who normally was very stern and skeptical, seemed in this instance quite positive and optimistic. He expressed hope and optimism in view of the fact that the drive motor was greatly unloaded and that the flames came out at the right place with seemingly great speed.

These tests indicated to me that the fundamental combustor investigations and systematic developments were necessary which would require time and money exceeding my private means. Again, Prof. Pohl came to my rescue. In a very cordial discussion he declared that he was convinced of the correctness of my considerations and of the great future potentialities of jet propulsion. However, he suggested that industrial support would be necessary. Prof. Pohl was willing to give me a recommendation letter to any company of my own choice. Intuitively, I thought that the engine industry would be negative toward a gas turbine de-

Figure 6. Max Hahn.

31

velopment; and therefore I suggested the Hein-kel Corporation, since Heinkel was the sole owner of his airplane company, and his uncon-ventional thinking and enormous interest in the development of high-speed aircraft were generally known.[1] Prof. Pohl wrote a letter of recommendation to Heinkel, and thereupon Heinkel invited me to come to his home in Warnemuende. He arranged a conference be-tween me and a group of his leading engineers about my jet engine proposals. The engineers were undecided. The fuel consumption of the jet engine seemed to the group extremely high, but the power-to-weight ratio of a turbojet was considered as potentially better than that of the propeller-piston engine. Heinkel's two top aerodynamic designers, Siegfried and Walter Guenther, emphasized the need for high power output per frontal area (more than 2000 equiva-lent horsepower per square meter of frontal area). They also acknowledged the importance of abolishing the propeller in view of future high-speed aircraft. I suggested that the jet engine also could be utilized for the generation of direct lift. The back-to-back compressor turbine configuration could lead to a flat "pancake" type engine suitable for wing installation. The thrust could potentially amount to several times the engine weight. Heinkel's engineers felt that this jet engine application was not attractive; however, since they did not altogether reject the idea of jet propulsion, Heinkel entered into an agreement with me. Upon my insistence he made two separate contracts, namely one royalty agreement and one employment contract (be-ginning on April 15, 1936). Max Hahn also be-came employed upon my request, after initial difficulties were resolved.

Heinkel wanted to keep the jet development apart from his aircraft organization with the goal to form a separate gas turbine division in the event that the early phases of jet develop-ment were successful. For this purpose he

---

[1] I learned later that my belief about a negative attitude of the engine industry toward jet propulsion was very true; even the Air Ministry had great difficulties to persuade the engine industry to accept generous contract offers for jet engine development.

made a clause in my employment contract that I would report and be responsible directly to him for the development of the jet engine. However, for reasons of security this development was called *Sonder-Entwicklung*, i.e., "Special Devel-opment" rather than jet engine development. For the same reason he wanted the location of the "Special Development" to be separated from the rest of his company, and so a kind of temporary small building with an adjacent semiopen test stand was erected a considerable distance away from the main building complex. This building provided working space for eight people. After the building was finished (early June 1936), Heinkel detailed Max Hahn and Dip. Ing. Wilhelm Gundermann with initially two draftsmen to the Special Development.

Heinkel explained to me that he wanted the jet engine development to remain his own en-terprise, not sponsored by the Air Ministry. He was extremely anxious to fly with jet propulsion as soon as possible, and gave me as a technical target an engine thrust of about 600 kp. He wanted me to begin immediately with the de-sign of such an engine suitable for flight. Ground testing should begin after a time span of one year, on about June 1937.

It became quite clear to me that my original plan to develop first a well-functioning com-bustor and then begin with an engine design was impossible in view of the political climate and my rather tenuous position in the corpo-ration and, most of all, the great impatience of Heinkel. On the other hand, it was also clear to me, from previous experience with my first model, that a poorly functioning combustor could result in a nonfunctioning engine which could well mean the end of the turbojet project. In this situation I decided to follow a twofold approach, namely (a) to build very quickly a simple jet engine of minimum risk, which would demonstrate the jet principle in a very convincing and impressive manner, and (b) to begin immediately with a systematic gasoline combustor development. I was convinced that after a successful demonstration of a jet engine I could win the necessary timespan for the de-velopment of combustor and flight engine.

The combination radial outflow compressor

and radial inflow turbine in my judgment was an ideal configuration for a jet engine of very low development risk. In order to also have a very low risk combustor, I chose gaseous hydrogen as fuel, which was known to have a very high diffusion speed and a very wide fuel-air concentration range in which combustion is possible. I had conceived a hydrogen combustor which I was sure would function very well and would not need time-consuming pretests. This hydrogen combustor consisted of a large number of hollow vanes with blunt trailing edges placed within the airduct between compressor stator exit and turbine stator inlet (see Fig. 7). The gaseous hydrogen was ducted into the hollow vanes and was injected into the wake downstream from the vanes through a number of small holes along the blunt trailing edge. My greatest attention was devoted to the calculations and layout of the hydrogen combustion engine and to the development of the gasoline combustor. Gundermann and Hahn worked on a design concept using spin-parts riveted to ring flanges. Gundermann particularly made the mechanical calculations of the sheet metal rotors and discs. The Heinkel Corporation was, as an airframe company, well equipped to produce quickly large spin-parts, but was unable to manufacture the ring flanges and the rotor discs. These parts had to be manufactured in a nearby shipyard.

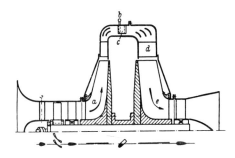

RADIAL TURBOJET (He S-1)
WITH HYDROGEN
(Built in 1936; tested in April 1937)

Radius of rotor - 1'
Thrust - 250#
10,000 RPM

Figure 7.

The gasoline combustor development program was as follows:

(1) Installation of a two horsepower Sirocco blower with controllable bypass.

(2) Investigations on segments of annular combustors
   • Influence of the shape of the combustion chamber
   • Flame holding mechanisms
   • Methods of gradual air addition
   • Factors influencing combustor volume for given pressure and fuel flow
   • How to obtain a low total pressure drop through the combustor.

(3) Gasoline vapor generation and injection into the combustor (generation of high pressure gasoline vapor by an electrically heated pressure boiler).

(4) Combustor utilizing atomized liquid fuel.

During 1936 we made only slow progress in the combustor development program because highest priority was placed upon design and construction of the hydrogen demonstrator engine He.S.1.

The He.S.1 engine was completed and installed in the test bed about the end of February 1937. I am not certain about the exact date of the first run of the hydrogen engine; it may have been in late February or early March.[2] During April most of our test runs were completed.

The apparatus fully met expectations. It reached the anticipated performance, it handled very well in acceleration and deceleration, probably because of the relatively small moment of inertia of compressor and turbine rotor and the great stability of the hydrogen combus-

---

[2] Heinkel wrote in his Memoirs that the first run of the hydrogen engine He.S.1 took place in Sept. 1937. This date is definitely wrong because I remember several comments in which nine months from the beginning to the first run were emphasized. In addition, I recall that water puddles in the vicinity of the jet made the demonstration very impressive. During March and early April we often had night frost, and prior to our first demonstrations to Heinkel's top engineers and important visitors, the test mechanic cracked the thin ice coverage of the puddles.

tor over the wide operational range. Most of all, the psychological effect was enormous. Heinkel and his engineers suddenly believed firmly in the feasibility of turbojet propulsion, and my position in the company was now very firm. It also was a considerable morale boost to my co-workers and to myself.

It should be noted that Whittle's engine made its first run at the end of April 1937; but in contrast to the Heinkel engine, the Whittle engine already operated with liquid fuel, and the first test run was witnessed and documented. For these reasons a comparison of the dates of the first test runs of Heinkel's hydrogen engine and Whittle's liquid fuel engine is, in my opinion, not meaningful.

After the successful demonstration of the He.S.1, Heinkel exerted a strong pressure for an accelerated flight engine program. We greatly intensified our combustor development efforts, beginning in May 1937; and in less than one year, in early 1938, a combustor with excellent operational characteristics and very low total pressure drop was achieved. These combustors worked best, however, with gasified fuel. The tests with atomized liquid fuel still exhibited some difficulties during starting and low-speed operation which were later overcome. Max Hahn had helped me most effectively in the experimental phases of the combustor development program.

I should mention here that Gundermann, Hahn and I worked as a team where each of us had an idea of strongest technical interest and competence: Hahn in manufacturing techniques and combustion experimentation; Gundermann in stress analysis and mechanical design. He also was head of the group of draftsmen. I gave the overall technical direction, such as utilizing hydrogen for the first test engine and establishing the program for the combustor development. I also made the layouts for the test engines, specifically the thermodynamic analysis and the internal aerodynamics, and became versed in the design techniques of axial flow compressors.

During the last months of 1937, the Guenthers began with predesign studies of the first jet propelled aircraft and specified as a necessary

thrust 500 kp. This aircraft was in many respects an experimental aircraft for demonstration of the principle and characteristics of jet propulsion, but had already provisions for some armament.

In late 1937, while I was working on various layouts of the flight engine, Max Hahn disclosed to me an idea of arranging the combustor in the large unused space in front of the radial flow compressor. He pointed out that this would greatly reduce rotor length and total weight. I thought that this was an excellent idea. I could see many additional mechanical and aerodynamical advantages. So I incorporated Hahn's suggestion in the layout of the flight engine and worked out the aerodynamics of the air ducts and the mixing of the flame gases with the by-pass air. (Figs. 8 and 9).

In view of the initial difficulties I had with Max Hahn's employment, it gave me great satisfaction to notify Heinkel and the Patent Division about Hahn's proposal. The company proceeded with an international patent.[3]

Aside from the combustor problems a major difficulty of the flight engine lay in the need for achieving a high massflow and high component efficiencies of compressor and turbine. The high massflow was obtained by an unconventionally large ratio of compressor rotor inlet diameter to rotor exit diameter. Normally such a compressor configuration would result in very large inlet losses caused by too high mach-numbers and too large inlet blade curvatures. I tried to reduce these losses by means of an axial inducer stage which gave the inlet flow both a precompression and a prerotation, thereby substantially reducing the mach number and curvature of the rotor inlet blading.

Since the flight engine had to be completed in a very short time (early spring 1939), we had to freeze the design in about early summer 1938. At that time the combustor with atomized liquid fuel injection was not working entirely satisfactorily; therefore, we used the system

[3] The Encyclopedia Britannica speaks of a joint patent of Max Hahn and Hans von Ohain. This is incorrect; Hahn was the sole inventor of the "Front Combustor" configuration. The von Ohain patents had been applied for several years prior to Max Hahn's patent application.

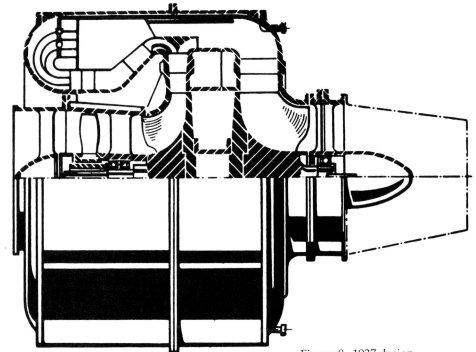

Figure 8. 1937 design.

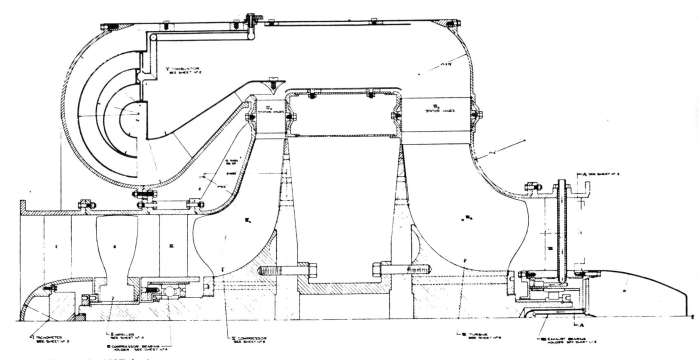

Figure 9. 1937 design.

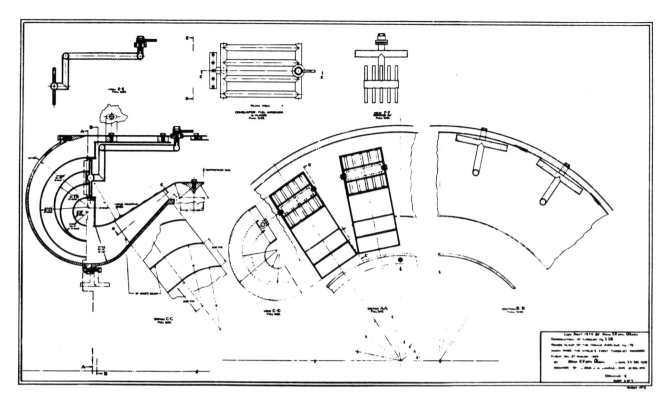

Figure 10. 1938 design.

with internal fuel gasification for the first flight engines (Fig. 10). It was planned to utilize an independent accessory drive for the first flight engines; for later engines, utilization of the atomized liquid fuel injection and a mechanical accessory drive developed by Gundermann was planned.

About early 1938 the detailed design of the He-178 began. Gundermann made essential contributions to the shape of the air inlet, and the air and exhaust gas ducts (Figs. 11 to 14).

In late spring of 1939 engine and airframe were completed, but the net thrust was considerably below the anticipated 500 kp; therefore, a take-off from the relatively short company air field was not possible. We made a number of internal engine adjustments, specifically in the exchangeable compressor-diffuser and turbine stator. In August the engine performance reached nearly the anticipated values. On August 27, 1939, Heinkel's test pilot, E. Warsitz, made the first successful flight.

Heinkel immediately informed high Air Ministry officials about this flight and invited them for a demonstration which took place in Fall 1939. To Heinkel's disappointment, his visitors were quite indifferent. Nevertheless, a few months later Heinkel's proposal for a jet fighter, the He-280 with two HeS8A turbojets installed under the wing, was accepted by the Air Ministry (Figs. 15, 16 and 17).

It is not the purpose of my presentation nor is it possible to give here a complete picture of the German turbojet development; however, a few facts and highlights may be appropriate.

In the early phases of the German turbojet development, from about 1936 to the early '40s, the higher echelons of the Air Ministry were skeptical or disinterested in turbojet development. In strong contrast to this attitude, the technical group of the Air Ministry headed by Hans Mauch and later by Helmut Schelp were from the beginning strong proponents of this new propulsion system. In fact, Schelp had personally investigated the best application regimes of advanced aeropropulsion systems including the propeller gas turbine, the bypass engine, the pure turbojet and the ramjet, which

Figure 11. Detailed design of the He 178 in 1938.

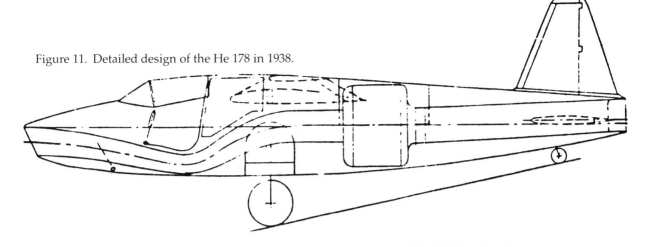

Figure 12. The world's first aircraft to fly purely on turbojet power, the Heinkel He 178. Its first true flight was on August 27, 1939.

Figure 13. The He 178.

Figure 14. The He 178.

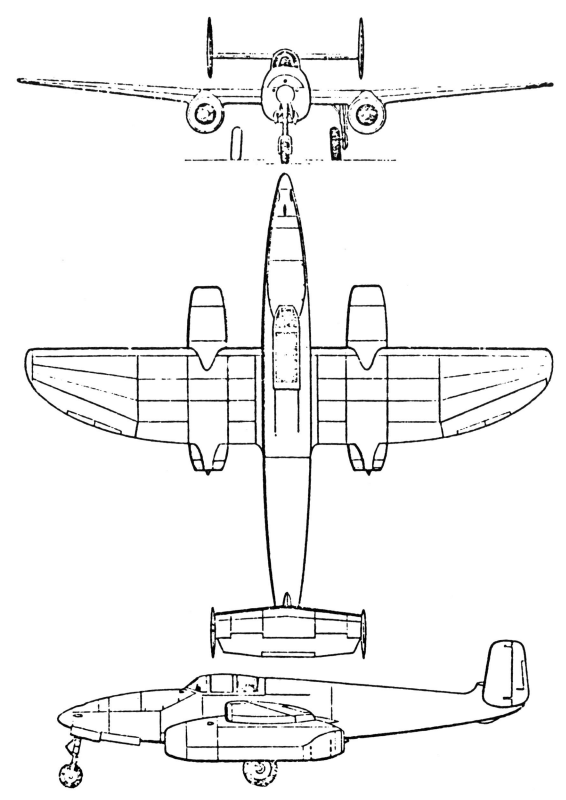

Figure 15. The He-280, the Heinkel jet fighter.

Figure 16. The He S8A

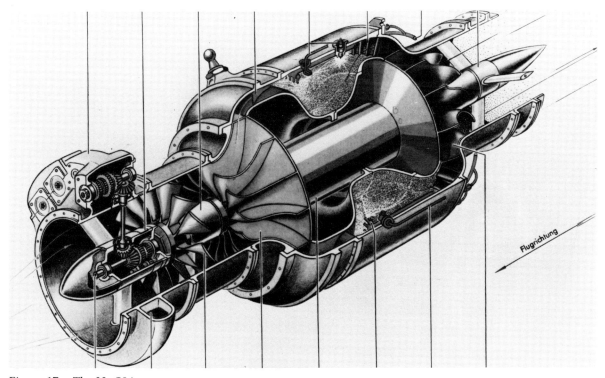

Figure 17. The He S8A

he presented to the German Academy of Aeronautics in the late 30s. He used the results of his study for planning and guiding purposes. Both Mauch and Schelp appreciated Heinkel's early efforts, which strengthened their position. However, they were concerned that Heinkel, as a pure airframe company, could not succeed with a production engine because of Heinkel's complete lack of experienced engine designers, facilities, and machine tools. Therefore, Mauch and Schelp approached the German aircraft engine industry in 1938 and offered contracts for study and development of turbojets. The aircraft engine industry, however, did not believe in nor was interested in gasturbine engine developments. After many initial difficulties Mauch and Schelp finally succeeded in their negotiations with Junkers, Bramo, BMW; and these companies accepted jet engine study contracts, while Daimler Benz ultimately refused. The Junkers' development of the 004 engine was headed by Dr. Anselm Franz who was in charge of internal aerodynamics and turbo superchargers, while Dr. Herman Oestrich became head of the 003 development team after Bramo and BMW had merged.

Heinkel's competitors had larger teams with great engine design competence and excellent facilities. Heinkel realized the need for an engine company and made an agreement with the Air Ministry to purchase the Hirth Engine Company — a side condition was that the He-280 should make its first flight in Spring 1941. The He-280 actually flew for the first time on April 2, 1941, and a few days thereafter Heinkel could acquire the Hirth Company.

In subsequent flight tests of the He-280, a top speed of 485 mph was attained at 20,000 ft. altitude, but higher speeds (about 550 mph) were expected once the anticipated engine thrust (1600 lbs) would be reached.

During the following two years, nine prototypes of the He-280 were built and tested at military proving grounds, and on various occasions flight demonstrations were made. In one instance a mock combat between the He-280 and a contemporary propeller fighter was arranged where the He-280 displayed clear superiority.

In the Spring of 1942, prospects for preproduction of the He-280 looked favorable, while the Messerschmitt 262 with axial flow turbojet Jumo 004 was plagued with several problems and delays. However, this picture soon changed when the main difficulties with the Me-262 were resolved by early 1943. The Me-262 proved to be superior over the He-280 with respect to both aircraft and engine performance and was chosen for future large-scale production. Therefore, in March '43, work on the He-280 was terminated. The performance of the Messerschmitt advanced rapidly and in mid 1944 a speed of 624 mph was demonstrated.

By the end of 1944, the BMW engine (003) was chosen for the Heinkel He-162.

For the Heinkel Corporation the most important result of the early flights of the He-280 was the acquisition of the Hirth Company. In 1942 I joined with my team the newly created Heinkel-Hirth Company. The former Hirth Company not only had excellent shops and facilities, but also outstanding scientific as well as practical engineers and support personnel. Integration of the former Hirth and Heinkel teams into a restructured broader organization proceeded very harmoniously. Top engineers of the Hirth group received leading positions in this new organization. One noteworthy example is Dr. Max Bentele, renowned aeromechanical engineer with a national reputation in turbine blade vibrations. Dr. Max Bentele became Chief of the Gasturbine Component Development Division in the newly-formed Heinkel-Hirth organization.

In Fall 1942, the Heinkel-Hirth Corporation received a government contract to develop a new turbojet, the HeS.011. The technical and performance specifications had been worked out by H. Schelp of the Air Ministry, who then had envisioned the future need for a higher performance engine for new applications as well as a replacement of the Jumo 004 and the BMW 003. Emphasis was placed on a high compression ratio of about 5:11 for greater fuel economy and aircraft range, a thrust of 3000 lbs, and no utilization of strategic materials such as nickel which called for a completely air-cooled turbine.

We abandoned the radial outflow compressor

Figure 18. Air cooled axial turbine devised by Max Bentele.

and radial inflow turbine, which are living on, however, in small gasturbines. Dr. Max Bentele devised a novel air-cooled axial turbine with a most efficient utilization of cooling air and extremely low manufacturing cost (Fig. 18). By the end of 1944 the specified performance had been met and transgressed, and production drawings had largely been completed. Beginning of production was scheduled for early summer 1945.

In Great Britain the early turbojet development was carried out by essentially one man, Sir Frank Whittle. His first turbojet patent in 1930 of an axial flow compressor followed by a radial inflow compressor represented a very advanced configuration. Although radial flow compressors in large turbojet engines have been abandoned for a long time, they may have an

excellent chance for a comeback as the last stage in a multistage axial flow compressor in large fan engines.

Whittle's first test stand engine, having a single U shape combustor, ran in April 1937, which represented the first liquid fuel aircraft gasturbine test run in the world. Sir Frank Whittle achieved his goals in the face of greatest adversities. His struggle and final success, and the early phases of Great Britain's industrial jet developments are excellently described in his book *Jet*.

In the United States, the Navy became interested in turbojet propulsion in 1938 and directed a high level advisory committee, composed of renowned engineers and scientists, to assess the potentialities of this new propulsion system. This committee gave a completely negative report on the usefulness of turbojets for aircraft propulsion. Since von Karman was particularly concerned with this report, I would like to quote again his Memoirs:

"On top of this, jet propulsion received a tremendous setback in the United States when a high level board of engineers set up by the U. S. Navy reported in 1938, after official studies, that gasturbines and compressors might be all right for ships but they were too big and ponderous for flight. Nor was the weight likely to be reduced in the foreseeable future, they added. So in 1938, the U. S. engine industry passed up jet propulsion and thus missed one of its greatest opportunities to become a pioneer in the field that in less than twenty years would revolutionize trasportation. Ironically, I was a member of that Navy-sponsored board, and I learned one lesson out of it that I have never forgotten. If you accept membership on a board, you should attend its meetings and read its reports. I was away in Japan at the time the turbine report was written, and I allowed my name to be used without reading it. When I returned to the United States and learned what had happened, I was furious with myself."

It is not possible for me to determine the extent of damaging effects this Navy report may have had on potential jet developments in the United States. In any event, such a damage was minimized by actions of the U. S. Army Air Corps. In summer '41, General H. Arnold became aware of the Whittle engine and its aircraft, the Gloster E 28/39, which had made its first flight in May '41. General Arnold recognized the enormous future potential of jet propulsion. After an agreement was signed between the American Secretary of War and the British Air Commission, the Whittle engine and drawings were shipped to the United States in late Sept. '41. Upon direction of General Arnold, a copy of the Whittle engine was to be built by the General Electric Company in Lynn, Massachusetts, because of the company's great experience in superchargers. At the same time a twin jet airplane powered by the G. E. engines was to be constructed by Bell Aircraft Company in Buffalo. A few months thereafter on March 18, 1942, General Electric built Whittle engine GE1A, ran on the test stand; and Oct. 3, 1942, the Bell Airacomet (XP-59A) equipped with two GE1A engines flew successfully at Muroc, California and reached flight altitudes up to 10,000 ft. For the United States the Jet Age had begun, and soon after this flight the U. S. industry was building jet engines of their own design.

In France, turbojet development was essentially dormant during World War II. After the war Dr. Oestrich and his team who had developed the 003 which ultimately had demonstrated outstanding performance characteristics went to France and laid the foundation for France's turbojet industry. The enormous know-how of this group and the advanced turbojet projects they transplanted to France minimized the effects of France's inactivity in aircraft gasturbine development during the war, and in the mid '50s the French Caravelle and the British Comet were the earliest mass produced passenger jet transports in the world.

In Russia, I believe, the acquisition of Rolls Royce engines has made a great impact on Russian jet technology; but the entire Russian turbojet evolution is not sufficiently known to me to assess this with certainty.

3. The early jet engines were simple and had a ratio of power output to weight far more favorable than piston engines (about two to three times greater), and were capable of greater flight flight speeds than propeller engines because the compressor elements were shrouded. However, lifetime, reliability, and overall fuel efficiency were substantially below the standards of propeller/piston engines.

Consistent with the initally stated thrusts, the broad goals in the gasturbine development can be briefly stated as follows:

- Improvement of Structural Integrity for Greater Endurance, Life Reliability, and Total Life Cycle Cost Reduction: Since the late 40s, a tremendous effort has been made to combat fatigue by analytical investigations of vibrations, creation of advanced diagnostics techniques, advanced materials and manufacturing processes. Through these efforts the engine life has increased from 20-40 hours in the mid '40s to currently 10,000 hours and more.

- Improvement of Overall Efficiency (Thermodynamic and Propulsive Efficiency) for Increasing Fuel Economy, Range, and Total System Cost: The first step toward higher thermodynamic efficiencies was increasing the turbine and compressor pressure ratio. From pressure ratios of 4:1 in the mid '40s to 10:1 in the '50s, 20:1 in the late '60s, and perhaps 40:1 in the future. Such high pressure ratios necessitate more than one spool compressors, variable stator vanes, better shrouds, seals, and possibly gap control. As a consequence of the increasing number of variable geometry engine components, the control systems became more and more complex and sophisticated.

  While the thermodynamic efficiency was continuously improved, the propulsive efficiency had to be increased also in order to attain highest overall efficiencies. For this purpose the ducted fan engine was employed by which the massflow of the jet is increased, while the average jet velocity is decreased, resulting in an improved propulsive efficiency. The first ducted fan engines were built in the mid '50s with relatively low bypass ratios (1:1 to 2:1). The problems associated with high bypass ratios, around 5:1 and possibly greater, were resolved in the early '60s with the help and support of the Aero Propulsion Laboratory, Wright-Patterson Air Force Base, especially of Cliff Simpson.

- Improvements of the Ratios of Thrust-to-Engine Weight and Frontal Area: Improvements in thrust-to-weight ratio have a strong impact on aircraft maneuverability, flight envelope, and speed capability. Unfortunately, the above described improvements in overall efficiency have inherently an adverse ef-

fect on the thrust-to-weight ratio of the engine. However, simultaneously with the efficiency improvements, strong efforts had been made to reduce engine weight. This resulted in the trends shown in Fig. 2 which indicate that both overall efficiency and power-to-weight ratio increased over the years. The weight reductions were achieved by the following means:

- Advanced designs constantly striving towards stronger and lighter structures.
- Lighter, stronger, and more heat resistant materials.
- Increase in throughflow per frontal area approaching the theoretical limit.
- High stage pressure ratio in compressor and turbine to reduce number of stages and thereby total engine weight.
- Higher Turbine Inlet Temperature: In the mid '40s, turbine inlet temperatures were around 1400°F. These temperatures were increased continuously through the following technological advancements: more uniform and suitable combustor exit temperature profiles, improved internal cooling methods, advanced materials and meterials treatment, such as directional solidification, and advanced manufacturing techniques. As a result, today's turbine inlet temperatures are nearly doubled.
- Increase in Engine Size: In the early '40s the engine thrust was ranging between 1000 and 2000 lbs. With the advent of the large jet transports and jet bombers in the early '50s, engine thrust rose to more than 10,000 lbs. With supersonic aircraft and still larger transports (C5A and Boeing 747), the thrust of the largest engines is now greater than 50,000 lbs.
- Constant and Variable Cycle Engines: For aircraft missions with constant speed over most of the mission time, for example a long-range transport with flight machnumber 0.9, the engine would be optimized for this particular flight speed.

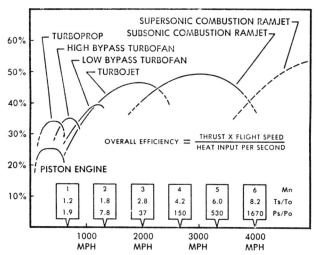

Figure 19. Trends in Aero Propulsion Efficiency.

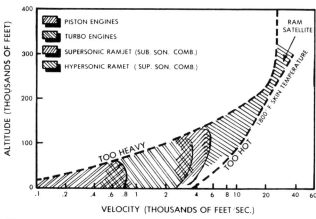

Figure 20. Speed and altitude regimes.

Efficiency trends of various types of aeropropulsion systems for single speed operation are shown in Fig. 19, which I will discuss briefly:

- For subsonic flight, the propeller-gasturbine with very high pressure ratio is the best propulsion system.

- For transonic flight the high bypass ratio ducted fan engine is the most suitable engine. At this flight speed the ram pressure begins to contribute to the engine efficiency.

- In low supersonic flight, M~1.5, a low bypass ratio ducted fan engine can be slightly better than the turbojet. Engine pressure ratio can be reduced due to high ram pressure.

- At higher supersonic flight speeds, Mach~2 to 3, the ram pressure becomes most significant and a low pressure ratio straight turbojet represents the best propulsion system.

- Beyond Mach 3 the ram pressure becomes so high that a turbojet would not contribute to overall efficiency, and the subsonic combustion ramjet is the best propulsion system.

- Beyond Mach 6 ram pressure and ram stagnation temperature are too high for a subsonic combustion ramjet. There-

fore, the air at the beginning of the combustion is decelerated only to a lower supersonic speed which led to the term supersonic combustion ramjet.

It is interesting to note that the overall efficiency of aeropropulsion systems increases as their operational flight mach number increases. The speed and altitude regimes for the various types of propulsion systems are shown in Fig. 20.

With the advent of supersonic flight, emphasis was placed on efficient flight operation, not only at one specific supersonic flight speed but over a large regime of flight speeds. For example, a supersonic passenger transport requires not only very efficient engine operation at supersonic design speed but also at transonic speeds for climbing, flying over the American continent, or crossing half the Atlantic in case one engine fails. Another quite different type of multimission would be a Vertical or Short Take Off and Landing (V/STOL) aircraft with efficient transonic or supersonic cruise requirements. Engines which have to operate efficiently in different flight speed regimes are often called "Variable Cycle Engines." In the broadest sense, they have the objective to achieve a reasonable compromise in total efficiency over a range of anticipated flight speeds. Of course, over this anticipated speed range, engine thrust must be matched to aircraft thrust requirements, and engine massflow to the massflow capturing characteristics of the inlet duct for avoiding spillover drag.

The idea of the variable cycle engine is more than two decades old, and some supersonic engines actually have what could be called variable cycle features. The variable cycle engine to its full entent is a future objective; it depends perhaps greatly on the ingenuity of a specific variable cycle engine concept—whether performance gains and fuel savings will outweigh the increased weight and complexity of engine and control system.

Broadly sketched, these were the ways the evolution of aircraft gasturbine engines progressed from the simple, low performance, short life turbojets 35 years ago to the complex, high performance long-life engines of today.

4. Now, I would like to addresss two questions which are often raised:

1. Is the current state of engine evolution at a point where further technological advancements are of diminishing returns?
2. Is the current gas turbine situation similar to that of the piston engine in the mid '30s, when a major breakthrough in form of a radically new engine was just around the corner?

To the first question, the answer is NO: Future technology advancements of strictly evolutionary nature will have an enormous impact on future propulsion systems. Specifically, beneficial effects will be obtained on the following engine characteristics: Reliability; operational characteristics; manufacturing cost; fuel economy; maintenance; range of engine applications; flight envelope; maneuverability. The compounded effects of these technology advancements over the next decades will give the impression of a technological breakthrough in comparison to our current state-of-the-art engines. The underlying estimates of technology advancement are as follows: The overall efficiency, which currently is already as high as that of a diesel engine, may advance by 15% to 20%, and the thrust to weight ratio may well increase by a factor two. Variable cycle technology

very likely will advance, which may furthermore contribute to fuel saving.

To the second question: It is not possible to predict or rule out the coming of radical innovations. One might speculate, however, in what areas radical innovations could have a strong impact on propulsion. Examples for such areas could be:

- Application of new energy sources and energy release processes to propulsion including Air-Rocket Hybrid systems for high speed propulsion..
- New methods of efficiently transferring energy to environmental air (current methods are limited to turbomachinery, and waves employed, e.g., in the complex).
- Radically new methods of functional integration of aero-vehicle and aeropropulsion system.

These examples should illustrate that "radical" innovation must not immediately be equated with "antigravity" or violation of the basic laws of Newton or of Thermodynamics.

To the other part of question 2, namely: is the current gasturbine engine situation similar to that of the piston engine in the '30s? The answer is No:

In the mid '30s, it was shown that the aero-vehicle could fly at high transonic and supersonic speeds, while the propeller/piston engine could not exceed about 450 mph, or at best 500 mph. Therefore, the new gasturbine propulsion system in the mid '30s unlocked a new frontier in flight speed. This situation does not exist today. Today, in any flight speed-altitude regime where an aero-vehicle conceivably can fly, an aeropropulsion system can operate. Therefore, whenever a major breakthrough in aeropropulsion should occur, it will not unlock a new flight speed frontier, but could lead to more efficient, less expensive, lighter propulsion systems, potentially with application for V/STOL.

Let us now discuss some other promising areas for future technology efforts:

Important future technological advancements can be expected from the area of Engine Airframe Integration. Currently, the major concern is to achieve a full understanding and finally a reduction of engine installation drag under all major flight conditions. An additional area which promises potentially great future gains is the area of "Functional Engine Airframe Integration." From this area evolutionary as well as radical innovations may emerge. The evolutionary efforts may be concerned with the following topics:

- Improved methods of preventing flow separation by boundary layer control through employing fan air without loss in overall propulsive thrust.
- Drag reduction and efficiency improvement through propulsion by boundary layer acceleration.
- Thrust augmentation; Thrust vectoring for V/STOL applications.
- Improved methods of engine induced supercirculation.

Another very important future endeavor is total cost reduction. Efforts will be directed toward improved manufacturing processes, design simplifications, reduction of maintenance time, increase in life and reliability, and also improved performance such as increased overall efficiency and thrust to weight ratio.

The last and most fascinating frontier may be the evolutionary approach toward supersonic and possibly hypersonic long-range transportation. Ironically, one major obstacle to high speed transportation is that portion of the journey which takes place on the ground between home and embarking the aircraft and between debarking and place of destination. In essence, remodeling the total airport system is one of the most important and challenging tasks for supersonic transportation to become more widely accepted.

Another obstacle, of course, is the economical problem of supersonic flight. Fuel is a strong factor and engines with variable cycle features will be needed. The solution will not come alone from the engine. Work on a better L/D of the airframe will be equally or even more important.

Finally, the environmental problems, whatever they may be, must be clarified and solutions must be found.

In my opinion, it is most likely that supersonic transportation on a much broader scale than currently with the Concorde will come, but it is difficult to estimate the time. We may have to think in decades rather than in years.

From the Wright brothers' first aircraft engine in 1903, the evolution of aeropropulsion systems progressed with ever-increasing vigor to the present. Ahead of us still lies probably a greater time span until this evolution reaches a plateau.

46

Jet Fighters

Walter J. Boyne and Donald S. Lopez

The words *jet* and *fighter* go together naturally since both connote power and speed. The jet engine with its raw power, its high power-to-weight ratio, and its relatively low frontal area was the answer to the fighter designer's prayers.

Fighter aircraft require high power-to-weight ratios to provide the speed and maneuverability necessary for their mission. During WWII fighter design was reaching the limit of performance available with the reciprocating engine and propeller combination. The advent of the jet engine opened a whole new range of performance for fighters. Top speeds have more than tripled since its introduction.

This photographic essay shows some of the steps in the evolution of the jet fighter from 1939 to the present.

As is so often the case, a major war led to a major technological development. Although the basic principles of jet engines had been known for many years, World War II spurred Germany and Great Britain to develop practical jet engines for aircraft. Hans von Ohain in Germany and Frank Whittle in Great Britain followed separate successful paths to propellerless flight.

On August 27, 1939, the first aircraft powered by the jet thrust of a gas turbine engine, the Heinkel He 178, lifted off the ground of the Marienehe Airfield in Germany. Not a fighter, this research aircraft's mission was to test the feasibility of this new mode of propulsion. The slim fuselage housed the Heinkel He S 3b engine designed by Hans von Ohain. The aircraft, a model of which is shown here, was designed by Ernst Heinkel.

The Caproni-Campini N. 1 was powered by jet thrust but did not use a true turbojet engine. The aircraft, shown in flight and during a ground test with the aft section removed, had very poor performance and was never considered for production. It first flew on August 28, 1940. It is now in the Italian Air Force Museum near Rome.

The Heinkel He 280 V-1 was the first jet aircraft designed as a fighter and the third jet aircraft to fly. The first flight took place on April 2, 1941. Although designed as a fighter, the Me 262 had superior range and armament and went into production in lieu of the He 280. It served mainly as a test bed for the Heinkel He S 8 engines. Note that the engines are uncowled in this flight due to cooling problems. Only nine aircraft of this type were constructed. The later models were powered by Junkers Jumo engines. *Courtesy Peter M. Bowers*

On May 15, 1941, the Gloster E.28/39 took off from the runway at Cornwall, England, the first Allied jet aircraft and the fourth jet to fly. Built around the Whittle centrifugal flow engine, the Gloster's sole role was to evaluate and demonstrate the capabilities of that engine. Its success prompted officials to order Gloster to proceed with the design of a jet fighter. The E.28/39 can be seen in the Science Museum in London.

As soon as the success of jet engines became apparent, the warring powers employed them in the design of combat aircraft. Their limited range and engine life dictated that they be used initially in fighters. Germany, desperate for a means of stopping the devastating Allied bombing raids, led the way followed by Great Britain, the United States, and, somewhat later, by Japan. After World War II, almost all new fighter aircraft were jet powered.

The first U. S. jet aircraft, the Bell XP-59A Airacomet, made its first flight on October 1, 1942, at Muroc, California. It was powered by two General Electric Type I-A turbojets developed from Whittle engines supplied by Great Britain. Sixty-six P-59's were produced, including the three XP-59A's, and the thirteen YP-59A's. Designed as a fighter, it was never used in combat and served primarily as a trainer in jet operations.

The first operational U. S. jet fighter was the Lockheed P-80 Shooting Star. The XP-80 was designed around the British de Havilland H-1 turbojet engine by a Lockheed team led by Clarence L. (Kelly) Johnson. The first flight was made at Muroc, California, only 143 days after work started. Production models were powered by General Electric (Allison) J33 engines. Although the P-80 did not enter combat in World War II, it was the standard U. S. fighter in the immediate postwar years. The trainer version, the T-33, continued in production through August, 1959. Of the almost 7500 P-80's built, 5691 were T-33's.

The first U. S. fighter powered by an axial-flow type turbojet, the P-84 Thunderjet, first flew in February, 1946. Of the almost 4500 of the straight-wing P-84's produced, more than 2000 were purchased for NATO Air Forces. P-84's were used for escort and general attack in the Korean War. In 1950, two P-84's equipped with probes for aerial refueling made the first non-stop jet crossing of the Atlantic. The Thunderjet was the first single-seat fighter capable of nuclear bomb delivery.

North American FJ-1 Fury, first in a line of jet fighters that led to the F-86 Sabre, became the first jet fighter to serve in an operational unit at sea. In March, 1948, Navy fighter squadron VF-5A, equipped with Furies, went to sea aboard the USS *Boxer*. Only 33 FJ-1's were produced due to the advent of more advanced fighters.

The first jet fighter to become operational was the Messerschmitt Me 262 Schwalbe (Swallow). It was first flown on July 18, 1942, powered by two Junkers Jumo 004 turbojet engines. High level indecision and engine development problems delayed its entry into combat until the fall of 1944. Although it was successful as a bomber interceptor it was introduced too late to have a major effect on the bombing raids. Only about 15% of the 1433 Me 262's built were used operationally.

The Gloster Meteor was the first operational jet aircraft in the RAF and was the only Allied jet used in combat in WW II. The first Meteor flight took place on March 5, 1943, in the fifth prototype, powered by de Havilland Halford H-1 turbojets. Later versions were powered by Rolls-Royce Wellands and finally by Rolls-Royce Derwents. Meteors were first used in combat against V-1 flying bombs and achieved their first victory on August 4, 1944. Meteors were first line RAF fighters until 1955.

On July 21, 1946, a McDonnell XFD-1 Phantom landed on the USS *Franklin D. Roosevelt*, the first pure jet U. S. aircraft to make a carrier landing. The Phantom powered by two Westinghouse J30 turbojets later became the first operational jet fighter of the U. S. Marine Corps. Only 62 of the FD-1's, later redesignated as FH-1's, were produced.

On October 14, 1947, USAF Captain Charles Yeager in the Bell X-1 became the first to exceed the speed of sound. Some of the first swept wing fighters were able to fly faster than sound in shallow dives, but not until the early 1950's were fighters able to exceed Mach 1 (the ratio of the aircraft's speed to the local speed of sound) in level flight. There were many problems in the relatively new field of super-sonic aerodynamics to be solved, including flight controls, inlet nozzles and airfoils.

The North American F-100 Super Sabre was the first fighter in the world capable of supersonic speed in level flight. The Super Sabre, with 45 degrees of sweepback (versus 35 degrees in the Sabre) first flew on May 25, 1953. The F-100C set the first supersonic world speed record when, on August 20, 1955, it was flown at 822.135 mph. F-100's saw worldwide use with the USAF and logged many combat hours in Vietnam. Almost 3,000 F-100's were built.

The Convair F-102 Delta Dagger was the first delta-wing aircraft to become operational in the U. S. Air Force. An all-weather intercepter, it was the first operational USAF fighter armed only with missiles and rockets. When first flown on October 24, 1953, the aircraft could not achieve supersonic speed in level flight. After several major design changes, including the application of the Whitcomb area rule, its performance improved markedly. More than 1,000 F-102's, including trainers, were built.

The English Electric Lightning, the first British supersonic fighter, replaced the Hunter as the first-line RAF fighter in the early 1960's. The sharply swept-back wings and the unusual over-under configuration of the two Rolls-Royce Avon turbojet engines give the Lightning a distinctive appearance in flight. First flown on December 2, 1952, some 230 Lightnings have been produced.

56

The versatile Dassault Mirage III made its first flight
on November 17, 1956, and became operational
in 1962. This delta wing fighter served in the air
forces of fifteen free-world countries, including
Australia, France, Pakistan and Switzerland. More
than 1,000 Mirages have been produced. The Mirage
V, a fighter-bomber, shown here, uses the same
airframe as the Mirage III.

As jet engines thrust fighters deeper into the transonic flight regime, their speed became limited by aerodynamics instead of by power. The swept-back wing was one solution for this problem. Widely adopted by designers, the now familiar bent wing appeared in all the major Air Force fighter forces. Most of the jet-to-jet combat in the Korean War involved the swept wing MiG 15 and the swept wing F-86 Sabre.

The Hawker Hunter was the principal RAF fighter from 1955 to 1962. It was first flown on July 20, 1951, and became operational in late 1954. Hunters were powered by either the Rolls-Royce Avon or Armstrong Siddely Sapphire engines. The final version, the Hunter F-6 used a 10,000 pound thrust Avon. More than 1,000 Hunters were produced for the RAF.

The twin-engine MiG-19 was the first Soviet fighter capable of level supersonic flight. The MiG-19 was first flown in September, 1953, and became operational in 1955. The wings have a sweepback angle of 55 degrees. It was used by all the major Communist air forces and by Pakistan in the 1965 war with India.

The Grumman F9F-6/8 Cougar was a swept-wing
version of the F9F-2/5 Panther. The Cougar used the
same fuselage and empennage as the Panther but
the wing was completely new. The Cougar first flew
on September 20, 1951, and became operational on
November 1952. They were the first swept-wing
fighters used by the Blue Angels. Almost 2,000
Cougars were produced.

The design of the first Soviet swept-wing fighter, the MiG-15, was based on German and Russian research. It was first flown in 1947 powered by a Rolls-Royce Nene turbojet engine. Production models used Russian modifications of the Nene. It was the primary opponent of the USAF Sabre during the Korean War. The MiG-15 was widely used by Soviet Bloc nations, being built in four countries and used by eighteen air forces.

The Dassault Mystere IV-A has been used in both the fighter bomber and intercepter role. The first flight of this aircraft was made on September 28, 1952, and the first production model was delivered in June 1954. The Mystere has been used in combat by the Indian Air Force and by the Israeli Air Force. More than 400 Mysteres were produced.

Originally designed as a straight wing fighter
similar to the Navy FJ-1, North American decided
to use the newly available results of German research and make the F-86 Sabre the first U. S. swept-
wing fighter. The first flight was made on October 1,
1947, using the Allison J35-C-3 engine and on May
18, 1948, the first F-86A, powered by the General
Electric J47-GE-1, was flown. The F-86 was much
faster than contemporary straight-wing fighters and
could exceed the speed of sound in a dive. The F-86
achieved a remarkable combat record against the
MiG-15 in the Korean War. More than 6,000 F-86's
were built.

McDonnell F-4J Phantom II

As jet engines produced more and more thrust and new roles were devised for jet fighters, aircraft designers employed many strange wing and fuselage forms to accommodate the requirements. Words like delta, double-delta, canard, manta, Coke-bottle, etc. were used to describe the shapes of these new aircraft. Some of the fanciful designs in the science fiction books were matched or exceeded by actual aircraft.

Vought F7U-3 Cutlass

Fairchild A-10 Thunderbolt II

Convair F-106 Delta Dart

MiG-21D (Fishbed-D)

Saab 37 Viggen

Grumman F-14 Tomcat

Saab 35E Draken

Douglas F4D-1 Skyray

McDonnell XF-85 Goblin

Gloster Javelin

Republic F-105G Thunderchief

Lockheed XF-104 Starfighter

The Development of the "Jumo 004" Turbojet Engine

Anselm Franz

With the introduction of the turbojet engine, an extraordinary advancement was made in aviation which had a revolutionizing effect on our entire world. This fundamentally new approach to aircraft propulsion made it possible to achieve a major improvement in overall aircraft performance.

The principle of the gas turbine has been known for a long time. Since the beginning of the twentieth century many attempts had been made to build a practical gas turbine powerplant. The great success of the gas turbine, however, came with its application to the propulsion of aircraft. For this application it seemed to be predestined not only because of its low weight and small dimensions but especially because with this engine jet propulsion could be realized and the flight speed limitation inherent in the old propeller drive could be eliminated. The principle of this engine, the turbojet engine, seems to have been proposed first in

DR. ANSELM FRANZ studied mechanical engineering at the Technical University of Graz in his native Austria. In 1936, he joined the Junkers Engine Company in Dessau where he eventually became Chief Engineer. In 1939 he designed the Jumo 004, the world's first axial flow turbojet and the first jet engine to be produced in volume production and to be used in combat. Most subsequent jet engines used the axial-flow principle. Following the war, he came to America where he first worked for the U. S. Air Force, and then for AVCO Corporation's Lycoming Division. He became Vice President of Lycoming, retiring in 1968, but while with the firm he designed a number of highly successful engines, including the T53 and T55 series of gas turbine engines, and the first T55 high-bypass turbofan engine.

1921 by Guillaume.[1] Serious efforts to develop a turbojet were begun in 1936, in England by Frank Whittle and in Germany at the Heinkel Aircraft Company by Hans von Ohain. Von Ohain's work is distinguished by the fact that with his experimental engine known as the He S-3b, the world's first turbojet-powered flight was realized on August 27, 1939. In spite of this early success, work at the Heinkel Company did not lead to a producible engine. Whittle's engine W-2 was the forerunner of the Rolls Royce Welland, which was produced in some numbers. Also in 1936, work to develop a turbojet was started at the Junkers Aircraft Company in a plant in Magdeburg by Herbert Wagner, the head of aircraft development. The engine they built, however, could not run under its own power and the project was abandoned in 1939.

At the Junkers Engine Company in Dessau, I began with a jet engine study late in 1938. In 1939, the Air Ministry wanted us to take over Wagner's engine, but I refused and in the Fall of 1939, we started under a government contract with our own design, the engine that became known as the Jumo 004. Both von Ohain's and Whittle's engine had radial flow compressors.

In the history of the development of jet propulsion, the Jumo 004 engine can claim to have been the world's first successful axial flow turbojet engine, a configuration that became

---

[1] French Patent 534801

standard in jet engine design. The 004 was also the first jet engine in volume production and combat service.

The design of the 004 had already many similarities with turbojets of today. As shown in Figure 1, the engine consisted of an 8-stage axial compressor, six individual combustion chambers, a single stage axial turbine which drove the compressor and a jet nozzle equipped with a movable center cone with which the exit area was automatically adjusted to various operating conditions. From the very beginning, this jet nozzle was designed for the incorporation of afterburning. For regulating the engine, a control was developed which was equipped with an isochronous governor that held the selected speed and, in connection with the jet nozzle control, the gas temperature approximately constant in the operational range. For starting and the low speed range, manual control was provided. The engine control and the other accessories were arranged on top of the compressor housing; the starter was placed in the compressor inlet hub fairing.

For the development of such an unorthodox engine, neither examples nor experiences existed. It was really an advance into unknown territory. In order to reduce the risk and insure success, I decided not to try for the maximum that seemed achievable but to set a rather conservative goal. I believe this approach was one of the main reasons why this completely new type of engine could be developed and put into production in such a short time. Of course, we also used existing knowledge and experience as far as possible, as for example in the design of the compressor blading where we relied on the work done by the AVA Goettingen,[2] and for the turbine where we used the experience in steam turbines of the AEG Berlin.[3]

At that time the entire Engineering Division of the Junkers Engine Company was under greatest pressure to develop and improve its reciprocating aircraft engines. It was not possible to get any engineers transferred to the new jet engine program. I, therefore, started this work with a few key people of my rather small department for supercharger and exhaust jet development and on that basis we gradually built up, mainly with newly employed young engineers, a new independent organization for the development of the jet engine. Over the years, this new organization, which grew from a few people to about 500 in 1944, also was equipped with quite elaborate experimental and test facilities including a material's laboratory, a general test field, test stands for combustor, compressor and engine testing and ultimately even with an altitude chamber engine test cell.

With an engine consisting of three major components as discretely different as the compressor, combustor and turbine, the logical approach would have been the systematic independent development of these individual components using special test stands. Such test equipment with the power supply necessary for compressor and turbine testing, however, was not available early enough. For experimental investigations and evaluations of these components, a complete running engine was required. We, therefore, first designed and built the experimental engine 004A which was intended to be thermodynamically and aerodynamically identical with the final product but was otherwise designed to obtain a running unit in the shortest possible time with no regard to engine weight, manufacturing considerations, or a restriction in strategic materials. Highly alloyed materials were used for all hot engine parts. Based on the results obtained with this engine, the production version 004B was to be designed.

The only component with which we were able to conduct a systematic bench test development was the combustor. While I felt that an annular design would be somewhat superior, we selected six can-type combustors. They seemed to present less development problems, but especially the necessary air supply was available for bench testing of a single can. The principle approach to the combustor design was to separate primary and secondary air and to provide in the center of the combustor can a

[2] *Aerodynamische Versuchs Anstalt*, Goettingen
[3] *Allgemeine Elektrizitates Gesellschaft*, Berlin

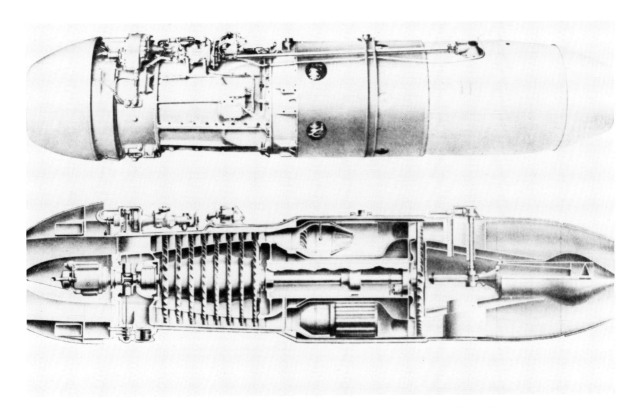

special flame chamber for primary combustion with close to stochiometric mixture ratios. In order to obtain good mixing and a short flame length, the primary air was introduced in this chamber with a swirl and the fuel was injected with a swirl nozzle against the airflow. This independent combustor development was successful and of high importance to the overall program. It provided the very first engine with an operating combustion chamber of known and quite satisfactory performance.

The design of the experimental engine 004A was completed in the Spring of 1940 and the engine made its first test stand run on October 11 of that year. In December, the engine was brought to full speed of 9000 RPM and in January 1941, a thrust of 430 kg (946 lb) was reached. At that time, a delay in the development testing was caused by vibration failures in the compressor vanes. With a changed stator design, however, the thrust of 600 kg (1320 lb) required by contract was obtained in August 1941 and in December of that year, a 10-hour run was accomplished and a thrust of 1000 kg (2200 lb) was demonstrated. The first flight of an 004A in an

Figure 1. Jumo 004 Turbojet Engine

Me 110 flying test bed took place on March 15, 1942.

The Me 262, powered by two 004A's, flew the first time on July 18, 1942.

Based on these extraordinarily promising results, the Air Ministry issued a contract for 80 engines of this type that was originally intended for experimental engine testing only. These 80 engines, rated at 840 kg (1850 lb) thrust, were to be used for further engine development and for airframe and application testing.

The 004A engine, however, was not suitable for real production not only for manufacturing reasons or because of its too high weight for a flight engine (850 kg/1870 lb), but also because it had much too high a content of strategic materials. The amounts of nickel, cobalt, molybdenum, etc., that were required for the heat resistant materials of this engine were simply not available under the conditions at that time. Therefore, when designing the production

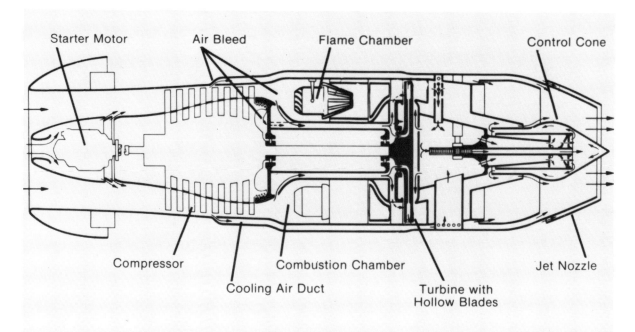

Figure 2. Air Cooling System of the Jumo 004

Figure 2. Air Cooling System of the Jumo 004

model 004B, besides changes for weight reduction and ease of manufacture, a far-reaching and very radical transposition was carried out from heat resistant materials partially to materials that were free of any strategic metal. Almost all hot sheet metal parts, including the combustion chamber and thrust nozzle, were changed to mild sheet steel SAE 1010. The surfaces of these sheet metal parts were protected against oxidation by an aluminum coating. New special solutions in design were required in order to keep the temperature of the sheet metal within acceptable limits by means of air cooling. As an example, the thrust nozzle may be mentioned here. Figure 2 shows schematically the design of the nozzle and it is indicated how the various parts of the nozzle including its inner control cone were cooled by air extracted from the compressor after the fourth stage.

The first production model was the 004B-O. Its weight was reduced from the 004A weight of 850 kg (1870 lb) to 750 kg (1650 lb) and the weight of strategic materials to less than half of that of the A-engine. The B-engine with its modular design also appeared to be quite suitable for production. With an additional modification of the first two compressor stages, the model that went into production, the 004B-1 engine with a thrust of 910 kg (2000 lb), was produced. The first B-1 engine was delivered in June 1943 and an Me 262 flew the first time powered by two 004B-1's in October. 100-hour tests were completed with several engines and an overhaul time of 50 hours was approved. During the Summer of that year, while testing this engine, vibration failures in the turbine buckets were encountered. Such failures occurred when, at full speed, blades with a rather low natural frequency came into resonance with an excitation caused by the six combustion chambers. Sometimes we used rather unusual methods. In this case, we hired a professional musician with perfect hearing who determined the natural frequencies of individual blades in assembled turbine wheels by means of a violin bow. The problem was finally solved by slightly increasing the natural frequency of the blades (increasing the taper) and by reducing the full speed of the engine from 9000 to 8700 RPM.

With this speed of 8700 RPM, the 004B-1 had the following characteristics:

airflow . . . . .21.2 kg/sec (46.6 lb/sec)

pressure ratio 3.14

gas temperature . . .775°C (1,427°F)

thrust . . . . .910 kg (2,000 lb)

specific fuel
    consumption . . .1.4 kg/kg hr (lb/lb hr)

The engine weighed 750 kg (1650 lb); it had a diameter of 760 mm (30″) and a length of 3860 mm (152″). The compressor blading was designed with zero reaction, i.e., the total pressure increase was performed in the rotor cascades. The turbine had 20% reaction. At the point of operation (static, sea level, full power), the adiabatic efficiency was 78% for the compressor and 79.5% for the turbine. The combustion efficiency was 95%. In altitude chamber tests the predicted altitude performance of the engines had also been proven. The tests showed that with the speed control combined with the automatic jet nozzle adjustment a full throttle operation of the engine with close to constant gas temperature was obtained (Figure 3).

From the beginning, it was intended to use hollow air-cooled turbine blades. But in order to get an operating engine quickly, the 004A was equipped with solid buckets and solid stator vanes. The 004B turbine had hollow air-cooled stator vanes from the outset but the production started with solid turbine blades while a parallel hollow blade development was conducted. Two different versions of hollow blades were developed, one manufactured with a deep drawing process and the other produced from conically rolled sheet metal by folding and welding at the trailing edge. While the material of the deep drawn blade, the Krupp alloy Tinidur, contained 30% nickel, Cromadur, the material of the sheet metal blade was free of nickel completely. This blade also appeared to be more reliable in operation and it was still somewhat

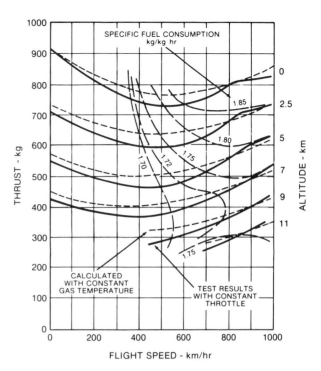

Figure 3. Maximum Thrust JUMO 004B From Altitude Chamber Test

easier to produce. With regard to suitability for volume production, of course, both blades were far superior to the solid buckets. As indicated in Figure 2, air extracted at the compressor exit was used as cooling air for these turbine blades and for the hollow stator vanes. The hollow turbine blades were introduced into production in the 004B-4 model late in 1944.

The results of all the efforts to reduce the strategic material content of the engine were quite remarkable. With the hollow Cromadur sheet metal turbine blade, a complete 004B engine contained no nickel and less than five lb chromium.

It should be of special interest that the model 004E was already equipped with afterburning. The fuel for afterburning was injected immediately in front of the turbine stator. With the turbine inlet gas temperature increased to 870°C (1600°F), the engine had a thrust of 1000 kg (2200 lb) without, and 1200 kg (2640 lb) with afterburning. After several 100-hour tests, the engine was scheduled to go in production in 1945.

Figure 4. Messerschmitt Me 262 Jet Fighter

The 004E was the first turbojet engine with afterburning.

Volume production of the 004B-1 started at the beginning of 1944 with delivery of the first engines. In spite of the extremely difficult conditions, the engine was built in steadily increasing quantities. Within a year, remarkable delivery numbers were achieved. For example, 950 engines were delivered in January 1945, 1100 in February and 1300 in March. Altogether, close to 6000 Jumo 004 engines had been built by the end of the war.

In addition to the Me 262, the Jumo 004 turbojet was also the powerplant of the Arado 234, a twin engine light bomber and reconnaissance aircraft that was produced in smaller numbers. Used for reconnaissance, this aircraft was quite successful due to its superior flight altitude and speed.

The large application of the Jumo 004, however, was the Messerschmitt Me 262 (Figure 4), which was in volume production towards the end of the war. This jet fighter was very successful thanks to its superior speed of 850 km/h (530 MPH). As mentioned before, the Me 262, powered by two Jumo 004 engines made its first flight on July 18, 1942. I remember vividly this significant event at the airport in Leipheim. Messerschmitt was also there. The plane was standing at the beginning of the runway, ready for takeoff with Fritz Wendel at the controls. The engines were turned on and Wendel carefully brought them to full power. Now he released the brakes, the plane rolled, and he held her down to the ground probably to the end of the runway which seemed endless. Suddenly, this airplane left the ground and, propelled by these two 004 jet engines, as seen from where we stood, climbed almost vertically with unprecedented speed until it disappeared in the clouds. At this moment, it was clear to me that the jet age had begun.

Power Plants — Past, Present, and Future

Gerhard Neumann

The rapid and dramatic growth of aviation over the past several decades is a matter of history with which we are all quite familiar. Integral to that growth has been the mushrooming progress in powerplant technology which, by necessity, is the lead factor in the development of aircraft systems.

This paper highlights some of the major milestones that have influenced the course of developments in gas turbine powerplants. It traces its origins in work done on turbosuperchargers, with discussion of the stimuli and shifts in requirements that resulted in various types of jet engines leading up to today's high-bypass turbofans. The natural quest to fly higher, faster and farther has reached a point of relative maturity in technology, so that today's efforts can now be directed more towards improvements in efficiency, reliability and ecological consciousness.

The future holds new challenges. It calls for new ways to control the spiraling costs of de-

GERHARD NEUMANN has been with the General Electric Company since 1948 where he developed the Variable Stator compressor system, now standard in most all jet engines of the world. A native of Germany, he originally went to China to maintain aircraft for the Chinese Nationalist Air Force. But with America's entrance into World War II he joined the U.S. Army Air Corps in China as an engineering specialist. He came to America in 1946, and during his years at General Electric he has served as General Manager of the Jet Engine Department and the Flight Propulsion Division, and in 1968 he was appointed Group Executive of the Aircraft Engine Group. Today he works on special projects for the Vice Chairman of the Company.

velopment and production of powerplants. In the face of higher and higher fuel costs, there is a need to strive continuously for lower fuel consumption, and at the same time, to study alternate sources of energy for gas turbines. And there is much yet to be done in making engines as clean and as quiet as the public demands.

Because today's climate is characterized by fewer new product opportunities, diminishing support for research and development, and cost/price inflation affecting both the manufacturer and customer, technology progress in the future may be less spectacular than in the past, but will be just as meaningful and beneficial to the future of aviation.

As we all know, the aircraft gas turbine—the jet engine—has had a tremendous impact on the course of aviation. To understand where we are today, it is helpful to trace briefly the history of the technological achievements that made our rapid progress possible.

It really started as far back as 1903—the same year as the powered aircraft—with a man named Sanford Moss (Fig. 1). As a graduate engineering student at Cornell, Moss shook the quiet Ithaca campus with his ear-splitting experiments. He succeeded in operating a turbine by burning fuel in a chamber under pressure. How were Moss's efforts received at the time? Perhaps his quote from his professor will give you an idea: "Whatever he thinks he is doing, it is not likely worth the noise, smokes and smells. In fact, it is very likely to be worth noth-

Figure 1. Sanford Moss

ing at all." The complaining professor was Dr. Durand who 15 years later, as the Chairman of National Advisory Committee for Aeronautics (NACA), would call on Moss and General Electric to develop a practical turbosupercharger.

So, the world was not exactly holding its breath waiting for the gas turbine in the early 1900's. To the best of our knowledge, the technology lay dormant until 1917 when the United States entered World War I. Due to pressure of the War, scientists in the U. S. and France were working feverishly on the development of a device that would enable reciprocating aircraft engines to operate at high altitudes. This device was the turbosupercharger which, as you know, boosted piston engine power by compressing air into the engine intake. By then, Moss had gone to work for General Electric as head of its turbine research department. He led an ambitious U. S. Army-funded program that culminated with a successful experiment conducted atop Pikes Peak in Colorado in 1918 (Fig. 2). It is interesting to recall that Moss in-

sisted that the competitive selection between the GE and French turbosuperchargers be based on tests in the intended operating environment and not merely on a test bench. Even in those years, the engine people were pioneering, trying to be as realistic in the testing of powerplant components as possible!

In 1920, a LaPere biplane (Fig. 3) equipped with turbosuperchargers broke the world altitude record at over 33,000 feet. It nearly broke the pilot as well: without heated clothing or oxygen he nearly froze; he passed out and only came to at 4,000 feet altitude, in time to straighten and land. The same plane broke the record again a year later by reaching 41,000 feet. In this same period, turbosuperchargers provided power boost for General Billy Mitchell's bombers in his effort to demonstrate that air bombardment would be more effective in sinking surface vessels than Naval gunfire. In fact, without the turbos, Mitchell could not have reached the altitude required to illustrate immunity from anti-aircraft fire.

Progress in the supercharger technology continued through the late 30's, and in 1939, a B-17 bomber equipped with turbosuperchargers set a cross-country flying record of nine hours and 14 minutes. By this time, the first "over weather" commercial flight between distant cities had been accomplished, thanks to the turbosupercharger . . . the maiden flight having been made in 1937 between the "distant" cities of Kansas City, Missouri and Dayton, Ohio in a TWA Northrop Gamma monoplane.

The dark pre-World War II days approached and, once again, another world conflict accelerated the progress of aviation.

By September 1939, both the English and the Germans had done work that showed that gas turbines had considerable potential for high-speed flight. In England, Frank Whittle (Fig. 4) had received a patent for a turbojet engine in 1930, when he was a 23-year-old RAF Flying Officer, but he had little luck in getting his designs approved for development. In Germany the first patent for a jet engine was awarded to an aeronautical engineering student, Hans von Ohain in 1935. Work to see what could be done with it was undertaken promptly, and the first

Figure 2. Three technicians, hand-in-hand, prepare to start a Liberty airplane engine equipped with the world's first turbosupercharger. The General Electric device, even at this high altitude, improved the performance of the engine from 230 h.p. to 356 h.p.

Figure 3. "The test vehicle and the men." Lt. John A. Macready, Dr. Sanford Moss, Major George E. A. Hallett and General Electric technician, Adolph Berger, standing, left to right, beside the LaPere Aircraft with supercharger installed.

Figure 4. Frank Whittle

engine to reach flight stage was a von Ohain 1,100 pound thrust turbojet that flew in the Heinkel He 178 on August 27, 1939, five days before the German invasion of Poland. In Italy, a Caproni "Jet" flew in 1940 with what could be called a Giant Geared Supercharger with bypass. Whittle's engine first flew in May 1941 in England.

German jet engine development progressed at a fantastic pace, indeed, with axial-flow compressors providing a very small engine frontal area, and with "Ersatz" turbine buckets formed of sheet metal, and liquid-cooled to survive the then relatively high turbine gas inlet temperatures. German ingenuity also developed a movable plug to modulate the turbine exhaust area, and introduced both a BMW and Junkers engine into the Luftwaffe by 1944. Soon, squadrons of German jet-propelled fighters challenged the fleets of American B-17's and B-24's (themselves equipped with turbosuperchargers) whose defending air crews simply could not

believe their eyes when heretofore secret, propeller-less airplanes swooshed by at the incredible speed of over 500 m.p.h.! Although major damage was done to Allied air fleets in the final months of the War, it was Hitler's personal reluctance to mass produce jet aircraft at an earlier date, and successful bombing of the German fuel-producing factories that avoided a near disaster to Allied air forces, at such a late stage of the War. Even the Japanese began to produce German-designed jet engines whose drawings and experimental hardware were transported from German-occupied France to Japan via submarine in a six-month long underwater odyssey! However, Japanese production of jet planes never got beyond the very beginning stage.

The U.S. lagged in its own jet engine effort until 1942. Whatever studies were made showed that gas turbines would be too heavy for aircraft use. Nevertheless, important component development work was going on at NACA's Lewis Research Lab—studies which would become useful later on. In fact, encouraged by results of a similar design by NACA, General Electric initiated design of an axial-flow compressor turboprop.

A visit by General Hap Arnold, Commander of the U.S. Army Air Corps, to the Royal Air Force in the U.K. in early 1942 resulted in picking up Frank Whittle's drawings and—with British approval—having jet engines produced in the U.S.A. Because of the obvious need for secrecy, General Arnold was unable to hold an industry competition to choose the firm charged with copying the Whittle engine. With its long experience in steam turbines, the development of turbosuperchargers and high temperature materials, General Electric was chosen to be the lead pony. There is still today—in the Lynn plant in Massachusetts—the first test cell of the first jet engine built in the U.S.A. The project was kept so secret that even the wife of a GE engineer with whom Frank Whittle stayed in Lynn—on a temporary assignment to help GE launch the jet age—had no idea of the Englishman's identity or what his visit was all about.

Although handicapped by the lack of critical manpower and materials shortages, the first

Figure 5. The XP-59A.

jet engine in the U.S. was built from British drawings and tested within six months of program go-ahead. Concurrent with the engine work, Bell Aircraft in Buffalo, New York, was building the XP-59A Airacomet aircraft. One year after the start of the project, the XP-59A (Fig. 5) took to the air in its successful first flight. The jet age was born in the United States! The engine was designated the "I-A" (Fig. 6) and produced 1,250 pounds of thrust. It weighed 1,000 pounds.

The early history illustrates a point connected with the origin of the aircraft gas turbine that is still valid today: it takes longer to design and develop and to bring into production a jet engine than it takes to produce a new airplane system. And it is primarily the advances made in engine work that make it possible to come up with an aircraft to do new and different jobs. The famous DC-3 was no different: this aircraft was dependent on Curtiss-Wright committing a 25-30% growth of the R-1820 engine, and had

Figure 6. The "I-A" engine.

Figure 7. The J47 engine.

to wait for this to come true before the airplane became available.

Through the 1940's, the U. S. Government was the sponsor for aircraft gas turbine work in the U. S. This period was characterized by a proliferation of military weapons systems. It was an experiment of sorts—and attempts were made to put the new gas turbine toy on almost every kind of airplane. The large diameter centrifugal compressor was abandoned in favor of the smaller diameter axial-flow one; steam turbine and farm equipment technology was discontinued in favor of real aircraft-type structures, lightweight flanges, compact controls, thin discs and short-cord blading. Soon came the first operational U. S. jet fighter, Lockheed's Shooting Star, which went into volume production with the GE J33 turbojet. GE's axial-flow J35 and J47 (Fig. 7) engines pushed thrust up to

6,000 pounds and power-to-weight ratings above 2:1. Concurrently, the first axial-flow engine was developed to drive a 1,000 hp turbo-prop; the advent of the Berlin Crisis and the Korean War caused the Department of Defense to order tens of thousands of J47's which were made with and without afterburners, to power a host of aircraft, including 2,000 B-47 Bombers (each with 6 engines), and thousands of North American F-86 Sabre Jets (which set speed records in excess of 650 m.p.h. and contributed to a 10:1 air victory ratio against the Russian MiG's in the Korean War). Even the giant B-36 with its six huge piston-powered propellers, sported four J47 engines under the wings for additional thrust when needed. Studebaker and Packard were enlisted to produce major engine components, and they did a tremendous job in a very short time. More than 35,000 J47's were produced in all, with the highest production rate of 1,000 engines in a single month! The average price of a J47 in

Figure 8. Navy fighters achieve Mach 2.

those days was $32,000—complete! And did you know that the J47 was the first jet powerplant to be certified in the U. S. for commercial aviation in 1949?

Then came the 1950's and a number of technological breakthroughs were made which provided even better weapon systems. In the United Kingdom, the birth of the commercial jet engine—a derivative of a military one—ushered in the Comet, a truly beautiful and remarkable airplane, but a plane beset by a string of bad luck. Industry, however, began to get a good feel for what a commercial jet could do, and what it could not do, resulting in the successful introduction of the American Boeing 707 which was a derivative of the KC-135 Tanker for the U. S. Air Force.

It is not possible to chronicle all the technical achievements of this period in which lines of supersonic fighters and bombers were created, but some of the most significant breakthroughs were the development of the Variable Stator

Compressor (permitting higher airflows and pressure ratios of single rotors), modulating afterburners, air-cooled turbines, front and aft-fan bypass engines. In 1954 General Electric even put on a test stand in Arco, Idaho, a nuclear-fuel powered jet engine which accumulated more than 100 hours of trouble-free running on nuclear energy alone. Air speeds for fighters (Fig. 8) and bombers of Mach 2 and above became routine, and commercial airliner speeds moved into the high subsonic range.

A personal aside that illustrates the persistence of our aerospace products. Just as Bill Littlewood's specified aircraft—the DC-3—is still going strong in some parts of the world "40-plus" years after first service, so will the J79 engine (Fig. 9) for whose prototype I had the design responsibility, outlast me. We expect to have the J79 in production through 1980 (that

Figure 9. The J79 engine.

will be more than 25 years) and expect it to remain in service well into the 1990's.

Other innovations in gas turbine technology during the 1950's saw the development of very small and light engines for helicopters and small turboprops for transports, engines whose compressor blades were no bigger than the nail of a small finger and whose rotor churned away at 25,000 rpm. Their bigger brothers, were also introduced in derivative versions for marine and industrial applications. Better materials permitted higher turbine temperatures, and titanium contributed substantially to lighter engines.

The 1960's saw the rapid growth of the commercial air transport systems and the relative decline in dominance of military applications, although in the year 1960 the U. S. Department of Defense was procuring 30 different military systems equipped with aircraft gas turbines—the result of the experimentations of the 1950's. Changes in the state-of-the-art became primarily of an evolutionary nature, and contributed to the very successful flights of the B-70 Bomber (Fig. 10) and SR-71 flying in excess of Mach 3. Advanced V/STOL systems were also created, the most notable of which was the Army's XV-5A where two large fans (with their axles in vertical position) were buried flush in the wings and were driven by the exhaust of conventional jets in the fuselage. In 1963 President Kennedy launched the American SST program; its related engine developments contributed substantially to the wonderful engines we are seeing today in subsonic transports: it was primarily the experience gained with the large fans in the XV-5A, and the turbine film-

cooling schemes developed for the SST, which enabled General Electric to develop an advanced technology engine core culminating in the creation of the first high bypass turbofan, the engine of today and the near future.

The high bypass turbofan demonstrated a cycle that improved fuel consumption by 30% over the best jets then available. As with any breakthrough in the past, the high bypass fan engine was born out of a need: the U. S. Air Force was studying the feasibility of a huge transport which would have the capability of handling a payload of 100,000 pounds, with a non-stop range of 6,000 miles. The powerplant would have to operate at efficiencies exceeding commercial transport requirements of that time. Power to drive such a huge transport required engines in the 40,000-pound thrust class—vs. 18,000 to 21,000 pounds thrust in transport engines then operational—with capability for growth needed beyond that figure. To get the high thrust and low fuel consumption necessary, the answer was the high bypass turbofan.

(And to think that it was as late as 1957 when the chief of a leading engine company wrote to the head of the largest airline in the U.S.A.: "There is nothing a fan can do that a jet cannot do, easier and better . . .")

General Electric's TF39 engine (Fig. 11) with an eight-foot diameter front fan coupled with an advanced technology core engine was selected for the world's largest airplane, Lockheed's C-5 (Fig. 12); the day of the supersized transport was with us.

As always when a new unproven idea is proposed there are numerous "can't do it" comments; for the high bypass turbofan they were: excessive nacelle drag, impossible turbine temperatures, too high pressure ratio.

Through the development of a novel turbine-

Figure 10. The B-70 Bomber.

cooling technique—film-cooling—turbine blade metals that heretofore limited gas temperatures to about 1800°F could now accommodate up to 700°F hotter gas in this new engine. Key to such an enormous breakthrough were two new manufacturing processes permitting the drilling of thousands of tiny holes into superalloys through which the cooling air could flow and thus shield the blade surface from the hot gas: the electrostream and laser beam drilling techniques. Another major challenge arose when compressor pressure ratios were increased. In the 1940's, when axial-flow compressors replaced centrifugal-flow designs, the ratios started to climb to 7:1. In the 1950's, single rotor compressors with variable stators, and dual rotor compressors were both capable of 12:1 pressure ratios. In the 1960's the combina-

Figure 11. The TF39 engine.

Figure 12. Lockheed's C-5.

tion of dual rotor and variable stators resulted in pressure ratios of 25:1 . . . two-thirds of that from the high pressure compressor alone, a record in itself.

The high bypass engine became the engine for the wide bodies and you have probably all enjoyed the benefits of this in air travel on a 747, DC-10, L-1011 or A300 Airbus.

The 20 years from 1950 to 1970 were an extraordinary time. Airlines were moving from reciprocating power to turboprops, to turbojets, to turbofans, and from using 50-passenger to 350-passenger aircraft. In the engine business, literally everything was tried:

- Nuclear-powered turbojets were developed and actually ran.

- We burned hydrogen, methane, coal, even boron enriched fuel was burned.

- Engines were built for tilt-wing turboprop, tilt-prop turboprops, tilt-pod turbojet, swivel nozzle turbofans, direct lift engines of ultra light weight, elaborate ejector cavities for lift augmentation, and lift fans—all to achieve VTOL.

- Fan power was provided for astronaut training to simulate landing on the moon.

- A range of air vehicles appeared, which spanned from the tiny jet pack turbojet to lift off one man to the SST efforts in Europe and the U. S.

- The industry was able to cut fuel consumption by over 50%, improve power to weight by a factor of five, improve reliability dramatically as measured by time between overhaul and keep the cost per pound of thrust nearly constant.

Where do we go from here? It is true that breakthroughs are still being made but they tend to be different in nature than those of the past. We became experts in making engines that go higher, faster, farther. Today, there are new and different requirements. The products that come along this decade will reflect selection, consolidation and refinement of the technology gains made in the 1950's and 1960's. It is painfully true that today's engines still have their problems: there is the puzzle of erosion of parts and in-service deterioration of performance. The mechanical reliability of blades, vanes, gears, lube systems, engine controls, thrust reversers, all need much improvement to allow the user desired availability status. And the total cost—Life Cycle Cost—must be controlled all the way from cradle to the scrap heap.

In getting to where we are today, the Free World aircraft gas turbine industry has grown to significant proportions to where we now:

- Employ more than 150,000 people.
- Operate in facilities worth more than $3 billion at replacement cost.
- Occupy more than 50,000,000 square feet of space.

Perhaps our biggest challenge for the future is how to manage these resources in what has become essentially a mature market for the product. We must do it in the face of some very interesting facts of life about this business. For instance, worldwide military strategy is highly variable, constantly shifting the amount of support given to aircraft engines. And the commercial market has essentially a "bite and digest" buying cycle. Airlines buy the airplanes, they then digest all of that capacity until they are ready to buy again . . . So we have up and down swings in the market. Added to these market characteristics is the fact that we face ups and downs of the general world economy as an overriding trend to the saleability and desirability of our product. Net result is that each segment of the served market is somewhat cyclical. Even though at times our military market is counter-cyclical, we still must accommodate the fact that we have those ups and downs.

In addition to these market considerations, long life cycle itself impacts greatly on how we must operate. I used as an example General Electric's J79 engine on which development work started in 1950. Production started in 1954 and is still continuing, and the J79 will be in

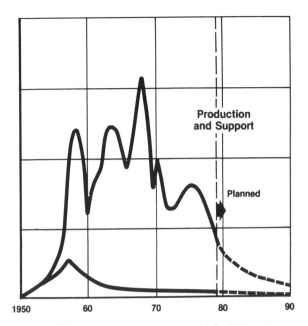

Figure 13. Production and support of the J79 engine.

service well into the 1990's (Fig. 13). At that rate, a 25-year-old engineer could join a company within a given engine project, retire at age 60, and have worked only on that one project. That gives you an idea of the long life cycle of our product. We had better do it right when we do it, because it's going to be with us a long, long time.

Next, there is the important overall question of cost of the technology. In terms of value of the engine, we have been able to deliver improving performance to the customer without commensurate increase in actual monetary cost. As one measure, if you divide engine industry sales in any given year (in constant dollars) by the number of pounds of thrust generated by all engines shipped that year (total power produced), it reveals that increasingly sophisticated products are being delivered at nearly constant cost to the customer (Fig. 14). One good example of technology payoff in terms of value lies in the high bypass turbofan breakthrough of the mid-1960's. Compared to former generation engines, the high bypass turbofan gave us a 30 percent improvement in installed thrust-to-weight ratios . . . in other words, more power for less weight, which translates into lower operating cost.

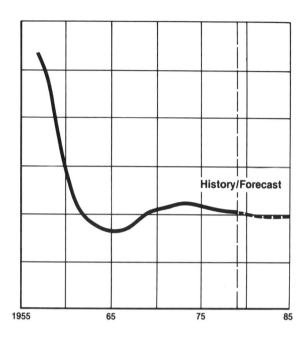

Figure 14. Engine cost to the customer.

In the future we expect further improvement in thrust-to-weight to come from the research we are now doing with materials. For example, the engine producers are doing extensive laboratory work with composite materials. These show great promise in that they enable the making of lighter weight and lower cost parts compared to metals. We can use them on lightly loaded, cooled portions of the engine, and they are proving to be highly reliable. But composites are not the total answer: hot gas is our energy source and the hotter the gas we can accommodate, the smaller, lighter and more efficient the engine becomes. These desirable improvements are achieved through advances in overall materials technology as well as through cooling systems designs. Materials development is taking on new directions as a result of changing requirements: for sure, performance and weight improvements still receive our attention, but most of the earlier progress has already been gained in this area. Now we are spending more and more of our emphasis on reliability, longer life and cost reduction. And we see the trend in this direction continuing.

Significant impact on the cost of engine development will be felt from application of the "design-to-cost" philosophy to every major program (Fig. 15). It is a well-known fact that unreasonable stretch in system requirements can lead to excessive costs. The goal must be to do what it takes to meet customer needs—yet without reaching beyond that just because it can be done technologically. In other words, it must be cost effective. Failure to do this will definitely hinder progress in delivering a better product for aviation.

While still on the subject of cost, I want to refer to the earlier point of the massive investment required of the engine manufacturer. It becomes literally a "bet-the-business" proposition for a single manufacturer to develop a new engine. In a climate where traditional military sponsorship for technology developments is tapering off, the solution to survival in this business seems to be more recourse to share-to-gain approach of participation in the free-world market. Through licenses, co-production and joint ventures, the companies involved can realize a better risk/gain perspective and the best of the strengths and resources of the part-

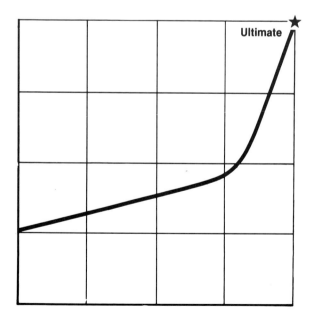

Figure 15. The "design-to-cost philosophy."

ners can be brought together to improve the value of the product for the customer. Granted, this requires a form of planned schizophrenia where otherwise vicious competitors become "loving partners" in certain narrowly defined limits but the industry has been able and will be able to make it work—and for a highly competitive industry like the aircraft gas turbine business, that is an accomplishment.

A good example of how international cooperation can work successfully is the CFM56 high bypass turbofan, co-developed by General Electric of the U.S. and SNECMA of France through a joint company, CFM International. This engine offers lower fuel consumption with reduced noise and emissions for aircraft of the 1980's. It has recently been chosen to re-engine some of the DC-8's now in service to extend their useful service life through the next decade.

Emissions. Another significant challenge is to meet the future requirements for protection of the environment. Efforts were initiated several years ago to reduce engine emissions. There has been a good measure of success: in modern engines, smoke emission has been virtually eliminated. Progress in invisible emissions is not so "apparent" . . . but is still significant. Even though the percent total pollution from aircraft is quite small—well under one percent of total pollution in areas near airports—we still must make improvements. The EPA has called for standards that will require significant decreases of harmful emissions. We are working toward meeting those standards. Through component and engine development work now in progress, I am confident the job will be done.

Noise. On the subject of noise as a "pollutant," dramatic achievements have been made already. Using the high bypass turbofan as a "technology breakthrough" example, today's wide-body jets fall well within what FAA has called "community acceptable" noise levels. Noise reductions have been achieved that are more than 15 perceived noise decibels lower than former generation engines (Fig. 16) . . . with powerplants having much more power. Some of this reduction comes from basic engine design and some from acoustic treatment. And research programs underway are aimed at

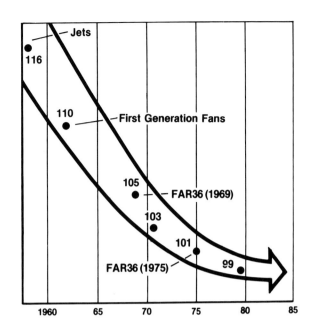

Figure 16. Noise technology trends at landing.

further significant improvements in both engine noise and emissions reductions for gas turbine engines.

Any discussion of the future would be incomplete without touching on the critical question of the fuel burned in aircraft engines. With shortages and high cost, economy of operation must be one of the major goals. Again, we have come a long way (Fig. 17). In terms of efficiency of transportation—and a valid measure is the fuel cost of transporting a passenger one mile—current wide-body transports are more efficient than any sports car, even than a Volkswagen bug with two occupants. And that does not consider the significant man-hours savings in air vs. automobile transportation.

As efforts are continued to make engines more efficient in use of fuel, considerable attention must also be directed to studies on nonpetroleum based energy sources. Unfortunately, it appears there is no quick relief from the problem. Dense hydrocarbons such as liquid coal and methane derivatives will be exploited for aircraft use as their cost and availability improve. But the outlook does not see this happening before the mid-1980's at the earliest.

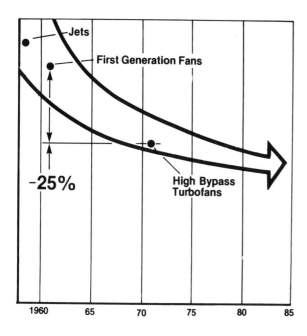

Figure 17. Fuel consumption technology trends.

There is also a need to accommodate fuels like Bunker C—first in our marine and industrial use of gas turbines and maybe later in the air—to save the conversion to light distillate energy lost in the cracking process.

As for hydrogen as a possible fuel source, it does not seem likely that it could become practical for aircraft use in the next 20 years. Although easily adapted to the aircraft gas turbine, the prime difficulty lies in storing and handling at the air-ground interface. Perhaps its earliest and most realistic benefit would be in hydrogen's development for use on the ground, thereby freeing up dense liquid energy for transportation use.

In looking at the future, several things seem clear:

• There will not be as many new systems developed and procured in any one time interval—and the level of research and development support will be less.

• The problems of life cycle cost (and productivity) will be uppermost in the minds of buyer and producer. The engine man

of 1990 may well be as much a financier as an engineer.

• The limitations (and cost) of fuel may well redesign, once again, the transport of the future: lowest drag, optimum speed, less wing sweep, more composites, variable cycle engines, higher bypass.

• A future SST will come only after the propulsion system concept is presented that allows low noise, good fuel economy, economic performance. Studies are underway under NASA sponsorship; the Concorde is providing helpful experience; there is a very dim light at the tunnel's end via a variable cycle fan of advanced technology.

• No matter where the factory is located, the market place will be world wide and the industry must accommodate the changes in approach necessary. Share-to-gain will not be an idle comment.

The aircraft gas turbine has come a long way in a relatively short time. As the lead element in making new systems possible, the technology breakthroughs have been dramatic in making the engine do more things and do them better. That progress will continue. As we look into the 1980's, we see military use expanding the boundaries of what the gas turbine can do. Commercial use will continue to grow and we see more derivatives for marine and industrial applications.

But in a relatively mature climate as far as the need for new types of engines is concerned, technology goals must be aimed at meeting changing requirements. The challenges will continue to be tough. Already, tremendous progress is being made in new directions. Such progress will continue, too. Engines will be produced at lower weight for the same power . . . at no more cost . . . engines that are more efficient and reliable . . . that are cleaner and quieter . . . that are simpler to maintain. The engine industry will make the changes and shift emphasis to accommodate the new excitement . . . "how to be mature."

Jet Bombers

Walter J. Boyne and Donald S. Lopez

The concept of jet bombers occurred immediately after jet fighters went on the drawing boards, for the eternal tug of war between fighters and bombers was not going to end simply because a new power plant had appeared.

The Germans were once again first, this time with the Arado Ar.234, a sleek single place aircraft that was really more useful as a reconnaissance plane than as a bomber. They also began work on a heavy bomber, the radical Junkers Ju.287, which had swept forward wings (now being considered for some aircraft of the 1980's) and six jet engines.

Similar development efforts were underway in England, Russia and the U. S., and shortly after World War II ended, a number of experimental types were flown.

The jet engines of the time were plagued by rather high specific fuel consumption, slow acceleration, and a tendency to flame out at altitude. Nonetheless, the great advantages in weight and power made them mandatory for the future, and the most obvious problem, an inherent deficiency in range, would be overcome by a technique that had been practiced for years, but had only recently come of age—inflight refueling.

For the very first time in the history of aviation, aircraft performance was going to be limited by airframe design instead of engine. As engines progressed, power increased dramatically, so much that limits had to be placed on straight and level flight speeds to avoid the possibility of structural damage. Bombers grew to be enormous, setting the pace and providing the technical basis for the later huge passenger planes.

Because of the improvement in anti-aircraft, with advanced surface to air missiles integrated with sophisticated radar systems, absolute speed became less important than the ability to hug the ground and fly below the perception limits of radar systems. As these defensive loopholes began to close, air launched missiles which could be launched from outside the defense system's perimeter came into prominence. The jet bomber, which began life virtually immune to interception due to its speed over the target, was relegated by improved defenses to a stand-off system. This development, ironically enough, has extended rather than curtailed the usefulness of the bomber fleet.

The Arado Ar.234 was the world's first operational jet bomber. Developed too late to have any practical effect on the war's outcome, the Ar.234 was nonetheless a magnificient achievement. Other than the drawbacks inherent in the jet engines of the time—slow acceleration, high maintenance, and low reliability—the aircraft was a delight to fly.

The Junkers Ju.287 was a German attempt at a heavy jet bomber. It incorporated swept forward wings, an aerodynamic feature being seen in many futuristic aircraft now on the drawing board, and six jet engines. A single prototype flew, and a second version was believed to have been completed in Russia after World War II.

The first American jet bomber was the Douglas XB-43, a straight-forward adaptation of the piston engine powered XB-42 "Mixmaster." Although not put in production, the KB-43 nonetheless served valiantly for years as an engine test bed, earning for itself the name "Versatile II."

The North American B-45A was the first U. S. production jet bomber. A conservative design, it provided a wealth of information on the tactical operation of heavy jets. The early models of the Tornado with four General Electric J35 engines had a maximum speed of about 575 mph at sea level.

One of the most significant designs in aviation history, the Boeing B-47 combined the company's unparalleled experience in building heavy bombers with the latest aerodynamic technology captured from the Germans at the end of World War II. The result was a magnificent six jet engine powered swept wing aircraft with an aerial refueling capability that permitted it to deliver a nuclear weapon anywhere in the world. When it appeared in squadron service, it posed an unsolvable problem for opposing defense systems, for it was extremely difficult to intercept by the jet fighters of the time. It directly influenced the design and development of the B-52, KC-135 and the famous Boeing 707 prototype, the 387-80.

Several highly efficient jet bombers were developed for the Royal Air Force. The most important of the three in terms of longevity in service and numbers built was the English Electric Canberra. The Canberra was a considerable departure from contemporary American practice, for it had a thick, broad-chord wing, and engines center mounted rather than on pylons. It became the first aircraft of foreign design adopted for operational use in the U.S. Air Force since the end of World War II, being built by Martin as the B-57.

Other English bombers of interest include the
Avro Vulcan, Handley Page Victor and Vickers
Valiant, which in their heyday constituted a potent
striking force for the RAF.

The Boeing B-52 was first flown on October 2, 1952; its missile carrying descendants are still expected to be a part of the U. S. defense triad in the year 2000. A 50 year life span as a first line combat aircraft is an incredible testimony to the soundness of the basic B-52 design. In its combat career, the B-52 has evolved from a high altitude nuclear strike aircraft to a low level conventional "iron bomb" weapon system to a sophisticated center for the release of an increasing variety of missiles. The process of adaptation has seen a series of changes in engine types, endless modifications to increase service life and defeat fatigue problems, and continuous improvement in systems capability.

Flown four years after the B-52, on November 11, 1956, the Convair B-58 Hustler was the world's first supersonic bomber. The mach 2 aircraft continued in service until 1970, when increasingly high maintenance costs forced their retirement.

The General Dynamics FB-111 is the only U. S. supersonic bomber. An adaptation of the F-111, one of the most controversial warplanes of all time, the FB-111 was designed as an interim replacement for the B-58 pending development of what eventually became the Rockwell International B-1.

The Rockwell International B-1, which probably had a longer development history than any other bomber, was dropped from production when it was feared that its cost would be too high. The aircraft, still under test, has performed well and may be considered to be the zenith of American bomber design to date.

Northrop YB-49

Martin XB-48

Martin XB-51

Convair YB-60

Avro Vulcan
and Boeing B-52

Figure 1., The Bell XP-59A Airacomet

Flying Jet Aircraft and the Bell XS-1

Charles E. Yeager

My first experience with jet aircraft was in 1944 when I was a pilot with the 357th Fighter Group, a P-51 Mustang outfit flying out of England against the Germans. I ran into my first jet aircraft in the summer when I was escorting a flight of bombers near Bremen, Germany. Having completed the escort mission, we were roaming around Germany looking for targets of opportunity at an altitude of around 15,000 feet. I had a flight of four aircraft. I spotted my first three jet aircraft; they were lower than I was, down around 8,000 feet going 180°. I spotted them somewhere around 12-15 miles in front of me. I really did not know what they were. We had been briefed on jet aircraft, and on some of their performance and characteristics, so it came as a complete surprise to me when I first saw how fast they were. I remember they were coming at around the one o'clock position going 180°. I put the nose of the P-51 down and went to full power on the engine. I was up to somewhere around 450-460 mph indicated. I pulled in and tried to get a deflection shot on the lead aircraft. I could get within about 1,000 yards on the deflection shot and got a strike or two, but he pulled away from me like I was standing still. However, I hung around the general area and finally spotted one trying to land on a field near Bremen. I split S and pulled in behind him. He had his gear down and was about two miles on the final to the runway when I opened fire at 200 yards and closed in very fast. He blew up as he approached the end of the runway, and I pulled up. That was my first association with jet aircraft.

After I returned from the war in 1945, I was assigned as the Assistant Maintenance Officer in the Fighter Test Section of the Flight Test Division at Wright Field in Dayton, Ohio. As a Maintenance Officer, it was my job to run functional flight tests on all of the aircraft in the Fighter Test Section when they came out of maintenance work. There I got to fly my first jet aircraft, the Bell P-59. Figure 1. The impression I got was how smooth the engines were, but the one thing that struck me was that the controls on all aircraft were about the same as a P-51 or conventional engine powered fighter. You push forward on the throttle and the airplane goes. The same thing happens with the jet aircraft, but a little bit slower on acceleration and a little bit touchier on landing, since the transition time from approach speed to touch down speed was a little longer in distance in the jet aircraft because you don't have the drag of the prop when you pull the power back.

Being in the Fighter Test Section, I went to

BRIGADIER GENERAL CHARLES E. YEAGER is the first person in history to exceed the speed of sound. A native of Myra, West Virginia, he became a pilot in the Army Air Force during World War II. He distinguished himself in aerial combat over France and Germany, shooting down 13 enemy aircraft, five on one mission, including one of Germany's first jet fighters. He later served as a test pilot at Wright Field. After the War he was assigned to Edwards Air Force Base as pilot of the nation's first research rocket aircraft, the Bell XS-1, and on October 14, 1947, he made history by flying it faster than the speed of sound. On December 12, 1953, he exceeded Mach 2.4 in the Bell X-1A. In 1975 he retired after 28 years in the Air Force, and he presently lives in Cedar Ridge, California.

Edwards Air Force Base—then Muroc Air Base —at Rogers Dry Lake in California on the first engine service test on the P-80. That August of 1945, I flew the P-80s and got to know them quite well. The development in jet aircraft in the first five or six years came hot and heavy. We went from the P-80s to the P-84. Our first operational jet, the P-80, was powered by the centrifugal compressor engine. The P-84, with the axial compressor engine, was the first airplane that I had flown that had the capability of hitting its critical Mach number straight and level, which was around .82 Mach number. The P-84 was the first aircraft in which I experienced some of the flying characteristics that later led, in my opinion, to the first supersonic flight in the Bell X-1. The P-84 would go straight and level at .82 Mach number, where the airplane would buffet and sort of pitch up, if you tried to go faster.

After the P-84 we got into numerous aircraft like the P-83, which was an enlarged P-59 powered by the two General Electric J33 engines. It was the first aircraft that was equipped with .60 caliber guns. I did a lot of firing tests on the P-83 flying out of Wright Field over Lake Erie. In the Fighter Test Section at Wright Field we also got our hands on most all of the captured German and Japanese aircraft that our opposition used in World War II. The Me-262 came into Wright Field and was flown on quite a few comparison tests against the P-80. One of the amusing things about the Me-262 was that it had practically the same rate of climb, the same top speed, acceleration rate and range as the P-80. We had three P-80s in Europe in 1944 but they all were lost in accidents and never did get to combat against the Me-262. The P-80 probably would have done a very good job against the Me-262, but it was never tried out. The thing that amazed me about most of the jet aircraft that we were flying in 1945, and in later years, was that the performance of the airplane depended a lot on how big the jet engine was. With the advent of afterburners which later increased the thrust of the engines we got a much higher performance. But in the early service tests on the P-80s we had a lot of engine problems and a lot of problems with pressurization. We also had a lot of

problems controlling the temperature of the air in the cockpits. We seemed to stress automatic control devices including automatic control devices for cockpit temperature. Fortunately, in most of the early jet aircraft when they installed a cabin temperature selector switch they also installed a four position switch that read automatic, high, low, and off. Of course, the automatic device never worked and we always were using the manual position. It took a few years to iron out the bugs and, of course, later aircraft temperature controls were quite successful.

But to go back a little to the problem of compressibility. I had my first association with compressibility in 1944 during combat, flying the P-51 against Bf. 109 and Ff. 190's. Normally during combat if you got on a 190 or 109's tail, if he had not bailed out, he would head for the deck wide open. The P-51 would get up to about .8-.81 Mach number going straight down from as high as one could get it, and you ran into compressibility as the shock wave formed on the wings and caused buffeting and a decrease in controllability of the aircraft. I personally did not know much about what caused compressibility, but in later years with the X-1 I learned very quickly. Of course, we had smart people in the Air Force and with Bell Aircraft Company and NACA who knew the problems associated with approaching the speed of sound and who conceived the idea of building an aircraft that would fly in the region of the speed of sound.

The contract was given to Bell Aircraft Company and they started construction in 1944 on the then XS-1. X meaning research, S meaning supersonic, and the 1 designation was for the first aircraft that was contracted for by the Air Force. The X-1 was an in-house program with Bell Aircraft Company, and the pilots were civilian test pilots for Bell who were assigned to the program. The aircraft was completed in early 1946 and the first glide flights were made by Jack Woolams at Pinecastle, Florida. They did not have the rocket engine available to install in the aircraft and the first few glide flights were made without the engine installed. They cut away the bomb bay of a B-29 which was specially equipped to carry the X-1 or XS-1. The X-1 was hooked onto a bomb shackle. They normally would haul the X-1 up to around 25,000 feet and dive the B-29 until you got above the stall speed of the X-1. You then pulled the release that released it from the bomb shackle and it fell away from the B-29. They later moved the XS-1 to Muroc Air Base, after they installed the engine. But in the meantime, Jack Woolams, who was the XS-1 test pilot, was killed in a souped-up P-39 in the Cleveland Air Races. Bell Aircraft assigned Chalmers S. (Slick) Goodland as the XS-1 test pilot. "Slick" made twenty powered flights on the X-1, taking it out to .8 Mach number and up to 40,000 feet. Tex Johnston flew the XS-1 one flight at the end of the Bell program. But, during the spring of 1947 there was a little bit of a hassle between Slick Goodland and Bell Aircraft Company about his pay and bonus money that was offered him to take the XS-1 to supersonic speed. The contract was rumored to be worth somewhere around $150,000 and Slick did not want it all paid in one year. He wanted it spread over a five-year period. Like all of us, he was interested in saving a little money from the tax bite. In the spring of 1947, Colonel Al Boyd, then Chief of the Flight Test Division at Wright Field, went to the Air Materiel Command and proposed that the Air Force take over the X-1 program because we had pilots who were as well qualified as the Bell civilian test pilots. Also the program was being delayed a little bit because of the dispute between Slick Goodland and Bell Aircraft Company.

The Air Force stepped in and took over the X-1. Colonel Boyd at that time screened most of the pilots in the Flight Test Division, and he tried to pick a pilot to assign to the XS-1 program as the primary pilot. He narrowed the field down to the fighter types because of their single engine, single cockpit type experience. It was then narrowed down to the fighter types in the Fighter Test Section of the Flight Test Division. As luck would have it, Colonel Boyd finally picked me as the primary pilot. In talking with General Boyd later, he said the reason he picked me specifically was because of my stability and performance in previous tests, and I also had a maintenance background, understood machinery, and never had much trouble maintaining an aircraft. He liked the way I flew. Although I didn't have the education and was not a West Pointer, as some of the officers in the Flight Test Division, I still had a great deal of experience in combat and experience in maintenance and running functional test flights on the aircraft. Also, I was selected in the spring of 1946 to go to the Test Pilot School at Wright Field, and I had completed that quite successfully.

After I was selected, Colonel Boyd selected Lieutenant Bob Hoover as my back up pilot. We devoted most of our time to learning the systems on the X-1. Bell Aircraft Company had given the Air Force the assistant crew chief on the XS-1. They let the Air Force hire him on Civil Service and this kept a great deal of continuity in the maintenance of the XS-1. Jack Russell knew the X-1 inside and out. They also gave us Dick Frost, who was a Bell test pilot and also probably knew more about the X-1 in both maintenance and flight test than any other individual. Colonel Boyd also gave us Captain Jack Ridley as the Flight Test Engineer on the program. Jack had a master's degree from Cal Tech, and had studied under Dr. von Karman. He was very smart and was also a very good test pilot. He added a great deal of continuity between me and NACA, which was in the program to obtain flight test data and to consult on advancing the speed of the aircraft. We went to Muroc in the late spring or early summer of 1947 with the X-1 and the B-29. I spent a great deal of time learning the systems and going over the flight test data that Bell Aircraft Company had gotten when Slick Goodland was pilot.

The X-1, in a typical flight, was backed down into a pit and the B-29 pulled over, and then the X-1 was hoisted up into the bomb bay of the B-29 and hooked onto the bomb shackle. After getting it hooked onto the bomb shackle, the B-29 was backed off of the pit and pulled up between the two tanks that held the fuel and liquid oxygen that the X-1 was loaded with. We carried in the X-1 somewhere around 288 gallons of liquid oxygen and approximately 300 gallons of a mixture of five parts alcohol to one part water as the fuel. As the power source in the X-1 we did not have hydraulic pumps or generators run by auxiliary power units or hydrogen peroxide generators, which we had in later aircraft like X-1A, X-2, X-15 and some of our space vehicles. The X-1 used as a source of power a very high pressure nitrogen gas which was pumped into small bottles that were manifolded together. In order to get this high pressure—some 5,000 PSI—we used liquid nitrogen and boiled it through an evaporator to increase the pressure and pressurize the manifold in the X-1. It took quite some time to get the pressure built up because we had to keep cooling the manifolds as they were pressurized. The best way to do it was to start pressurizing the manifold on the X-1 a day prior to the flight. This gave us all night to cool, and then we would top off the pressure to get it up to 5,000 PSI. To use this 5,000 pounds of nitrogen gas, we ran it through a single stage manifold regulator, a dome regulator that I was familiar with from the natural gas fields in West Virginia where my father was a drilling contractor. As a child I disassembled and assembled and cleaned and put new diaphragms in dome regulators and knew them like the back of my hand, so it was no problem understanding the operation of the system in the XS-1. This first stage dome regulator reduced the 5,000 PSI which we started with down to 1,500 pounds of pressure. We used this 1,500 pounds to raise and lower the landing gear and the flaps. Then we reduced the 1,500 pounds through two more dome regulators, reducing the pressure to about 300 PSI. We used one dome regulator to pressurize the liquid oxygen tank at around 300 pounds, and the second dome regulator to pressurize the water alcohol fuel tank at somewhere around 290 pounds per square inch. Then we further reduced the 300 pounds through a manual regulator to approximately 100 PSI and ran this 100 pounds of nitrogen gas back to the tail of the aircraft where we had a jackscrew that ran through the leading edge of the horizontal stabilizer. This gave us the capability of moving or changing the angle of incidence of the horizontal stabilizer. We had an air motor on top of the jackscrew and an air motor on the bottom. We could run the jackscrew one way, which would cause the leading edge to go up, or run it the other way with the other motor to cause the leading edge to go down. The way I controlled

it was by two Solenoids that were connected to an electrical switch in the cockpit on the control column. I will cover the changing of the horizontal stabilizer later because this turned out to be a very important capability built into the X-1. We further reduced this 100 PSI down through an orifice in the cockpit to some four pounds per square inch and used this four pounds of nitrogen pressure through the gyros to run the eight ball flight indicator and the needle in the needle and ball turn and bank indicator. Then we dumped that gas as it came through the flight indicator into the cockpit to pressurize the cockpit with somewhere around 4 PSI. So we had a 100% nitrogen environment in the cockpit. We were flying with one oxygen mask and one oxygen system in the X-1, and no redundancy and no back-up system.

On a typical flight, after fueling the liquid oxygen and water alcohol tank and pressurizing the nitrogen system and loading it under the B-29, the X-1 pilot did not take off in the cockpit of the X-1. The reason was because the climbing speed of the B-29 was around 180 miles per hour. The X-1 number 1 with the 8% wing and the 6% tail, had a stalling speed fully loaded around 240 miles per hour. We figured that since I had no way of getting out of the cockpit of the X-1 once you were in, you were pretty well sealed in and that if we had an inadvertent shackle release or had to drop the X-1 anywhere under 12,000 feet you would end up in a spin at too low an altitude to recover from the spin. So I rode in the B-29 during take off. When we got up to around 12,000 feet, I went back into the bomb bay of the B-29 where we had a ladder in the right side of the bomb bay opposite the entrance door on the right side of the X-1. I would get on the ladder and they would let me down into the slip stream just opposite the door on the X-1. I would slide into the X-1, feet first, wearing a seat type parachute, primarily to sit on, and get squared away in the cockpit. Then they would lower the door. Jack Ridley would normally come down on the ladder with the door and hold it against the right side of the X-1 and I would lock it from the inside. Once I got squared away with my oxygen mask and helmet, I got hooked up to the communications system and talked to the B-29

Figure 2. Yeager and the Bell XS-1

pilot and the two chase pilots, going through the check list during the climb to 25,000 feet. Prior to drop, I would load up the first stage, getting 1,500 pounds in my manifold for the gear, and then I would load up my second stage regulators, pressurizing the liquid oxygen tank and the water alcohol tank. I would bleed off the liquid oxygen manifold, getting the gas out of the manifold until I got liquid oxygen through the bleed valve, and then I would shut it down. I was ready for drop and ready to ignite the chambers of the rocket engine.

Usually the B-29 pilot would climb within gliding distance of Rogers Dry Lake until we got to about 25,000 feet; then he would back off to about Victorville, some 40 miles away, still within gliding distance of the lake bed, and pick up speed with the B-29. This meant dropping the nose and diving it somewhere around a 15-20° dive angle. Once they got up to 240

miles per hour indicated, he would give me a countdown of 10, 9, 8, 7, 6, on down to 0, and release the shackle that dropped me out of the B-29. After drop, once I knew I had fallen clear of the B-29, I would level the aircraft out and ignite one of the chambers of the rocket engine itself.

The rocket engine consisted of four chambers, and each chamber would put out 1,500 pounds of thrust, or a total of 6,000 pounds of thrust with all four chambers on. With roughly 588 gallons of propellants, I could burn up all of the propellants in 2½ minutes, if I ran all four chambers. Five minutes with two running, and ten minutes with one single chamber running. On all of the flights that I made on the XS-1, we never landed with any fuel aboard because the gear was not designed to take that additional weight. The X-1 empty weighed somewhere around 6,800 pounds, with instrumentation and pilot aboard. Fully loaded with fuel it ran close to 13,000 pounds. So at the end of a run if I had not used all of my fuel, I would jettison the remainder of the liquid oxygen and water alcohol and then come on down somewhere 5,000 or 6,000 feet above the lake bed at somewhere between 300 and 400 miles an hour. I would fly over the point where I wanted to touch down at 400 miles an hour, break left or right, whichever the wind predicated, and roll the airplane out on downwind, put the gear down at around 250 miles per hour. The flaps would come down with the gear. The airplane, now empty, stalled around 190 miles per hour. So I held it around 220 on the base leg, flew a final at 220 and flared the aircraft and touched down at around 190 miles per hour on the lake bed. We had a roll out of about three miles on the lake bed if I did not use brakes. With Rogers Dry Lake having a runway some eight miles long and five miles wide, I would normally pick a spot in the middle and aim for it so that if I undershot or overshot two or three miles it did not make much difference. Figure 2.

We started out in the X-1 program and, if you remember, I had flown P-80s and P-84s straight wing jets up to a Mach number of .82, and .83. I knew what buffeting was; I knew the flying characteristics of the aircraft. On my flight, I did not make a powered flight. I made three glide flights without any propellants in the aircraft to get the handling characteristics and a feel for the aircraft on landing. On the glide flights, Bob Hoover chased me in a P-80 and Dick Frost flew a P-51 chase aircraft or a P-80 chase aircraft. After the three glide flights, I felt pretty much at home in the aircraft since it flew very nicely —quiet, controls were good, coordination was good. I felt at home in the cockpit by then, having spent a lot of time on the ground runs, on the engine, and learning the aircraft.

We then started off on our first powered flight. Prior to a flight we would have a meeting with NACA, Walt Williams, Dee Beeler, and some of the instrumentation people. Jack Ridley and Bob Hoover and Dick Frost and myself repre-

sented the Air Force. We would sit down and talk about what we were going to do on the first powered flight and come up with an aim for Mach number. I figured we might as well aim for .82 Mach with no indication of any problem. So, on the first powered flight, after drop at around 24,000 feet, I fired one chamber, then fired off the second chamber, and turned off the first, fired the third chamber, turned off the second, fired the fourth chamber and turned off the the third, which showed me that all my chambers were operating. I pulled up and did a roll with the aircraft. Being a typical pilot, when I pulled the nose up and did the roll, I decreased the g's to about zero. This caused the rocket engine to quit running and I could not figure it out until later when I got on the ground and we found that the liquid oxygen in the fuel tank was cavitating when we went to zero g. That, of course, would interrupt the flow of liquid oxygen to the rocket engine and we would get a flame out. But once you rolled out again, the chamber would re-ignite. I shut off the rocket engine, came down at 450 miles per hour in a steep dive across the field and pulled up and ignited all four chambers. The airplane really took off. I got up to .8 Mach number quite fast. In order to keep the aircraft below .82 which was our aim for mach number, I pulled the airplane almost into a vertical climb. I was doing sort of a modified barrel roll going straight up. But as I went through 38,000 to 40,000 feet, and dropped the nose a little bit, the first thing I knew I was up to .84 Mach number with no indication of any problems. So I shut off and jettison the remainder of my fuel and came on down and picked up my chase aircraft, and landed on the lake bed.

Jack Ridley and I sat down and wrote up the flight test report on how we had gotten the airplane up to .82 Mach number, and we sent the flight test report back to Wright Field. In return came a hot letter from Colonel Al Boyd, my Chief, wanting to know why I had exceeded .82 Mach number when he specifically told me not to. Jack Ridley and I sat down practically all night trying to figure out a good answer. I told him I felt good in the airplane and probably had exceeded .82 Mach because I felt that nothing was going to happen and that I was a little bit elated in flying the X-1 under power for the first time. He accepted it after a terse telephone call telling me to pay attention to what I was doing. And so we continued.

Each flight that I made in the X-1 increased the Mach number some two or three hundredths of a Mach. We ran into our first buffeting at about .88 Mach number. The first X-1 (46-062) had an eight percent thick wing and a six percent thick tail—those figures being the thickness-chord ratio of the surfaces. #2 X-1 #6063 which we had flown there at Muroc Air Base, too, had a 10% wing and an 8% tail. The #2 got into buffeting at about .84 Mach number because of the thicker wing and tail. But I flew the #1 X-1 out to .88 Mach number where we ran into our first buffeting. At the end of each run, when I got to .88 Mach number, I would roll the Aircraft over, and pull 2 or 3 g's. This gave me a feeling of what I would run into on the next flight at a higher Mach number straight and level. As we went through .9 Mach number, our buffeting increased and the airplane got a little squirrelly, meaning that the stability began to break down laterally and directionally a little bit as the shock waves were becoming more intense and moving back on the wing and the fuselage and the tail. After some seven or eight powered flights, I had worked the airplane up to .94 Mach number. As I recall, at .94 and at some 40,000 feet, I rolled the airplane over and pulled back on the control column and nothing happened. I would flop the control column back and forth and the airplane would not respond in any way. So I raked off the rocket engines and decelerated back down to where I had elevator control and jettisoned the remainder of the fuel, glided on down, and landed on the lake bed.

I was a little bit worried about the outcome of the whole program, because it had been predicted that the X-1 would either pitch up or pitch down when I got in the region of the speed of sound. Now I had run out of ability to control the X-1. We got NACA and all of the engineers together and had a talk about what was happening with the X-1. We did have in the instrumentation monometer pick ups where they had drilled small ⅛ or ¼ inch holes on the wing,

a foot or two out from the fuselage. They also drilled holes in the horizontal stabilizer. They connected tubes to the internal recorder, recording the pressures in all of these holes. The pressure recorder showed where the shock wave had formed over the thickest part of the wing at about .88 Mach number, as well as the thickest part of the horizontal stabilizer. As we were increasing our Mach number, this shock wave was moving back and laying down. At .94 Mach number, the shock wave was right at the hinge point of the elevator. Under this condition I had completely lost my elevator effectiveness.

I showed the most concern because it was my life that was on the line with the X-1. I talked to Colonel Boyd back at Wright Field. He told me that safety was the primary factor and if I did not like the program I could quit any time. We would call a halt to it because the British had killed a couple of pilots in the DH-108, the de-Havilland Swallow. We did not want to jeopardize our whole research and development program by wiping out our X-1 and the crew and causing a lot of concern about our program in the United States.

We looked at the systems on the X-1 and the capability built into the XS-1 of moving the horizontal stabilizer or changing the angle of incidence of the horizontal stabilizer. We had not used this system during any flight until this time. We checked out the system on the ground and went through it, and got it operating properly to where I could control or change the angle of incidence of the horizontal stabilizer in increments of about ¼ of a degree. After practicing on the ground, we set it back to where we were previously carrying it at some 2 degrees leading edge up or nose down trim, and we made a flight. We went out to .8 Mach number, and I changed the angle of incidence of the horizontal stabilizer about 1 degree nose down from normal, and the airplane pulled about 3 g's. Of course, I still had elevator control and could control the pitch. I retrimmed it back to where we had it previously, accelerated out to .9 Mach number, and made the same change of 1 degree leading edge nose down, and the airplane pulled about 3 g's, as it did at .8 Mach number. I retrimmed it back and accelerated out

Figure 3. Historic First Supersonic Flight XS-1, Oct. 14, 1947

to .94 Mach number, where I had lost my elevator control, made the same change of 1 degree leading edge nose down and the airplane pulled 3 g's. I retrimmed it back, came on down, and landed.

As far as I was concerned we had the thing licked because, although I had lost my elevator effectiveness, I still could control the X-1 with the horizontal stabilizer; and as far as I was concerned that was good enough for me.

On the next flight, we took the aircraft out to .96 Mach number and sat there in relatively heavy buffeting and the Mach meter was fluctuating at around .96. As I accelerated up, the Mach meter jumped from .96 to 1.05. Figure 3. I would like to say that they really did have a lot of confidence in our program because the Mach meter only went to 1.0. It sat there and fluctu-

ated and then jumped off the scale. If you extrapolated, it worked out to about 1.05 Mach number. The buffeting quit, I got back a little bit of elevator effectiveness, and the airplane flew quite nicely. I shut off the rocket motor after about 20 seconds beyond Mach 1 and came back through the speed of sound, got into the same buffet, the same instability, and the loss of elevator effectiveness. I jettisoned the remainder of my fuel and liquid oxygen and came on down and landed.

That date was October 14, 1947. We were quite elated that we had accomplished what we had set out to do with the XS-1. There were a lot of happy people, including Larry Bell and Colonel Al Boyd and all of the generals at the old air materiel command.

I went on and made some 40 flights in the X-1. I took it out to 1.5 Mach number, which was the max somewhere around 1,000 miles per hour. The airplane got up to around 70,000 feet. Later, after completing all of the flights, it was retired to the Smithsonian in 1950 where it still hangs today.

Finding out that we needed a controllable tail or horizontal stabilizer on an aircraft if we expected to operate within the region of the speed of sound was probably one of the most important things that came out of the whole XS-1 program, apart from finding out you could fly beyond the speed of sound without the airplane disintegrating. During the whole X-1 program that data we were getting from our flight test work was being reduced by NACA and given to all of the major aircraft contractors, such as Boeing, North American, Lockheed, General Dynamics and Republic. Once we got the aircraft up to supersonic speed and found out that we need a flying tail, it just so happened that the F-86 was on the drawing board at North American. The built a trimmable horizontal stabilizer on the F-86 and later a flying tail. That F-86 was used against the MiG-15 in the war in Korea. We had a kill ratio of about 12 MiG-15s for every F-86 lost. We knew our pilots were not that much better than the North Korean and Chinese pilots, so there had to be some reason. In 1953 when I went out with Tom Collins and then Major General Al Boyd to Okinawa to fly the MiG-15, it was quite obvious the advantage that the F-86 had over the MiG-15, because the MiG-15 had a fixed horizontal stabilizer. When you got the airplane up to about .93 Mach number, it began to buffet. It would buffet right out of the dive and completely lose elevator effectiveness. Knowing this and finding this out with the X-1, we had that capability in the F-86 some three to four years after finding it out with the X-1.

Figure 4. Brigadier General Charles E. Yeager

The First Forty Years of Jet Aviation

Najeeb E. Halaby

The fortieth birthday of jet flight gives us a moment in history to review progress and to anticipate prospects. The 75th anniversary of the Wright brothers' flight has been celebrated elegantly and well, the 50th birthday of Lindbergh's heroic transatlantic crossing has received its full affectionate respect. Now, we focus on the import and impact of the jet on aviation in America and the world since that first jet powered flight in October 1939 in Hitler's Germany by Luftwaffe Flugkapit än Erich Warsitz with Dr. Hans von Ohain's turbine.

Measured by its achievement of man's fundamental goals, jet aviation has been a great success. Militarily, the jet has attacked and defended nations in the lethal cycle of man's suicidal tendencies but on balance has served more than it has slain. We in the West can be thankful that air defense has kept war from our heartland. More benignly, the jet transport has greatly reduced the non-productive time in getting from here to there, conserving human resources, facilitating production of more goods and services, creating new technologies and jobs, freeing more leisure time, easing universal social contacts and meeting emergency needs. All the while the risk and the price of jet transportation have steadily declined. More than 154 million passengers have flown across the Atlantic in the past 30 years—about 140 million of them flew in jets in the past 20 years without a fatality over or into the Atlantic. During this same period, the first class fare in 1967 dollars has dropped from $900 to $364 while almost everything else but the long distance telephone call has soared in price. There is unevenness, however, and much left to be done to optimize man's use of the airspace, one of our planet's greatest assets!

First, a personal note. Jet flight came alive for me during the period 1943-1945. Three bits of nostalgia will refresh recollection of the new frontier of the jets. The first was the excitement of a young U. S. Navy Reserve Lieutenant on being selected in 1943 as one of the first naval aviators at the Naval Air Test Center, Patuxent River, Maryland, to be a jet test pilot. The second was flying the first American-built jet, the YP-59A Airacomet which is hanging in the National Air and Space Museum, then more a test bed than an operational aircraft, to its maximum attainable altitude of 46,660 ft. To the best of our knowledge, this was a world record for manned jet flight at that time. This was done empirically, by exhausting the fuel supply and landing dead stick from that dark and forbidding height to and almost into Chesapeake Bay! Having lost electrical power on the way down—

NAJEEB E. HALABY, a graduate of Yale Law School, learned to fly in 1932, and during World War II he served as a Navy carrier pilot. In 1944, at the Naval Air Test Center, Patuxent River, he was one of the first naval aviators to fly as a jet pilot. After the war, he served President Eisenhower as Deputy Assistant Secretary of Defense for International Security Affairs; and then President Kennedy as Federal Aviation Administrator. He became Chief Executive Officer of Pan American World Airways, presiding over the introduction into service of 33 Boeing 747s. Today, he resides in Alpine, New Jersey, and is President of Halaby International Corporation. Still an active pilot, he has flown all of the principal modern airliners, including the early versions of the 747.

dressed warmly in my fleece-lined suit, boots and helmet—I cranked down the landing gear with the final welcome sound of the gear pins locking on final approach.

My third spectacular event was in May 1945 when, during the first transcontinental jet flight, I slowed down my Lockheed YP-80A Shooting Star briefly to fly formation on the right wing of an American Airlines DC-3 as we both let down toward Nashville Airport. The total amazement on the faces of the pilots and the passengers as they peered at this winged apparition personified the dramatic contrast between prop and jet.

Few today can remember what the problems of the jet age were.

The first was whether we could rely on the jet to work. Could you get it started? Would it burn up everything and everyone in its wake? Could you get it restarted if it flamed out? Could you accelerate and decelerate it in the instantaneous manner in which aviators had been accustomed with the "retaliating" engine particularly for aircraft carrier approaches? Dozens of my most anguishing aerodynamic hours were spent as the project test pilot for the Westinghouse axial-flow turbine, the Navy's answer to Frank Whittle and General Hap Arnold who brought the English centrifugal flow engine to the United States. This highly activated drop tank was slung precariously and unstably under the belly of the FG 1 Corsair and burned 100 octane gasoline for the first time in a jet. I tried diving, cruising, stalling, anything to start that engine in flight but to no avail. Flame-out was the first fright of jet flight. So, the first problem was to get this new fangled turbine started and keep it going. Those great turbo jet inventors wrestled confidently with this problem but I will tell you pilots had their doubts.

After the X-1 program we got into the X-1A, and on December 12, 1953, we took it out to 2.5 Mach number at around 78,000 feet. Other research aircraft followed and you know their accomplishments, such as the X-2, X-15, and of course our space program. The jet aircraft evolved into F-100s which could fly at supersonic speeds straight and level; into F-104s which could operate beyond twice the speed of sound; into the aircraft that we have today, such

as the F-15 and the F-16, aircraft that can sit there at supersonic speeds and pull 6, 7, 8 g's and never bleed off speed. Tremendous performance and capability! Weapons systems have increased to where you can do pretty well anything with a fighter aircraft in the way of air to air gunnery with guns or missiles, and air to ground with smart bombs, guided missiles, and the like. The jet aircraft that we started with back in 1944, the Me-262s and P-80s, have evolved into these highly technical, high performance jet aircraft we have today. There is no way of predicting what jet aircraft will be in the future, ten or twenty years from now. Figure 4.

It is my opinion that in the not too distant future, say eight to ten years, we will develop new jet engines. We will develop jet engines that have the capability of operating or propelling passenger-carrying aircraft out to Mach 3 or Mach 4. It just is not economically feasible to operate a supersonic transport with today's engines and the cost of fuel. When these new engines are developed somewhere around ten years from now, it will then be economically feasible to design and build passenger-carrying aircraft that will operate somewhere around Mach 3 or Mach 4 and do it on a paying basis.

Then, there were the problems of high altitude flight. Very few flights had been made over 25,000 ft. forty years ago. There was great concern about the pilot's life when he ascended above 20,000 ft. Hypoxia and euphoria not acrophobia, aeroembolism not cynicism were the terrors of the time. Very little work was under way in the field of cabin pressurization and positive pressure oxygen breathing was the fix. In particular, we spent hours and hours in the pressure chambers at Lockheed and at the Naval Aeronautical Laboratory in Philadelphia testing the first pressure breathing mask to force enough oxygen into the lungs in order to sustain life at the new jet heights.

The next great concern was the speed of the jet aircraft. The maximum speed of prop driven craft was then about 350 mph while the jets were designed to cruise at these speeds and to dive at much higher speeds. Less vibration and noise, better bubble canopies all made high speed flight deceptively simple but higher wing loadings required a higher takeoff and landing speed and increased the risk. So speed, as always the challenge to the aviator, had also been heightened.

The next was the range—these early jets had very short range so the fuel shortage was a most agonizing part of any flight plan and the flights were usually measured in minutes rather than hours. The fuel consumption varied tremendously with altitude and when one descended to the lower altitude, one was pretty much committed to land—very promptly.

The next great concern was that the turbine wheel would disintegrate and treat the plane and pilot more like sausage than helmeted hero. Many of you will recall the great lengths to which the German, British and American engine pioneers went to make sure that the turbine and compressor blades and wheels were tested to destruction before they were permitted on the aircraft. Vulnerability to gunfire was also of deep concern. Oddly enough, I do not believe there has been a fatal civil accident directly due to turbine blades escaping orbit although that was a primary fear in the early days.

Another question related to the meteorology of aerospace. Little was known about the weather conditions above 30,000 ft. and even less about radiation and health at these altitudes and so this was of great concern.

On the ground we were bedevilled by jet intake sucking up ice, rocks, tools—yes, even underwear though there were few lady mechanics then! At the other end we feared the jet wake would burn wooden carrier decking or melt macadam runways.

Finally, there was just superstition. If it has a wing on it, it will fly but if it does not have a propeller on it, there was real superstition that it might not fly. So, if those passengers on the DC-3 were not only startled but stunned by this propless bird, you can imagine what it was like to land this still classified YP-80A at the civil airports of El Paso, Fort Worth and Nashville—which were the longest hops between Muroc and Patuxent River one could make. Taxiing to the ramp produced absolute astonishment for everyone in sight.

There were others on the land side of jet flight who were amazed. When I landed at Nashville, for example, it had taken my Navy advance men a week to collect enough bulk kerosene to complete the flight to Patuxent. Poor people used it for lighting and heating and it had to be collected in a gasoline truck and filtered and made ready for the YP-80A. What a tribute, by the way, to the currently besieged international oil companies that they could shift from gasoline to jet fuel so quickly and economically in the early '60s.

Another groundling astounded by the sound of this bird was the airport neighbor. Not that it made as much noise compared with a B-26, for example, but that it made a different noise, a noise that was ominous by its strangeness. Finally, the air traffic controller had to adjust to a faster pace as he received unbelievable ETAs between the range stations over which I flew. Since it was a classified flight, they had not been informed that it was a jet cruising around and they repeatedly inquired if I had—like early aviators would—doubled the speed and halved the distance! So, these were some of the threshold problems, you might say, of jet flight. Several of them persist today.

In addition to the early technology and threshold operating problems, I will dwell on the politics of jet aviation—the various competing and intersecting interests, the legislation, the regulations, the human and institutional transients and reactions. I will confess at once my personal perspective: namely, where the relation between private enterprise and public control has been both balanced and dynamic, the greatest progress has been made. Where the government has stifled the development, and certainly, where the government has taken over the civil aviation industry, the least progress has been made for the benefit of the passenger, the shipper and the neighbor of the airplane on the ground. So my emphasis will be upon whether and if so how we have achieved a creative balance between the interests of the public, the government, the manufacturers and the operators of jet aircraft.

But, let us go back to the end of the first all-military jet period—1948—to see how it appeared then.

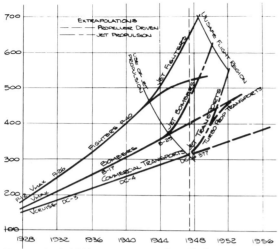

Figure 1. A 1948 perspective of jet flight.

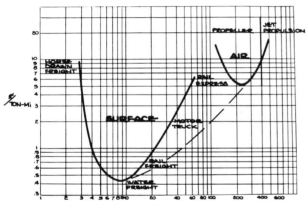

Figure 2. Comparison of direct operating costs.

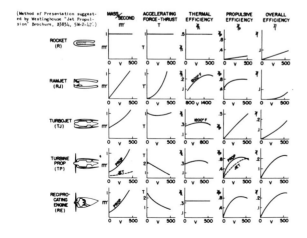

Figure 3. Diverse powerplant perspectives.

Fortunately, God has given civil aviation an ample number of pioneers and prophets and one of those, Robert Hage, gave a lecture at Princeton about jet propulsion in commercial air transportation. As a design engineer he gave us his 1948 perspective of jet flight. In Figure 1 he showed speed on the vertical line and time along the horizontal line, the fighters, the bombers and commercial transports growing through the years 1928 and 1948 and his extrapolations and comparisons between props and jets into his "wild blue yonder" of 20 years ago. Then in Figure 2 we see direct operating costs versus speed for the horse, the ship, the train, the truck, the prop airliner and the jet airliner. Finally, we see in Figure 3 the diverse powerplant characteristics—the range from reciprocating engine to turbine propeller, turbo jet, ram jet and rocket. I think it is fascinating that at the very moment he was giving his lecture, my friend and compatriot, C. R. Smith, the President of American Airlines, was saying that only when the British Rolls Royce Nene engine had attained a 500 hour reliable span of operation between overhaul, would America be ready for a high speed jet transport. Mr. Hage concluded that "a medium range turbo jet transport carrying 25-30 passengers and flying at a cruising speed of 500-525 mph is an extremely likely development for the use on the routes of the major airlines between major centers of population by the close of the year 1950." Prophetic he was, although 1950 proved a bit early for widespread use of turbo jet transports. Interim turbo prop aircraft like the Vickers Viscount and the Lockheed Electra briefly beguiled the air transport tycoons. The commercial jet age assumed a fast pace and grand dimension in 1958 with the de Havilland Comet and the Boeing 707, the latter pioneered by William Allen and Juan Trippe and Pan Am, followed by the DC-8 produced by Donald Douglas and introduced by United Air Lines' William Patterson. Then followed the pure jet British Aircraft 111 and the French Caravelle which enjoyed a surge of temporary success in the early '60s.

If the dawn of the jet age was 1939, then surely the bright midmorning was in the early 1960s when the large jet transports began to appear

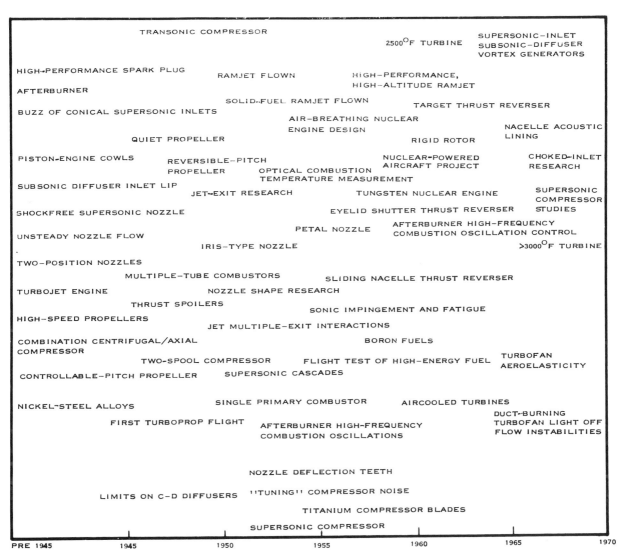

Figure 4. Selected advances in propulsion research.

and they brought to the universe a new system of magnificent mobility for mankind that may be the most significant achievement of the jet engine—the system spawned by the turbine. In turn, of course, this led to another dawn and another day of the space age which built upon the system of jet transportation in the atmosphere.

I would like to discuss the significance of the *system*—what we might call an international jet transportation system. The turbine produced a thrust of new life through the dead-end of the piston and it introduced a new era of reliability. There were, however, fundamental innovations in the airframes of the jets. Sweepback, landing flaps, power controls had already been in use but what was revolutionary was the system. As the aircraft got heavier, the take-off distances got longer, almost every major airport in the world had to be lengthened and enlarged to accommodate the new jet transports with their greater loads. The main emphasis of the political executives was on the runway rather than all the other facilities for handling the flood of new passengers—we found to our later discomfort.

The second component of the system that needed transformation was the airways. Not only did the aircraft take off and land at higher

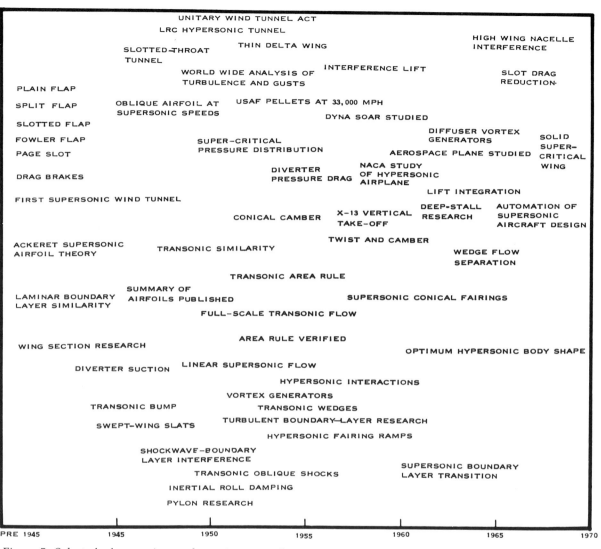

Figure 5. Selected advances in aerodynamics research.

speeds but climbed at higher speeds, approached at higher speeds and cruised at higher altitudes with enormously greater closing rates. The risk of collision terrified us all in the airspace of the 1950s where the rule of the air was: "see and be seen and avoid." The turbine has induced over the last two decades in the United States and Western Europe a multi-layer airspace system of great complexity and great efficiency but also with continuing risk of collision. If one looks at the airspace as one of God's gifts, one also looks at it as a layer cake—the prop layer, the turbo prop layer and the high jet layer extending for military and reconnaissance aircraft all the way up to 75,000 ft. The cake is cut and managed by the civil aviation administrations in the Western world. Some perform remarkably well; others lag dangerously behind.

A third component of this total system is that of general aerospace technology. The advances in thermodynamic and aerodynamic efficiency induced by the simplicity and economy of the jet age have been extraordinary not only in the turbine but in related fields of avionics, testing, maintenance and spare parts. The fact that the computer came into its own in roughly the

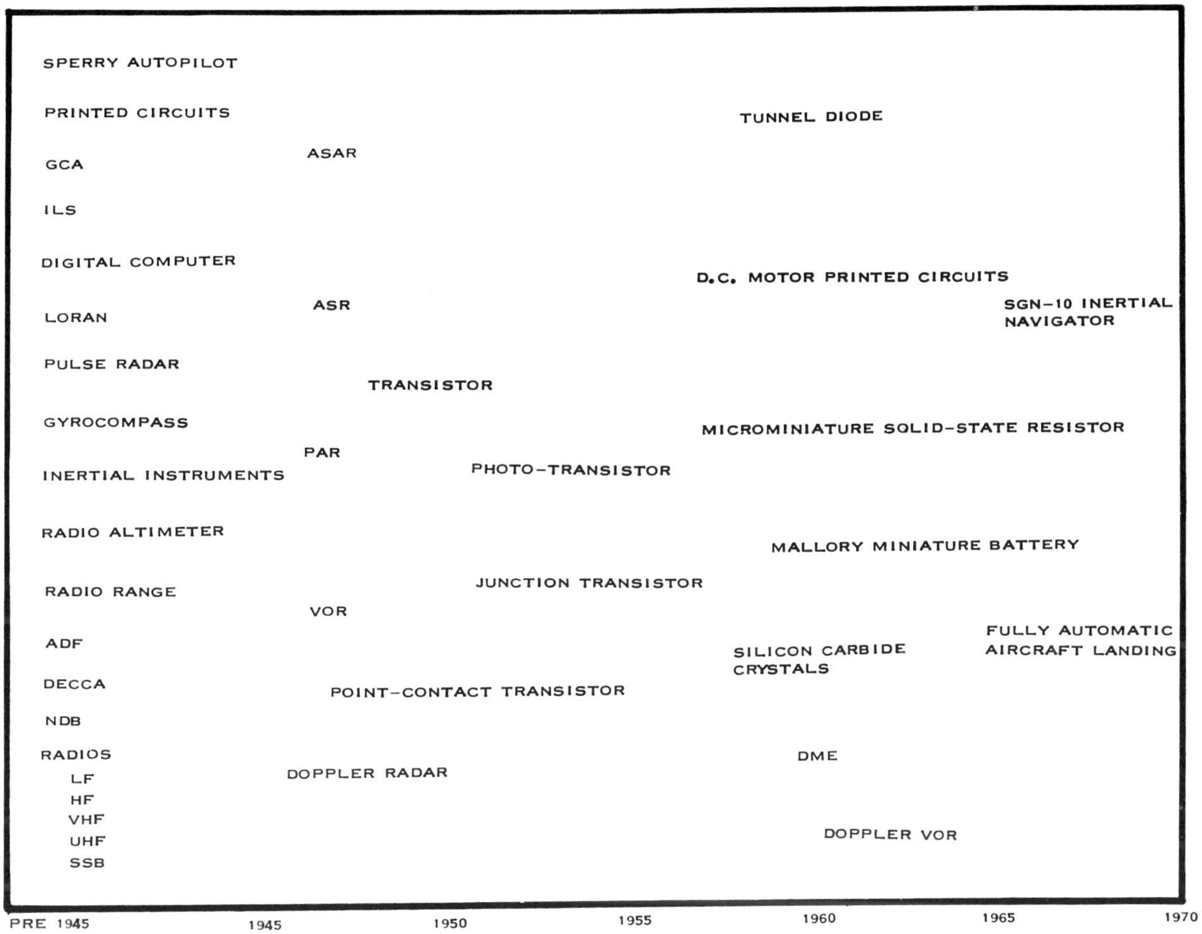

SPERRY AUTOPILOT

PRINTED CIRCUITS   TUNNEL DIODE

GCA   ASAR

ILS

DIGITAL COMPUTER   D.C. MOTOR PRINTED CIRCUITS

LORAN   ASR   SGN-10 INERTIAL
                                                                    NAVIGATOR

PULSE RADAR
                       TRANSISTOR

GYROCOMPASS   MICROMINIATURE SOLID-STATE RESISTOR
                  PAR
INERTIAL INSTRUMENTS   PHOTO-TRANSISTOR

RADIO ALTIMETER   MALLORY MINIATURE BATTERY

RADIO RANGE   JUNCTION TRANSISTOR
                  VOR

ADF   FULLY AUTOMATIC
                                          SILICON CARBIDE AIRCRAFT LANDING
DECCA   POINT-CONTACT TRANSISTOR   CRYSTALS

NDB

RADIOS   DME
   LF   DOPPLER RADAR
   HF
   VHF
   UHF   DOPPLER VOR
   SSB

PRE 1945   1945   1950   1955   1960   1965   1970

Figure 6. Selected advances in avionics research.

same period as the jet has made the air transport industry one of the most computerized of all industries. Without real time high speed calculation, where would ATC be today? The transistor coming again in the same developmental era made for a whole revolution in maintenance where the plug-in module replaced the techniques of the past.

But, better than my memory, let us scan developmental history as documented in 1971 for NASA and the FAA by Booz, Allen Applied Research, Inc. In Figure 4, there are selected advances in propulsion research depicted against the 25 year period, 1945-1970. Then in Figure 5 there are selected advances in aerodynamics research for this period and in Figure 6 selected advances in avionics research. Figure 7 shows selected advances in human factors research and Figure 8 selected advances in safety research.

The reason for presenting this swift sweep of the growth of technology is to illustrate what the inventors and engineers had suddenly poured upon the heads of the policy makers— they had first to define what the legislation and regulation had to cope with. I have always been of the belief that you had to understand before you could control, that you had to articulate the problem before you could solve it. For example, a survivable DC-8 crash plus hours of on-the-ground crash tests enable us to require airframe configuration and crew procedures to assure full passenger evacuation within two minutes after an accident. It became necessary not only to analyze but to extrapolate the operating prob-

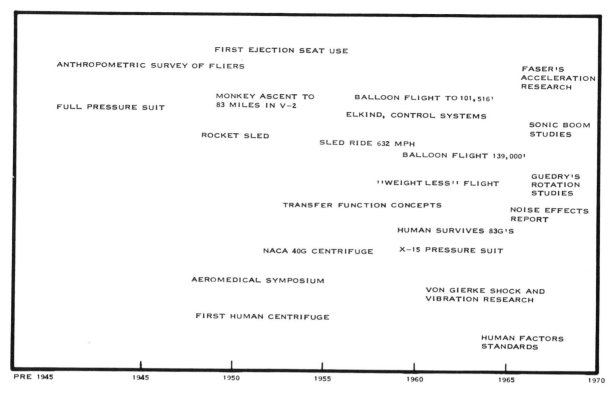

Figure 7. Selected advances in human factors research.

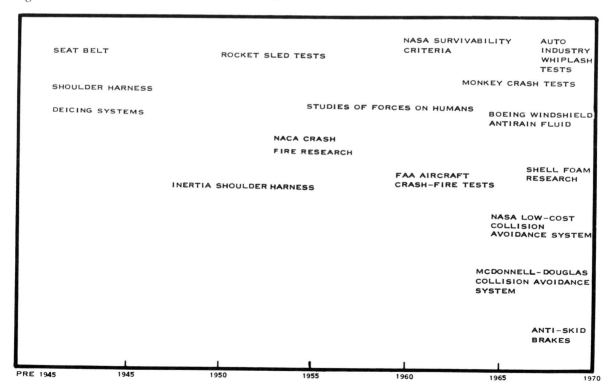

Figure 8. Selected advances in safety research.

lems before providing a regulatory framework for them. Thus, we see the thrust of civil aviation technology very powerfully fueled by military research and development. Hardly any of these developments could have been funded and facilitated as rapidly as they were without military research and development money since there was available only small amounts of civil agency and private corporation funding. Qualitatively, some of the private inventions and developments were far more important than the amount of funds devoted. In each case these developments induced elaborate and expensive facilities which in turn converted the airport into an industrial complex in order to provide the infrastructure on the land side of jet aviation. In turn, this produced communities clustered around airports—jet cities—a whole new era of noise abatement and community interaction with the jet pioneers. Meanwhile, the speeds and range of jet aviation required much more nearly instantaneous communication and the jet induced accelerated development and application qualitatively as great as that of World War II.

Speed and size required that the old low frequency, four-course radio range and non-directional beacon system be replaced by static free VOR — TACAN — VHF system. The primitive "groping for the airport through the fog" was replaced by the precise instrument landing system and by the time the big jets arrived, joint use of military and civil radars was a necessity along with nearly all weather take-off and landing capabilities. All of this had to be internationally compatible and procedures standardized among nations by the International Civil Aviation Organization (ICAO).

As with the jet, British and American competition sharpened the race of electronic technology. So, it may be said that the jet accelerated airways development from bonfires to beacons to radars and toward computers. Then, in the past 20 years, computerization, inertial navigators, airborne radars and a complex ground environment of facilities have given us a measure of automation in navigation which would not have occurred so rapidly. We were taxiing toward a modern flight support system

with the DC-7 and Stratocruiser but the DC-8 and 707 added thrust and several tragic midair collisions spurred more rapid progress—with a periodic royal commission required to prod and push the bureaucracy into innovations.

As aviation got more complex and voluminous, the rules of the sky had to be reviewed and revised and in a threshold period, the Federal Aviation Act of 1958 was passed in the 20th year of jet aviation. All the rules of the sky were recodified and brought up almost but not quite to speed with the new technology. In short, the jet brought major transformations and interlinked together a series of subsystems into a national jet transportation system such as we have today. There are, of course, discontinuities.

Recent collisions around crowded airports have indicated the need for accelerated work in improved communications and control of the skyways. Collision on the ground on a fog-shrouded Atlantic airport indicated the terrible consequences of lack of cockpit and tower discipline and unavailability of surface radar. The horrible waste of precious time at airport parking lots and ticket and baggage queues indicates the unevenness of the transportation system. The lateness in developing noise reduction technology is another social shortcoming of the system and, of course, the uneconomical development of the supersonic transport indicates how the technicians rushed out ahead of the economists and produced a tour de force but not a viable new dimension of the jet transportation system.

In the race between inventors and engineers in developing aviation and the lawyers and politicians in regulating aviation, the record will show that lawyers are much slower and cheaper than engineers! The record also dramatizes what I call political lag—the agonizing time required for politicians to catch up with technicians! But thanks to Icarus and others, we receive promising surprises at times, such as deregulation and authorization of use of airport trust funds for modernizing the airways system.

It is important to remember that in 1939 American aviation was coping with the Civil Aeronautics Act of 1938. We were more concerned with the growth of our airline companies and their competition and the need for an air traffic control and airport system that would accommodate the fabulous DC-3 and forthcoming DC-4 than we were with jet transportation and a war on the horizon. The Civil Aeronautics Act had three primary purposes: (1) to promote aviation, primarily at that time through subsidies to selected airlines and to control competition among the mushrooming operators, (2) to regulate the safety and (3) to establish and maintain a system of airways and air traffic control. The Civil Aeronautics Act created the Civil Aeronautics Authority, a tripartite organization with (1) a five-member board responsible for economic regulation and safety rulemaking, (2) an Administrator responsible for promoting air commerce, controlling air traffic and establishing airways, and (3) a safety board responsible for investigating accidents and determining their probable cause. In 1940, President Roosevelt by Executive Order broke up the Authority into two separate agencies: (1) the Civil Aeronautics Board, which assumed the quasi-legislative and quasi-judicial powers of the five-member board and the safety board and (2) the Civil Aeronautics Administration, which assumed the operational and technical activities of the Administrator. The legislation provided a regulatory framework for the period up to the introduction of jets. Then, 20 years later, the Federal Aviation Act of 1958 established an independent technical/operating regulatory agency, the FAA, and continued the CAB as the economic regulator. Thus, the Congress of the U. S. set up a system of rules and controls that has persisted for the first 40 years of jet flight. On the whole, it has worked remarkably well and although there is political lag behind technology always, the Airline Deregulation Act of 1977 suggests that our system of government is capable of coping effectively with changing economics and technology.

The economic regulation of the air carriers is the stuff of a whole series of other lectures in other places but a question which we should address is whether we have kept the principal engines of progress in civil aviation in good working order, timing and in balance. The primary force, of course, is the marketplace itself. The public demand for low cost, safe transportation on the one hand and the thirst for profit of the suppliers on the other hand is in the American system the most powerful force for progress—at least most of the time. The military aeronautical research and development where our national security has demanded a high level of technology and operating efficiency from principally the Air Force and Naval aviation has been a major boost. The third force, that of civil government, has been one of constraint rather than impetus in most cases. The economic regulator in the beginning fed subsidy to the trunk carriers and more recently to the local service carriers so that in a semi-monopolistic air economy they can survive and provide widespread service to the public. Later, the CAB emphasis was on control of entry into an unsubsidized market and a control of rates and routes both domestic and international so as to restrict destructive competition and to prevent a monopolistic tendency. Reams have been written on whether the CAB has strangled or facilitated airline transportation. As Chairman of Pan Am, newly in command of a jumbo fleet of 33 Boeing 747s in 1972, I felt passionately that we had the worst of both worlds—excessive regulation and excessive competition. But, history will probably judge, in general, that the balance between competition and regulation has been maintained better in the United States than in other nations and it has produced a successful technological growth in view of the fact that more than 75% of the world's airliners have been manufactured in the United States and the fact that the safety record of these airlines has been constantly improving and the cost of transportation improving in relation to the cost of all other necessities.

Compared with our superpower rival, the Soviet Union, we have managed remarkably well in civil aviation.

Whether this balance between private enterprise and public control has been good enough and also comparatively how have we ranked with our principal collaborator and competitor in civil aviation, Great Britain, merits a brief look at the British experience with the Comet, the BAC-111, Trident, VC-10 and the Concorde and, I suppose, comparatively speaking the Lockheed Electra, DC-8 and the Boeing 700 series.

In the British stream of development, the Government has had the role of funding and the appointment of manufacturing and operating officials. The operators of British aircraft have been as good as any; the engineers and manufacturers are too but they have had to cope with their own brand of state socialism and bureaucracy and to compete with the regulated free enterprise system of the United States and, generally, without as much of a motive or as much freedom to innovate. The Comet demonstrated the inventiveness and ingenuity of the British in the creative mode of Sir Frank Whittle. They were the first to fly a commercial jet aircraft but the Comet's safety assurance systems both in the manufacture and in the oversight of the Aircraft Registration Board permitted the introduction of cabin pressurization and fuselage component that failed in flight and caused the aircraft to fail economically. The BAC-111, on the other hand, scooped the world's market for medium range turbo jet transportation and during a period of the 60's had a fatality-free U. S. service record and was a limited commercial success. The French medium-range airliner, the Caravelle, was also a minor short-term success and some of both types are still flying today. The VC-10 has been restricted to Commonwealth carriers.

In each case the British manufacturer was required to use a powerplant developed and manufactured within the country. In each case, the amount of developmental funds available was limited by Parliament and, therefore, the designers and engineers were constrained by political and fiscal factors rather than market forces and private financing. I believe the same thing could be said about the Concorde as the others. Namely, there was not a body of experience with a large size military supersonic aircraft. The designers were forced to use a British engine and aluminum as the metal. They were also in a sense forced to collaborate with the French although that may have been synergistic and, finally, they were tightly paced by the an-

nual availability of funds. So, we have seen the perils of political plane making.

To some extent the failure of the United States SST is attributable to similar reasons—dependent entirely on Congressional funding, pressed forward in the beginning and then delayed by the government's inability to select the manufacturers and then caught up in a budgetary and environmental crisis. On balance, however, you can probably conclude that the system worked to prevent us from a disaster, the final and probable cause of which would have been the quadrupling of fuel price in 1973. We now realize we must stop short, look long and listen slowly before we develop any kind of supersonic or hypersonic transportation. At the same time we must give full credit to the designers and manufacturers and those dedicated safety regulators in the Aircraft Registration Board and the FAA.

On the lighter side, we should note with pleasure the extraordinary, widespread success of the business jets—mostly developed by and for private enterprise. The very first small private jet was the Morane Saulnier which I flew and enjoyed very much at White Plains in 1954 —only now is the four to six small passenger jet becoming fashionable. The Marcel Dassault Mystere or Falcon was a gifted child of a Franco-American union. The Hawker Siddeley, the Grumman Gulfstream, the Lockheed Jetstar led the way for safe and convenient business jet aviation that interlinks the world of international business. So, too, the helicopter has enjoyed a boost from the jet in lower weight, smaller size, enabling multiple turbines and greater reliability.

The lessons the air transport world has learned in these four jet decades may be summed up in a brief case history of the introduction of the first Pan Am Boeing 747—perhaps, the most successful introduction in the history of a large new jet aircraft. During her first four years, she had no fatal accidents— subsequently none of the five fatal accidents has been attributable to a failure of the engine, airframe or avionic systems. So, we are learning. Some believe this giant step was too large too soon but no one can deny that it forced the growth of what might be called the "airfra-structure," which is my name for the entire system of facilities and services that support the jet engine and the airframe. This aircraft was again fathered by the jet engine—the availability of the very large JT9D and the CF6 turbo fan high bypass engines out of the military competition for development of very large cargo transports.

Contemplating in 1966 an annual traffic growth rate of 15%-20%, William Allen at Boeing and Juan T. Trippe at Pan Am, old friends and buccaneers of the air, conceived of their final technical triumph—a 500 passenger aircraft cruising above all the weather and past all competitors with intercontinental non-stop range. While searching for the U. S. SST with FAA funds, they decided to put their own money on the 747—the largest order in airplane history was awarded to Boeing by Pan Am. I believe Mr. Trippe, approaching mandatory retirement, conceived this as the final great contribution to airplane innovation and William Allen in a similar mood wished to retire on upward wing. To them go credit for a very high risk investment; to Allen's disciples at Boeing and to Captain Harold Gray and John Borger, Chief Engineer, at Pan Am go credit for the engineering and the technical pioneering of this giant aircraft. That great bird fell in my lap when I became Chairman and Chief Executive of Pan Am in May 1970 with the challenge of actually introducing the aircraft into scheduled service. As with the early jet pioneers, we faced some similar problems. The one that seemed the most formidable was the safety of as many as 400 souls and the loss of a $25 million investment on a single flight. This focused our attention on the flying characteristics of the leviathan of the air and the flight managerial qualities of the crew, airborne and ground-based. Therefore, the selection and training of the commander of each great ship seemed of the greatest importance. We set up a comprehensive training system with the full collaboration of the FAA. A special base at Roswell, New Mexico, under the command of an outstanding airman, Captain James Waugh, gave concentrated attention to its safe and efficient operation under all worldwide conditions. We had to solve union seniority problems in selecting Captains but we were determined that no feasible step towards safety would be overlooked regardless of the cost of the new simulators, evacuation equipment, eliminated seats and high-priced technical hours required.

The size and weight of the aircraft required new runway and taxiway strengths and widths. Competing airlines and airplane manufacturers were determined to slow down the introduction of the aircraft and a thousand reasons were dreamed up why it should not be allowed to enter various airports and airspaces. For example, our brothers in Britain would seek to ban it from Heathrow—presumably until British Airways had one in operation!—on the grounds that it made too much noise, so large an aircraft would destroy too much or too many on the ground, the jet wake would endanger other aircraft in the airways and the flood of passengers would inundate their facilities. They could not refuse airworthiness for such a superbly engineered and tested aircraft but they could inhibit its operation.

Early troubles with the Pratt and Whitney JT9D engine—exemplified by a shutdown on the inaugural flight due to the sensitivity of engine airflow to a tail wind while taxiing—was seized as a reason for claiming the aircraft was unreliable.

The tremendous jet votex was a great concern to the FAA. The tornado power of the jet wake blew over equipment and facilities on the ground and threatened light planes in the airspace. It required greater separation between aircraft on approach to busy airports.

In terms of the private airfrastructure, Pan Am had to build a new jet center to service the engines, airframe and a whole new avionic subsystem with the most sophisticated test and maintenance equipment. We had to build a new passenger Worldport at JFK. In fact, the combined expenditure for the 33 Boeing 747s, the new terminal and overhaul center was just about $1 billion and almost more than the world's most experienced airline could lift financially.

And then in the very moment of introduction,

the economic regulators let loose a flood of additional competition from U. S. and foreign carriers, freeing the charter carriers to conduct semi-scheduled competitive service. Within a year one of its most serious recessions hit the American economy with the traffic growth rate dropping from 17% to less than 5% in the early 1970s. The technicians were out in front of the politicians and economists again!

It can be said the 747 was ten years too big and too soon but in terms of its operating record and the safety and success of its introduction, it has been the greatest ever.

A word about the impact of the press on aviation. As the drama of the jet, its pace, sleekness, dangerous beauty swirled about the world, it became symbolic—to a poor peasant tilling with his wooden plow in Changchou a faraway wonder; to a German miner a plaything for the rich; to a terrorist a target of great opportunity for recognition; to an author the stuff of a thousand novels; to a politician a symbol of noise and danger to run against, to investigate; and to the falcons of the press a rabbit to chase.

The impact of the campaigning politician and the competitive pressure on the development of civil aviation is worth a lecture itself as The Electra Story and The Saga of the DC-10 have revealed. Regrettably, the spectacle sells more than the quiet routine performance of the system and there are fewer and fewer aviation editors and journalists who understand and articulate the crash or the innovation for the edification of the public. In my experience with the passing of the aviation columns in the major dailies and the rise in space stories, we have lost many of the careful critics and accurate reporters who were so helpful in the first two decades. Now the aviation press is composed of a few professional trade pressmen more often than not captive of either advertisers, seductive public relations men or local industry or the amateur writing spot stories in a superficial and misleading manner on a short deadline to a headline writing editor who yearns for the spectacle of the day. Praise be to the precious few who still dig for the truth and lay it out honestly!

Now as we look ahead we recognize the possibilities for great new developments even as some of our aviators become antique and some of our institutions and forces at work reach maturity or is it the other way round? We need vigilantly and constantly to emphasize safety at every stage—design, engineering, manufacturing, quality control, maintenance and operations. Even more safety assurance is required as complexity increases and utilization of aircraft intensifies. The fine line of responsibility for the integrity of the airplane needs redrawing as between manufacturer, operator and regulator. For example, perhaps the FAA should have one of each active transport aircraft withdrawn from service at 10,000 hour intervals, torn down and exposed to total testing for corrosion, fatigue and design and manufacturing failures that may appear after only extended use. Clearly, the technical and operating lessons we have learned must be better spread all round the world—transfer of technology, safety data and continuing education and training become ever more important as volume and complexity of worldwide operations increase. ICAO's role, likewise, becomes more significant. Where civil and military aviation are out of communication or in conflict, we must learn to live together in the airspace; domination must yield to collaboration, patrimony to partnership.

We need a lower cost, safe and quiet intercity transport. Because of short hauls and short runways, there are fewer cities served by scheduled jets now than 1970. Whether it is V/STOL or otherwise, we know it is technically feasible.

Obviously, we need more work on the airport and intra-city transportation—as a component of the world's air transportation systems.

We obviously need a generation of very high speed air transports to compress the world to approach that of satellites in orbit.

Clearly, more work is required on fuel economy and it is within technical reach to achieve a 30% improvement in hydrocarbon fuel economy. But even this won't be good enough when we run out of oil or price jet fuel out of the sky. Even now, we must start thinking new fuels such as hydrogen.

Maybe, most of all we need a lively and enlightened constituency supporting civil aviation in the countries of the world. We have to convert passengers into lobbyists, employees into advocates, experts into educators, if we are to continue to get a favorable balance of competition, private enterprise and public control and support; if we are to get a constant and steady public funding of aeronautical research and development; if we are to keep the pressure on for civil-military partnership and for unification of the public agencies involved in air transportation and, therefore, more rapid decision making. Productivity in all sectors of the system will have to continue to increase lest energy and labor costs price the service out of the market. At the same time, we must never forget the fundamental purpose of serving and protecting the passenger, the shipper, the neighbor and the men and women who make and operate the system. This demands we pause and think and work toward ways of making it more humanistic than mechanistic; more not less considerate of the well being of the individuals involved.

If we can help those well educated, experienced and thoughtful people in the world's legislative, journalistic and regulatory bodies to understand and to keep pace with the technology, we airmen of the world can adapt the technology to best serve the public and ourselves. If we can climb to these altitudes, then surely man's dominion over the airspace will continue and will produce veritable progress for all mankind.

In closing, you will enjoy a quotation from Charles A. Lindbergh's "Spirit of St. Louis" which may help us re-fly the first 40 years of the jet:

> "Aviation combined all the elements I loved
> . . . I began to feel that I lived on a higher
> plane than the skeptics on the ground;
> One that was richer because of its very
> association with the element of danger
> they dreaded, because it was freer of the
> earth to which they were bound."

Jet Airliners

Walter J. Boyne and Donald S. Lopez

The advent of the jet engine provided airline planners with entirely new opportunities, as well as entirely new problems. For the very first time aircraft performance was going to be airframe-limited rather than engine limited. Passengers were going to be carried in larger numbers than ever before, with the consequent loading and unloading problems at terminals. And, because of the high investment, utilization would be more important than ever.

As things turned out, the airline operators adapted to the problem better than could have been expected and almost overnight it seemed that the great fleets of DC-7's and Constellations were superseded by 707-s and DC-8's.

Each new aircraft—Comet, 707, 727, L-1011—was the sum of the dreams of a thousand men, and each one had challenges to overcome. Oddly enough, even though speed was nominally the *raison d'etre* of the jet plane, airline cruising speeds have not changed markedly since the 707 prototype first flew on July 15, 1954. But there has been a marked increase in passenger capacity (if not in comfort) and in productivity, reliability, and ease of maintenance. Jet transport progress has been sparked by improvements in jet engines as the following photo essay will stress.

The English led the way with turboprop transports, and the Vickers Viscount was an immediate success in Europe. It had the further distinction of being the first British aircraft to enter service in the U. S. when Capital Airlines inaugurated service on the Washington to Chicago route on July 26, 1965. The four Rolls Royce Dart turboprop engines provided a cruising speed of about 310 mph, and the aircraft became immensely popular.

Another foreign design, the 1955 Fokker Friendship, was built under license in America by Fairchild, and began service with West Coast airlines on September 27, 1958. Slightly smaller and slower than the Viscount, but less expensive to operate, the F-27 replaced DC-3's on many of the nation's local service airlines.

The era of pure jet airline service was inaugurated with the sleekly beautiful de Havilland Comet, which made its first flight on July 27, 1949, and entered commercial service on the London-Johannesburg route on May 2, 1952. Years ahead of competition, the 36-seat, 500-mile-per-hour airplane proved to be highly reliable and wildly popular with its passengers. The aircraft was flawed, however, by a basic design problem which the testing and certification procedures of the time were unable to anticipate. The cycling of the pressurized cabin created fatigue failures which resulted in catastrophic accidents and the removal of the other-wise excellent plane from airline service. De Havilland made valiant efforts to recover by creating a later series of Comet 4 aircraft, which inaugurated jet transatlantic service on October 4, 1958. Sales were not sufficient to keep the firm competitive, however, and the Comet dropped quietly into history.

The Avro "Jetliner," which first flew on August 10, 1949, less than a month after the Comet, was a straightforward attempt to adapt piston engine airframe design concepts to four Rolls Royce Derwent jet engines. Essentially a compromise, the Jetliner did not go into production.

The Boeing Company, fully aware of the risks involved, was guided by its experience with the B-47 and B-52 bombers to proceed with a jet powered transport rather than experimenting with turbo-props, as many in the industry advocated. In 1952 a decision was made to build, with company funds, a commercial prototype, one which Boeing hoped would be attractive to the military as a tanker. The prototype of the 707 series, the 367-80, made its first flight on July 15, 1954, launching a dynasty of Boeing-built airliners which would dominate the market place for the next quarter century.

Douglas Aircraft responded to the 707 with the DC-8, which made its first flight on May 30, 1958. Douglas had been the principal supplier of passenger aircraft to U. S. carriers, and was no little dismayed by the rapid acceptance of the Boeing design. The DC-8 was an excellent aircraft, but it was unable to gain back the firm's previous dominance in the field.

One of the most unfortunate corporate gambles of the century was the Convair 880/990 series. Begun despite the fact that Boeing and Douglas had already sewn up most of the market, the 880 was slightly smaller and slightly faster than its competitors. Convair persisted in development through an agonizing series of engineering and corporate difficulties, but was forced ultimately to discontinue production. Ironically, some observers believe that the decision to halt the project was made at precisely the time when the market conditions were changing sufficiently to have salvaged the program.

To this point all passenger jet aircraft might be considered "first generation" in that they were powered by the same turbojet engine types (primarily Pratt and Whitney JT3s) which powered military bomber and tanker aircraft. These engines, while much more powerful and efficient than large piston engines, were characterized by a relatively high specific fuel consumption and high noise levels

The second generation of engines, the low by-pass turbofan, had better fuel consumption and was less noisy. They did have some additional maintenance problems, however, which gave operators some initial difficulties.

The Boeing 707-300B, Boeing 727 and DC-8-61 were among the aircraft to use the new engine type. While speed increases were nominal—in fact the speeds at which aircraft cruised changed very little over the first twenty-five years of jet transports—there were great improvements in productivity.

The Convair 990 shown here used G.E. CF-805-23 engines. The "speed bumps" on the trailing edge of the wing improved airflow patterns. Top speed was 640 mph.

The Boeing 727, which was once called a "billion dollar gamble" by popular historians, will go down in history as one of the greatest airliners of all time. Still in production, it is estimated that more than 2,000 of the type will have been built before production is halted. The excellence of the basic design is attested to by its continuous development, which can be traced even to the 757 design. The 757 is intended to compete with the wide body transports of the 1980's.

Part of the 727's success, and indeed, the success of almost all modern transports, is the use of complex leading and trailing edge devices to provide greater lift at lower speed and improved control of drag.

The second generation of transports were "stretched" to accommodate more passengers and to take advantage of the weight savings in fuel allowed by the low bypass turbofan engines. Long fuselage "plugs" were inserted to increase the passenger capacity, and the wings, landing gear and other components were beefed up accordingly.

As jet aviation matured, a new market requirement for short haul aircraft opened. The British offered the BAC-111, while Douglas responded with the DC-9. This twin engine aircraft gained wide acceptance, and was promptly challenged by the Boeing 737, known as "Fat Albert" due to its comparatively wide fuselage.

The third generation of transports used the high bypass turbofan engines like the Pratt and Whitney JT9D or the General Electric CF-6. These powerful engines, which were characterized by greatly improved specific fuel consumption figures and lower noise levels, made the gigantic wide body transport possible.

The first of these, the Boeing 747, weathered initial problems to become the world's leading transport.

McDonnell Douglas and Lockheed chose not to compete directly with Boeing, and instead sought to divide a more limited market for a smaller, three engine wide body type. The Douglas DC-10 emerged first, and has gained a large percentage of the market.

The Lockheed L-1011, after a rather rocky start, now appears to be appealing to a broader market, and sales of its later models are promising.

The Anglo-French Concorde is a striking example
of international cooperation. The joint product of
twin development lines of the French Aérospatiale
and the British BAC companies, the Concorde has
consistently pleased passengers and appalled
economists.

America dropped development of its own SST
for a variety of reasons, including oppostion by
environmentalists, but it turned out to be a fortu-
itous decision. The vast increase in fuel prices
ruled out any chance of the design being
commercially successful.

Lockheed C-130

The jet engine had applications other than for bombers, fighters and transports. It made an unsurpassed military air transport system possible by its application to the three Lockheed aircraft, the turbo prop C-130, the large C-141 StarLifter, and the huge C-5A Galaxy.

Similarly it brought a world of utility to the executive aircraft fleet, beginning with the turbo prop Grumman Gulfstream, and then expanding with a series of pure jets like the Gulfstream II, Learjet, Jet Commander, Sabreliner and JetStar.

Finally, the Strategic Air Command simply could not have accomplished its mission were it not for the military development of the 367-80, the KC-135 tanker.

Two other important areas of jet application are trainers and helicopters. Jet trainers are vital for the training of jet pilots, while the gas turbine engine with its smooth operation and high power to weight ratio is largely responsible for the wide use of helicopters today.

Lockheed C-141

Lockheed C-5A

Grumman Gulfstream II

136

Learjet   Aero Commander 690

North American Sabreliner   Lockheed Jetstar

Boeing 367-80   Boeing KC-135

Figure 1. The B-47.

Jet Aviation Development: A Company Perspective

John E. Steiner

The profound changes in our world civilization during the last forty years have been significantly affected by aviation, which in turn has been cornerstoned by the development of the jet engine. On the commercial side, a combination of technological factors has produced an air transportation system which is having a fundamental effect upon our civilization. In fact, air transportation is considered now by many to be the second greatest single contributor to economic development, exceeded only by education. It has affected our methods of doing business, our pursuit of leisure, and the development of our young people.

On the military side, control of the air has emerged as a decisive military necessity. Operations have become global in nature and geographic isolation has gradually eroded so that no portion of the world is very distant from the rest. A surprise military confrontation 4000

JOHN E. STEINER, a graduate of Massachusetts Institute of Technology, has worked for the Boeing Company in Seattle since 1941, and he has been active in the development, design, testing, certification, product evaluation, and program management of virtually all Boeing airplanes in that period. He was in charge of aerodynamics and requirements during the development and testing of the first U. S. commercial jet transport prototype 707 and its derivatives. He was Vice President, General Manager of the production of the 707, 727, and 737 airplanes; and Vice President, Product Development during the initiation of the Model 747 Program. Mr. William M. Allen, former Chairman of the Board of the Boeing Company, calls Mr. Steiner "the dominant figure in the 727 program." Mr. Steiner represents the U. S. air transport industry around the world, and he is currently Vice President Corporate Product Development at Boeing.

miles distant can be effectively countered by rapid airborne support, with the delivery of thousands of tons of materiel accomplished in a few days—or really a matter of hours. While we maintain intercontinental ballistic missile deterrent systems, the day-to-day peace-keeping function depends very heavily upon jet aircraft—of both military and commercial types.

It has been Boeing's good fortune, as an aerospace company, to be involved in the development of the world's largest military and commercial jet aircraft. Such development has been spread over almost the entire forty year period, and has involved development of eleven major military and commercial jet types, with either a new type, or major derivative introduced on an average of about every eleven months over this time. Credit, if due, must accrue to those men, nations, and companies who participated—for our role was small in relation to the total, and the developmental opportunities, as we shall see, were often thrust upon us.

It is the purpose of this paper to review these developments—to identify the conditions which produced them, and where possible, to identify the reasons for the degree of success achieved—in the belief that a review done in this manner will form a fabric, the pattern of which may contain threads of interest, and perhaps of importance in extending them into the future.

This discussion is an examination of Boeing's involvement in aviation history, according to the wishes of Smithsonian conference planning. As such is it illustrative, but in no way complete. Several other industrial companies and

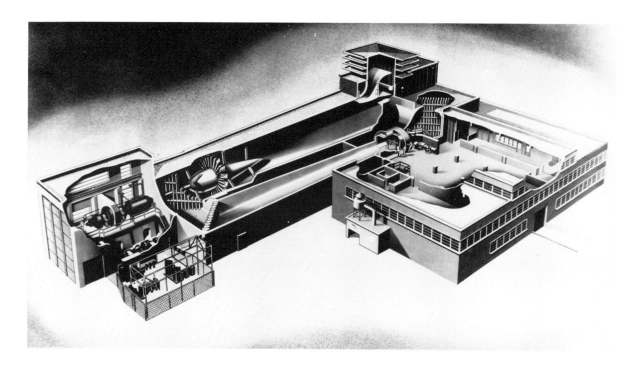

Figure 2. The Boeing wind tunnel.

government organizations participated in jet aviation development in about an equal degree.

Boeing's first involvement with jet engines was like that of other U. S. bomber manufacturers, when in late 1943 the Bombardment Branch of the Army Air Forces put out study contracts to five manufacturers for a medium-weight jet bomber design. The intention was to examine a variety of jet bomber concepts with the possibility of buying prototypes from each manufacturer. North American's efforts produced the straight wing XB-45; Convair the straight wing XB-46; Martin developed the straight wing six-engine XB-48; and Northrop the tailless XB-49. As the contract study period neared its conclusion, Boeing asked to be allowed to study the subject further. The problem, as we saw it, was that none of the airframes being examined had speed (Mach number) characteristics that fully exploited the jet engine performance potential. We were thus in the midst of a deeply frustrating development process when, in early 1945, the wing sweepback phenomenon came to light.

Bob Jones of NACA (now NASA) at Langley

Field Research Center invented wing sweepback, and George Schairer, Boeing's chief aerodynamicist, first heard of it from that source. Although unknown to NACA and Boeing, sweepback had been discovered earlier in Germany. You may recall that, as World War II drew to a close in Europe, the U. S. sent combined military and civilian technical groups to ascertain the latest level of German technology. Mr. Schairer joined the Dr. von Karman team and arrived at Reichsmarshal Goering's Aeronautical Research Institute at Braunschweig the morning Germany surrendered. United States, British, and other personnel were involved in the trip, and the examination of the wind tunnel files gave even greater credibility to the NACA development than the Americans had been exposed to. The Boeing bomber team at Seattle was redirected by George's letter sent May 10, 1945, which told us to investigate sweepback, which we did, although not without the usual resistance from within the organization.

The effects of wing sweep on transonic aerodynamics had been discovered in 1935 by Dr. Adolf Busemann in Germany and had actually been published but not remembered in the U.S.,

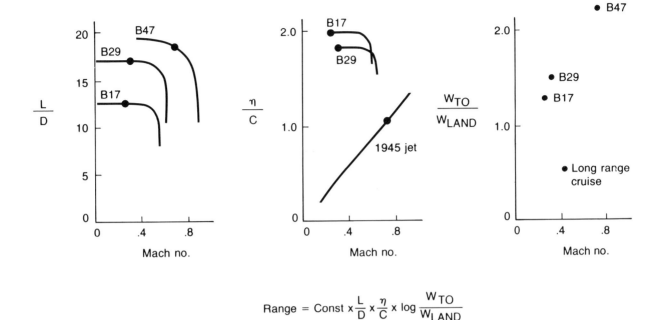

$$\text{Range} = \text{Const} \times \frac{L}{D} \times \frac{\eta}{C} \times \log \frac{W_{TO}}{W_{LAND}}$$

Figure 3. The challenge and the response.

U.K., or elsewhere outside Germany. Actually, sweep was not of significant interest until the advent of the jet engine which increased its efficiency radically with speed. The Germans had their first swept-back airplanes in operation at the end of World War II.

The B-47 depicted in the photograph in Figure 1 first flew at Seattle on December 17, 1947, the 44th anniversary of the Wright brothers' first flight.

You now know where the sweepback came from, but there was a great deal more to the breakthrough than that. Under Schairer's sponsorship, Boeing started development of its own wind tunnel in 1941. It was completed and put into service in 1944, and at the time was the largest and fastest privately owned facility available. The test section was 8 feet high, 12 feet wide and 20 feet long. It was powered by an 18,000 horsepower synchronous motor driving a 24 foot diameter single stage 16 blade fan.

The velocity range was from zero to .975 Mach number with a bare test section. The models were supported upright by either a two or three strut mount which was attached to a six component external balance. The structure was reinforced concrete and was vented to the atmos-

phere at the end of the fan diffuser. The general arrangement is shown in Figure 2.

Use of that tunnel on a maximum effort basis resulted in a great many more developments. There was no real "body of data" applicable to jet aircraft at that time, so the dedication of that research facility to the B-47 solutions resulted in a truly remarkable achievement.

The scope of the problem is shown in Figure 3. The propulsive efficiency term was about one-half of that of B-17 or B-29—and to get even, this one had to go to Mach number speeds beyond those formerly practical. To compensate, the other two terms—lift over drag and takeoff weight over landing weight, had to be radically increased.

With this large a problem, solutions required innovation, wind tunnel testing and both emperical and calculated solutions. Jet engines wanted to go fast, but conventional airframes did not. Furthermore, determining how to mount jet engines on an airplane was anything but a solved problem. Many configurations were tested, among them those shown in Figure 4.

Early Boeing bomber configurations incorporated the more bulky centrifugal compressor jet engines. However, most B-47 designs were done

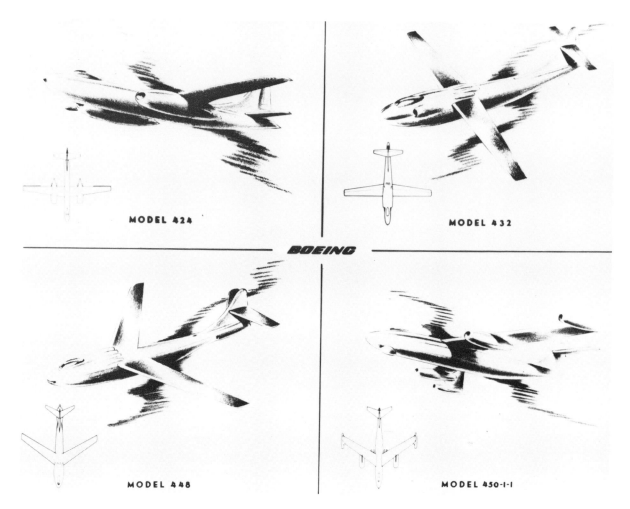

MODEL 424

MODEL 432

MODEL 448

MODEL 450-1-1

Figure 4. Evolution of the B-47.

with the higher fineness ratio axial flow machines. Engines in the body were tried, as were engines close underneath the wings. Podded nacelles on the aft end of the body beneath the horizontal tail were tried, and they were to become popular years later. Podded nacelles above and behind the wing, somewhat similar to those in recent aerodynamic developments, were tried. In addition, German data on podded nacelles was examined. In the course of all this experimentation and study, it was determined that an underwing podded nacelle with the engine moved forward so that its pressure field did not interfere with the wing's pressure field gave the best solution. The design grew to have double pods forward of the inboard wing and a single podded engine on the wing tip. The reason for the six engines was purely a need for thrust, since the early J-47s were rated at only 5000 lbs. thrust each. Tips were later extended out beyond the engine in an even greater effort to gain performance.

In the process it was realized that the configuration had structurally become very elastic. Much of the science of aeronautical structural dynamics as we now know it emerged as a result. An example of wind tunnel tests of an aeroelastic model is illustrated in Figure 5.

The impracticality of cutting the wing torque box for the landing gear was recognized early, and this aeroelastic consideration, plus aerodynamic considerations, led to the use of a bicycle gear with wheels mounted in the fuselage. A bicycle gear maintains constant aircraft attitude for takeoff or landing, and the aircraft

Figure 5. B-47 structural dynamics model.

cannot be rotated for takeoff or landing when on the ground, leading to poor braking at high speeds.

The combination of low thrust engines and a bicycle landing gear led to installation of JATO bottles for takeoff use when necessary and to a drogue parachute deployed at landing. The B-47 configuration also led to the development of a wheel antiskid system not unlike those used today to sense impending skids, since the bicycle gear did not allow rapid weight transfer to the wheels during deceleration.

However, this was not all. The XB-47 had a flight control system composed of rigid feedback loop hydraulic power controls with automatic manual backup, a system similar to that used on the 727 fifteen years later. It had a flaperon control which varied the Fowler flap asymmetrically to augment the ailerons; and it had

leading edge slats, also similar to, but much smaller than, those used fifteen years later. The slats were eventually removed from the production configuration. The B-47 did not use spoilers, but spoilers were developed on an experimental B-47 aircraft.

The B-47 wing was long and thin. Its 9.43 aspect ratio is still the highest ever used on a swept-wing airplane. The airfoil was 12 percent thick from root to tip. In addition, the bomb bay was sized to carry the "fat boy" atomic bomb, which, surprisingly, none of the competitive machines could do. In addition, the B-47 drag was substantially better than estimated.

High sweepback gave the B-47 high effective dihedral and unacceptable dutch-roll characteristics. This was corrected through the use of a full time stability augmentation system consisting of a rate gyro which put in corrective rudder motions—a mechanism also similar to those used on the 707 and 727 airplanes over a decade later. It was probably also the first production use of a full time stability augmentation system.

The XB-47 was not immediately heralded as the enormous breakthrough that it really was. Tests of the other prototypes had left much to be desired, and the Air Force had become skeptical about the range ability of a jet bomber. The XB-47 was, of course, late in the prototype competitive game, but its spectacular flight performance eventually attracted wide attention within the Air Force. In the end, more than 1300 were manufactured by Boeing and nearly 700, in addition, were built by Douglas and Lockheed under license. Boeing's president, Mr. William M. Allen, who took charge in 1945, became a confirmed jet enthusiast as the B-47 was developed. It was his leadership and his confidence in the future of jet transportation which spearheaded our later developments.

The B-52 was also developed out of an airplane competition, but one of a different kind. The circumstances were approximately as follows: In 1941, President Franklin Roosevelt and Prime Minister Winston Churchill met to discuss the problems facing the U. S. if Britain fell. The two agreed that British collapse would require North American bases for strategic bombing of Germany and that the U. S. would develop airplanes for this capability. This agreement resulted in the B-36: a six-engine, propeller driven, reciprocating engine intercontinental bomber, capable of carrying a large bomb load for a long distance. Later, somewhat in parallel with the medium bomber jet prototype program, a competition was held to develop the second generation of long range heavy bombers. At the time, there was not the slightest doubt in the minds of those in the Army Air Force that this had to be a big straight wing turboprop aircraft. In June 1946, Boeing was advised that it had won the design competition for the new long range, heavy bomber.

One must remember that at this time, several influences were simultaneously at work. An at-tempt was being made to match the jet engine with a medium range bomber airframe with no real hope that it could be successfully extrapolated to an intercontinental bomber. Simultaneously, the heavy bomb load, for which the B-36 had been designed, had been reduced to the weight of one atomic bomb. Finally, the big propeller airplanes had more than their share of propeller trouble, and the turboprop did not promise any relief from this.

Again using its excellent wind tunnel facility, Boeing diligently performed two years of development to meet the objectives. The objectives were a 10,000 pound load carried 10,000 statute miles, or, by Air Corps rules, an operating radius of three-eights of this (or 3300 nautical miles). Boeing studied both turboprop and turbojet aircraft, but concentrated on the Air Force desired turboprop. An attractive turboprop airplane was developed and a design team arrived at Wright Field to present their findings for approval in October 1948. The nagging problem was that the engine and propeller manufacturers estimated that it might take as long as four years to develop the necessary power plant.

German technology stepped in again in the person of Dr. Waldemar Voigt, who was at that time an advisor to the Bombardment Branch. Dr. Voigt advised Col. Pete Warden that he ought to have Boeing try a swept-wing jet bomber, using refueling if necessary, to accomplish the desired range. Col. Warden, with only a cursory glance at the latest turboprop study results, asked Boeing to make a hurried assessment of the jet bomber concept that he could use in discussions at the Pentagon. This shocking disclosure was on Thursday, October 21, 1948. What followed was no less than incredible.

There are many myths in the aviation business, but the story that the B-52 was designed in a Van Cleve Hotel room at Dayton, Ohio, happens to be true. The team worked around the clock, and by Monday presented Col. Warden with a three view drawing, estimated performance, and a model of the airplane carved out of balsa. Reproductions of the actual hotel room drawings of the three view and the profile, signed by E. C. Wells, Boeing's chief engineer, are shown in Figures 6 and 7, Based on a pre-

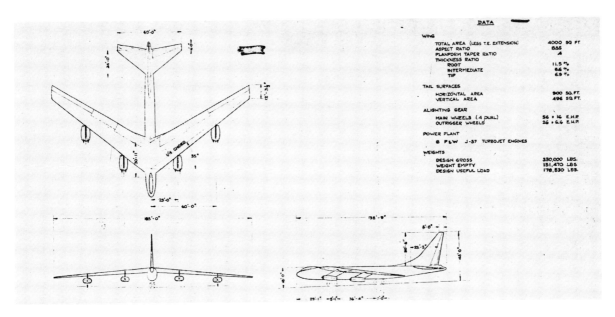

Figure 6. General arrangement of the XB-52.

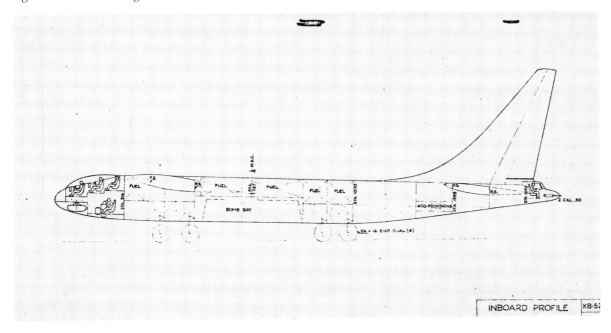

Figure 7. Inboard profile of the XB-52.

liminary review of the package, Warden instructed Boeing to make significant reductions in the turboprop effort in Seattle and to proceed with the jet activity. He then confirmed this decision during a Pentagon visit.

The tortuous path leading to the XB-52, and then the production B-52, is shown in simplified form in Figure 8.

The events of October 1948 dampened the large propeller development program in this country. By this we do not mean that propellers for major airframes will not come back—they

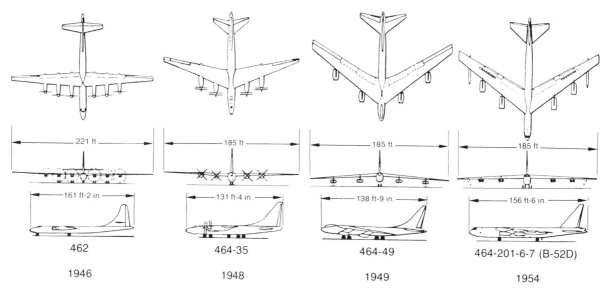

| 462 | 464-35 | 464-49 | 464-201-6-7 (B-52D) |
| 1946 | 1948 | 1949 | 1954 |

Figure 8. Early days of the B-52 evolution.

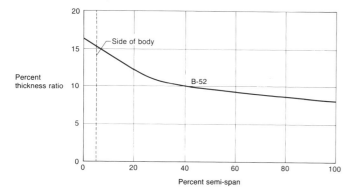

Figure 9. B-52 wing thickness vs. span.

might. But if so, it will be after a lapse of about 30 years.

The B-52 borrowed much, of course, from the B-47, which established the technology base. However, it added one very significant piece to the technology which is illustrated in Figure 9.

Again, by massive empirical wind tunnel effort, using the Boeing wind tunnel, we had found that the wing root thickness could be increased substantially without significantly degrading its high Mach number drag characteristics. This had an extremely beneficial effort on weight empty and thus on the airplane's struc-

tural efficiency and payload range. It also reduced undesirable aeroelasticity, and improved the high Mach number stability.

However, these empirical results were not particularly welcome at a time when NACA had just proved that the way to get high Mach number was by "Coke-bottling" the body at the wing-body intersection. This seemed totally incompatible with the slab-sided body and thickened wing root that Boeing was using. The Air Force wanted it explained throughly before Boeing could proceed, and so a Boeing team arrived at Wright Field in October 1949, ready to defend their thickened-root plus an airfoil distribution which moved the point of maximum thickness forward (in percent chord) as it approached the body. Again, German technology experience came to the rescue and Dr. Bernhard Gothert, who was by then an advisor at Wright Field, confirmed that, in theory, the Boeing approach would work.

The original Westinghouse J-40 engines were replaced by Pratt & Whitney's new J-57 before the XB-52, illustrated in Figure 10, was built and flown in April of 1952. The original tandem cockpit on the XB-52 was changed to a side-by-side cockpit in the production model and the body was lengthened to near its present length.

From 1952 to 1962 a long series of B-52s emerged. The airplane that was built to fly in

Figure 10. The XB-52.

Figure 11. The B-52 Stratofortress.

smooth air at high altitudes also became a low-level terrain follower with structurally redesigned wings. The vertical tail was reduced in height and, finally, new fan engines were installed. A picture of a late model B-52 is shown in Figure 11.

Now, over 30 years after its original design,

B-52s remain the backbone of our western world strategic bomber inventory. With new engines, new structure and a totally new avionics package, little is left of the original other than its name and general appearance. The B-52 has truly become a legend in its own time.

Let us discuss for a moment the background of

the 367-80, a prototype, which was, of course, the first U. S. jet transport. By 1950, The Boeing Company had become convinced from its B-47 and B-52 activities and from the development of the improved efficiency Pratt & Whitney J-57 axial flow turbojet, that the way of the future was in turbojets and not turboprops. During 1950, we attempted to sell to the world's major airlines a commercial airplane which had a scaled-down B-52 wing and was powered by four J-57's. We called it the Model 473. Even though the British Comet had pioneered the jet transport route before us, we were unable to obtain sufficient airline interest to continue that commercially-oriented transport program in spite of our visiting every large airline in the United States and Europe.

During 1957, we attempted to sell the same concept to the Air Force as a tanker, but only were successful at wearing our shoes out treading the halls at Dayton. At that time, Dayton's view was that military transports must have truckbed height, high-wing and body-mounted gear—"the new look." Even though the KC-97, and before that the KB-29 and KB-50, had pioneered the way for a tanker derived from a bomber, Wright Field did not look kindly upon a 35-degree swept-wing jet for the tanker mission.

Thus, in the spring of 1952, we decided to privately finance and build a commercial prototype which we initially called the 707. (The 500 and 600 model number were reserved for "pilotless aircraft," missiles, and non-aircraft products, so we were forced to the 700 series.) Wright Field had not been receptive, but we still wanted to sell our 707 concept as both a commercial airplane and as a tanker. At the last minute, Mr. Allen changed the model designation to 367-80. Actually, 367 was the model number of the KC-97, and -80 was simply the 80th version that had been developed under that generic model number. So our prototype was launched—with a non-applicable model number from a previous military tanker airplane. There were lots of other problems, including the happenstance that our wind tunnel was shut down for conversion to a NACA-developed, slotted test section, 58,000 horsepower transonic configuration. The

Dash 80 wing was really the well-developed 25-degree sweepback (1951) tanker wing swept an additional 10 degrees which we checked out in the Cornell tunnel. Figure 12 is a photograph of the airplane in flight.

Building a big prototype airplane with one's own money was not a very common thing, either then or now. The Dash 80 gamble staked about one quarter of the Company's total net worth on our conviction that "jet was right." Other companies had not yet come to that conclusion, as evidenced by the fact that the first turboprop Lockheed Electra was not delivered until late 1958. The Douglas heavy transport, the C-133, also powered with propellers, was delivered in 1956. Thus, it was a big day when our "one-of-a-kind" rolled out as it pictured in Figure 13.

A major technological change in the Dash 80 was the return to a conventional tricycle landing gear. Unlike the B-47 and the B-52, the Dash 80 was a low wing airplane to facilitate a long body deck for carrying passengers or possibly freight. We felt it had to fly more or less like the airplanes the airline pilots were used to, so it had to have a tricycle landing gear allowing the pilot to lift the nose at takeoff and to depress the nose at landing. It was no easy task to fit a tricycle gear on a swept-wing airplane. The gear development had its troubles, including a main gear collapse during a taxi trial. A picture of the landing gear is shown in Figure 14.

In addition, the Dash 80 flight control system, except for rudder and spoilers, returned to the aerodynamic controls historically associated with commercial airplanes. There were many additional developments designed to make the airplane fly like commercial airplanes had flown. Spoilers were necessary to get the weight on the wheels and increase the drag during deceleration. A better yaw damper was a requirement. We also knew we had to face up to thrust reversers and noise suppressors, but we could delay that for a little while.

Soon after the gear repair was made, the Dash 80 made its first flight on July 15, 1954. Like its predecessors, it was successful.

In the 1930s, U. S. transcontinental travel took about 18 to 20 hours and it was not a lot less

Figure 12. The 367-80.

Figure 13. The rollout of the "Dash 80."

Figure 14. Landing gear of the 367-80.

Figure 15. The 367-80 uses triple flaps in a flight test.

than that in 1940. Then with the advent of the DC-6 in 1947, it came down to about 12 hours, and with the DC-7 to about 10 hours. In the autumn of 1955, the prototype Dash 80 startled the nation with a transcontinental flight from an airport near Seattle to Andrews Air Force Base, Maryland, in three hours and 58 minutes eastbound and four hours and 21 minutes westbound.

The Dash 80 went on to father the KC-135 tanker and then the long line of 707 commercial transports. It stayed with The Boeing Company for many years as a flying test bed doing yeoman work as depicted in Figure 15.

It was the first airplane to test-fly a triple-slotted flap. It became an aft-engine testbed.

Then with NASA help, the airplane was altered to an externally blown flap configuration. Over the years, the Dash 80 tested many concepts, and these are just illustrative. The Dash 80 was presented to the Smithsonian Institution in May of 1972.

Boeing had become a supplier of heavy tankers many years earlier. The mission was of course the supplying of fuel in large quantities to long range bombers and to fighter aircraft. The flying boom refueling system was developed by Boeing to allow the use of a straight-through metal pipe, rather than a flexible hose, which was satisfactory for fighters but not of an adequate transfer rate for bombers. Our parade of tankers is shown in Figure 16.

The emergence of the B-47 and B-52 had led to a jet tanker requirement—the sort of thing we tried so desperately to start in 1951. By 1953, the

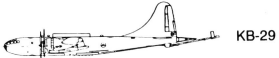

KB-29

KB-50

KC-97

Figure 16. The lineage of the KC-135.

Air Force held a jet tanker competition in which the Boeing Company participated. Ironically, we lost the competition. However, by the time we had our Dash 80 prototype up and flying, we could make delivery guarantees that no other company could match. The Air Force found this to be irresistible , and in late 1954 a contract for the KC-135 was awarded. The first KC-135, illustrated in Figure 17, was delivered in 1957.

The KC-135 was a substantially different airplane from the Dash 80. It gave the engineers a second chance, and as we all know, that can well mean a complete revision. In addition, we saw this as an opportunity to obtain tooling commonality with a commercial derivative. Among other things, we changed the body width as shown in Figure 18.

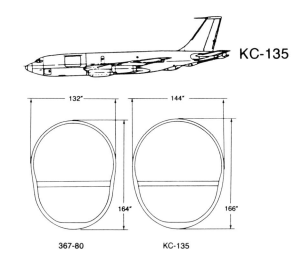

KC-135

367-80   KC-135

Figure 18. A body cross section comparison.
Figure 17. The KC-135.

Figure 19. The KC-135 as a tanker.

A great many commercial mockups had shown that a diameter of 144 inches should be optimum for 4-, 5-, and 6-abreast seating. This part of our plan did not work, as I will describe later.

The KC-135 went on to be an airplane of many uses—not only a tanker, shown in Figure 19, but a reconnaissance airplane, an electronic countermeasures airplane and a military platform for a large number of other missions. More than 800 were built.

Like the B-52, the KC-135s have continued for years as the nation's primary tanker fleet. And, with improvements and possible re-engining, they may continue as such for many years to come.

Even the most skeptical airlines were impressed by the performance of the Dash 80, and since we owned the airplane, we could make airline demonstration as we saw fit.

We even made one demonstration that was not planned—or approved. Seattle in those days held a major powerboat race on Lake Washington for unlimited hydroplanes and it was common practice for us to take our airline and military customers out in boats to watch it. Our chief test pilot could not pass up the opportunity to show off his airplane in front of 200,000 people or so. With a full test crew aboard, he made a cou;le of barrel rolls at altitude, then came down to about 200 feet and barrel-rolled over the speedboat course, returning to do the same thing in the other direction. A lot of people went home thinking about jet transports instead of hydroplanes. Perhaps we demonstrated that companies can risk their financial future on something they believe in—and chief test pilots can risk their jobs on something they feel very strongly about.

The commercial transport business had been dominated by the Douglas Company for over two decades, and a majority of the airliners flying were Douglas built. Naturally, Douglas did not take kindly to the upstart Boeing Company building a jet transport prototype, and proceeded to do considerable developmental work. However, I do not believe they really became serious until they saw the Dash 80 in actual existance.

The first big domestic airline competition was for the United Airlines order in 1955. We thought we were ahead—we had demonstrated everything. However, Douglas had built up great confidence on the part of United Airlines and others, and they also focused on points where they thought we were weak. Their DC-8 had a larger wing area, less sweep back, and a slightly wider cabin cross-section. The wing did not decide the United question, but the body cross-section did—in the DC-8's favor for an order of 30 airplanes.

After losing United, we made the decision to forget the commonality objective with the KC-135 and widen the cabin as shown on Figure 20.

To this day, all KC-135s and C-135s, and all 707s have four inches difference in their body diameters. Not only were we unable to use the KC-135 body tooling, but extensive investigation into the airline situation led us to structurally change the wing, so the KC-135 and 707 had even less commonality.

The real test came with Pan American and its intercontinental requirement. Pan Am had announced on October 13, 1955, twelve days before the United Airlines order, that they would buy 25 DC-8s and 20 707s. The DC-8s were to be powered by JT-4 (J-75) engines, rather than the lower powered JT-3 engines we were using. This, combined with the DC-8s larger wing and higher gross weight gave the DC-8 a non-stop Atlantic capability, which was not matched by the initial 707. Pan Am told us they were buying the 707s because of their earlier delivery date and considered them to be interim equipment. The scene this time was the Ritz Tower Hotel in New York, instead of the Van Cleve Hotel in Dayton, but the results were similarly traumatic. Over a weekend, we decided we had to meet the competition or face failure. We laid out a new wing and made aerodynamic estimates in the hotel room. Ed Wells then went back to Seattle to re-orient the program while some of us stayed in New York to tell Pan American what we were doing. The result was a two-model program, with two different wing areas, two different engines, and two different body lengths. A comparison of the wings is shown in Figure 21.

On November 8, 1955, we received an order

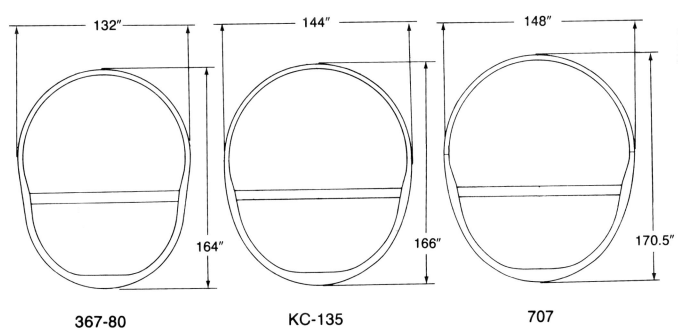

367-80   KC-135   707

Figure 20. Cross section evolution.

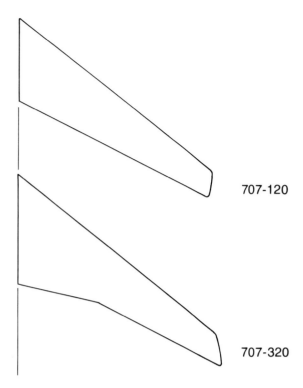

Figure 21. Wing plan form comparison between the 120 and the 320 of the 707 series.

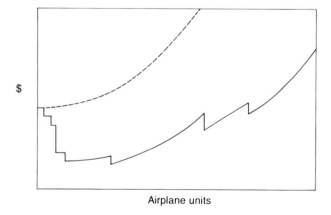

Figure 22. Risk and break even chart of the 707/720 program.

from American Airlines for 30 of the smaller 707s, but with the wider body diameter—which was now one inch wider than that of the DC-8.

Eventually all of Pan American's order was shifted to our larger 707-320 except six, which Pan Am retained due to their earlier delivery date. In the end Pan Am standardized on Boeing 707s.

There thus came to be a head-on competition between the DC-8 and the 707. As a result of the competition, both aircraft became better—a good illustration of the value of competition in the development of quality products.

Not having the equivalent of the Douglas customer base, we had to put additional money into our gamble. When Qantas Airways of Australia wanted a special long-range small model, we shortened the body. No other airline ever purchased that body length, but we eventually produced 13 for Qantas. When Braniff needed a special highly-powered airplane for South America's high altitude fields, we put a larger engine, the JT-4, on the smaller airframe. Braniff's airplanes were the only ones ever to combine the original small 707 size with the JT-4 engines. Each such model, of course, not only had design and manufacturing changes, but required a recertification program.

The upgraded Boeing wind tunnel became significant, and since we knew we were about out of money and would not have another chance, the design of the 707-320 was carefully honed. If you remember the range equation contains L/D and the log of the weight ratio. The combination of L/D and weight ratio of the 707-320 was not equalled for over 15 years afterwards.

The financial side of the 707 grew very dim indeed. Shown on Figure 22 are two items, the upper line is an illustration of a "normal" commercial airplane program in which the risk of the full development is taken when the first contract is signed. One expects after the first delivery to repay the investment gradually, finally crossing zero at what is called the break-even point. What actually happened in the 707 case is illustrated by the lower line, adding model after model and risk after risk. This plunged the Company deeply into debt, and stretched the 707 breakeven point far to the right.

However, we kept hard at it, using improved engines, raising the gross weight, selling freighter and combination versions, and adapting the airplane for many uses. We have built

Figure 23a. Civilian use of the 707.

930 707s, and the airplane has seen both military and civilian uses, as shown in Figures 23a and 23b.

The airplane now forms the aircraft platform for the E-3A Airborne Warning and Control System, the most sophisticated such system in the world. Photographs of the original 707 commercial airplane compared to the modern E-3A military system are shown in Figure 23.

The 727 story started in May of 1958 when a program task force was formed, reporting to the general manager of all commercial activity, with the job of identifying the program, technology, and configuration that would make a successful short-to-medium range commercial jet. The number 727 was chosen because the 717 had become the KC-135. The date was of interest because the first Electra, a turboprop airplane optimized for the short-to-medium range role,

Figure 23b. Military use of the 707.

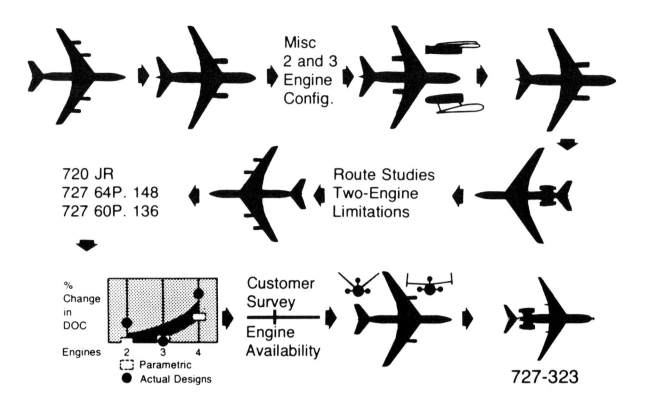

720 JR
727 64P. 148
727 60P. 136

Misc
2 and 3
Engine
Config.

Route Studies
Two-Engine
Limitations

%
Change
in
DOC

Engines   2   3   4
☐ Parametric
● Actual Designs

Customer
Survey
+
Engine
Availability

727-323

Figure 24. Development of the 727.

was not delivered until October, 1958. Our first 707-100 was also delivered in October, 1958. Convair's 880, which was an all-new jet airplane designed to do the short-to-medium range job, was delivered in May, 1960, and Boeing's answer to the 880, the 720 (which was a short body 707 derivative), had its first delivery in April, 1960.

Go-ahead was not actually made on the 727 until December, 1960, and the accomplishments during the intervening period of time are roughly shown in Figure 24.

We started with the obvious miniaturized 707 just as our competitor—Douglas—started with a miniaturized DC-8, which they called the DC-9. They had "sold" the four-engine DC-9 to United Airlines long before we sold United the 727. However, the sale was contingent on Douglas obtaining another major customer, which was never obtained, and the program died.

The Boeing Board of Directors similarly insisted that we have orders from two of the four major U. S. domestic airlines (which at that time were United, American, Eastern and TWA) before we could start the 727 program. Part of the problem depicted in Figure 24 was the near impossibility of fulfilling that requirement. TWA was not in a financial condition to buy anybody's short range airplane. American had already purchased a large number of Lockheed Electras and had no interest in taking on another airplane.

United, as in the case with Douglas, was willing to buy a four-engine airplane, but because of their high altitude Denver situation were, at that time, unwilling to consider a two-engine airplane. Eastern, even though they also had purchased a fleet of Electras, perceived the advantages of the jet and were willing to entertain the purchase of a jet replacement for the Electra, providing its economics were competitive. They believed that such economics could only be obtained through the use of two engines.

Thus to launch the 727 program, we had to, in some way, find a middle ground between United's desire for four engines and Eastern's desire for two. The middle ground proved to be a three-engine airplane, and it was this, more than any other factor, which led to the three engines on the 727.

There had not been a commercial three-engine airplane built for 25 to 30 years (although one, the British Trident, was in work), and in attempting three engines we felt we had to have all the arguments we could muster. In the lower left corner of Figure 24 is a chart comparing the economics of two-, three-, and four-engine aircraft. Previous Rolls Royce work had shown that the economics of a medium-size and a medium-range three-engine airplane while not as good as those with two, were much better than those with four. In fact, the Rolls work showed that the three was economically better than the two, if one overpowered the twin to meet high altitude takeoff objectives. We independently confirmed the same general conclusions. These conclusions were applicable to engines of that day and do not necessarily hold for today's new engines. The physical size of the 727-100 was always about the same as that of the Electra, as illustrated in Figure 25.

In the two and one-half years available, the task force completed several thousand hours of wind tunnel work attempting to fully understand the difficult 727 design requirements. The airplane was specifically designed to meet the usable 4860 feet of the instrument runway 4-22 at New York's LaGuardia Airport and fly out of that field nonstop to Miami. This required guarantee led to the use of the triple-slotted flap and leading edge slat combination which is still the highest non-powered lift system ever used on a swept-wing airplane. However, there were many other problems. To achieve the difficult economic capabilities of the turboprop Electra, the airplane had to climb fast, fly fast and descend fast. One of the advantages of the "T" tail was that it permitted deployment of wing spoilers without airplane vibration, leading to very high usable rates of descent. There are ways of obtaining this with a low tail (using spoilers outboard of the stabilizer tips plus some forms

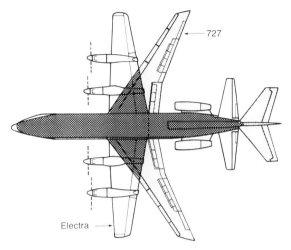

Figure 25. Size comparison of the 727.

of pitch correction) but we did not know them at the time.

We tested low, medium and high tails. We tested landing gears in wing pods as well as folded into the body. We tested high lift systems, both in the wind tunnel and in flight, with the use of the Dash 80 test ship. We combined the technology of the B-47 flight control system with the technology of the Electra control system to obtain a three axis control balance far superior to that of the 707. From the start, the 727 had to be a "pilot's airplane" and this meant a refinement of flight control systems that we had never before attempted. As a small example of this, the stick force per "g" between extreme forward CG (center of gravity) and extreme aft CG on the 707 and DC-8 has a variation of about 7 or so to 1, whereas the 727 has a mechanical computer that senses center of gravity position, and alters stick force to achieve a stick force per "g" variation of only about 2 to 1 over its center of gravity range. This was important on an aft engine airplane where wide variations of CG would be encountered.

A serious argument existed for a considerable time as to whether the best configuration

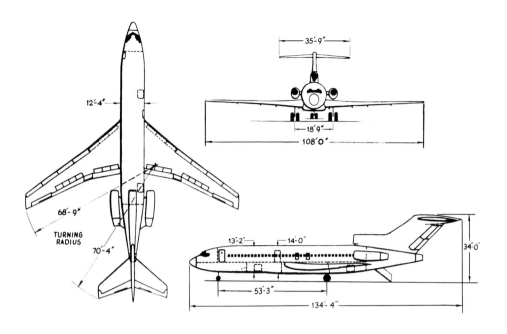

Figure 26. General arrangement of the 727.

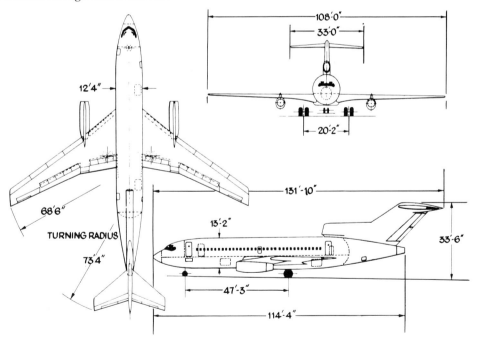

Figure 27. Alternate configuration of the 727.

was three engines located aft, or two on the wing and one aft. We set up competitive teams and assigned them to optimize the airplanes shown in Figures 26 and 27. In the end we found that there were advantages and disadvantages to each. The loadability of an aft engine configuration was definitely more difficult, particularly as future stretch models were envisioned. However, there was some evidence of a drag improvement, particularly when short field and very high lift versus wing area trades were considered. Wing area, of course, affected economics. There were even some indications that the aft engine airplane was slightly cheaper to build, because its systems were more concentrated. None of the effects was decisive, but we finally opted for the aft engine configuration. A minor additional defense of this configuration is that it results in a very quiet front half of the passenger cabin during takeoff and climb, an advantage which becomes more or less lost as cruise speed is gained.

By this time, we had our 58,000 horsepower transonic tunnel fully operational, and we took the structural dynamics and aeroelastic situation one step further—by testing aeroelastic models not only at low speed, but at transonic speeds, such as was the case for the partial model shown in Figure 28.

Boeing was not unique in perceiving the need for a new technology short-to-medium range airplane. Douglas had seen it in the original four engine DC-9. Lockheed had seen it in the Electra. British de Havilland Aircraft Corporation saw it in the Trident, and Convair saw it in the 880. What was unique was that, in the middle of the 707 financial dilemma, Boeing decided to go into a large production program involving an extremely advanced state-of-the-art airplane without a prototype—for the first time ever at Boeing. Such is the force of a competitive environment.

An oddity in the 727 development was the engine choice. Boeing selected a Rolls Royce Spey derivative (the ARB 963). United went along. Eastern did not, and the Pratt & Whitney JT-8 program was hastily born—so hastily, in fact, that flight test failures were common. Nevertheless, P&W "made it right" and the JT-8

Figure 28. Transonic model for the 727.

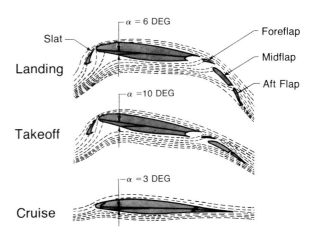

Figure 29. The high lift systems of the 727.

went on to become the world's largest jet engine program ever. Figure 29 diagrams the wing flap system used, the elements of which spread out fore and aft as they lowered. The system worked, and the takeoff and landing guarantees were met. In addition, the airplane flaps-up cruise drag turned out about 10 percent less than predicted—partly because the technical staff chief, Bill Cook (who had experienced leaky slats as a chief designer of the B-47) secretly put

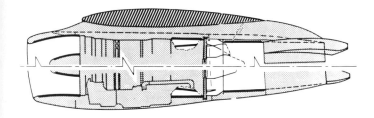

Figure 30. Nacelle of the 737.

drag for leaky slats into the performance calculations, while at the same time driving the project to seal them better.

The 727 has really had two lives. The first life began in 1963 on initial delivery. The second life began in late 1970 when it was recognized that a combination of U. S. domestic competitive frequency requirements and system development and route proliferations could not be as economically addressed by the larger widebody airplanes. The domestic system really needed a smaller, but modern, airplane. We used the longer body model developed in the late 60s; redesigned the aircraft, improved its noise characteristics, gross weight and payload range; put in a new interior which looked like a "wide body" and proceeded to sell it in large quantity. Today, almost 20 years after the original design, the airplane is being built at a rate of 12 per month, has over 1600 firm sales, and will very likely increase to 2000 for an all-time record.

There was obviously a market for an airplane below the size of the 727, and British Aircraft Corporation (BAC) had flown the BAC-111 in August, 1963, to serve that market. Since much of the market was in the United States, the Douglas Company perceived a real threat to its traditional market and delivered the DC-9-10 in late 1965 to counter that threat. Both airplanes employed two engines aft and a "T" tail. Boeing continued technical work but was reluctant to be third in the marketplace. However, by 1964, a unique design concept had been developed.

The key to the 737 configuration was the so-called "stream tube" nacelle used on the outboard location of the B-47. The fundamental idea was that if the nacelle were long and thin with respect to the wing cord, its pressure peaks

would occur forward and aft of the airfoil pressure peaks and would thus have almost as good a drag situation as the forward lower-podded position (this is why the outboard B-47 nacelle worked). This, then, permitted a low tail and a shorter airplane and made the use of a relatively wide body (e.g., the same width as the 707/DC-8) somewhat easier. The actual nacelle used is shown in Figure 30. The original 737-100 had about a 90 foot wing span and a 90 foot overall length and flew about 90 passengers in a mixed class configuration. A conditional initial sale was made to Lufthansa German Airlines. However, the real key to a large market was perceived to lie within Eastern Airlines and United Airlines, both of whom were uncommitted. Douglas, seeing its market again threatened, went back to the drawing board and offered Eastern a very substantially improved DC-9, the DC-9-30. Eastern bought it, and we responded by offering United a new improved 737-200. United bought that, and the horse race was really on, but with Douglas having a time advantage.

The "little airplane that could" is shown in Figure 31 as it takes off from a gravel field. It was small for the number of passengers that it held (now up to about 100, two class) with the wing span of a DC-3 and with a length only slightly greater than the span. The fundamental advantage was that it had the same body width as the 707 and DC-8 and would, therefore, handle the cargo or passenger accommodations of either airplane. It was recognized that in this sector of the marketplace, reliability and maintainability were all important, and extensive attention was devoted to those goals. For this reason, for example, the 737 has no main landing gear doors except the one attached to the strut to cover the hole in the lower surface of the wing.

Unfortunately, the 737 turned out to be a battle ground for the two-man versus three-man cockpit; with United and Western signing union contracts for three-man crews. Some assumed that since the DC-9 and BAC-111 both operated exclusively with only two men, the 737 would die due to economic penalties incurred. Now, 15 years later, 80 737 customers use two-man

Figure 31. The 737.

crews (as DC-9 and BAC-111) and only three use three.

At about this time, the world market in the lesser-developed countries was beginning to become important, and combination passenger/cargo airplanes that could serve its short and poorly surfaced fields had advantages. Boeing's first experience with gravel runways was on the 727-100 in Alaska and later in the Micronesian Islands of the Central Pacific. The 737 configuration was more difficult, but with a lot of technical development, a multi-element gravel kit was developed and the airplane certified for either gravel or grass fields. Elements of the kit are shown in Figure 32.

While the U. S. market absorbed (and is still absorbing) 737s, the place where the airplane shows its greatest superiority is in the less-developed areas of the world. In many of these, the combination passenger/cargo 737 has become the daily link with the outside world, and the ability to carry pallets and igloos that have been air-freighted into main ports of entry on 707, DC-8 or 747 freighters (or otherwise shipped) has become very significant, as illustrated by Figure 33. Today, about 15 years after the first 737 sale, the production rate is at 8.5 per month. The airplane has been substantially improved in the intervening time period and

Figure 32. The multi-element gravel kit for the 737.

Figure 33. A combination passenger/cargo 737.

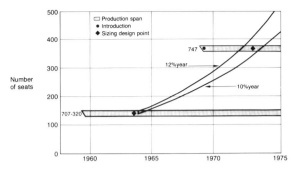

Figure 34. Sizing of the 747.

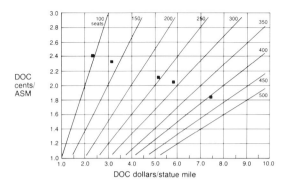

Figure 35. Direct operating cost comparison.

will probably be produced throughout the 1980 decade and beyond.

The 737, again, was a product of competitive forces. All the airplanes improved. Even the U. S. government benefitted when it later bought military versions of both the DC-9-30 and the 737-200.

By the mid-60s, airline traffic was growing at over 15% per year. Airports and airways were becoming glutted for the then current air traffic control system. The idea of air travel vacations for the masses was catching on, and a whole new dimension was being added to the market. This dimension, however, was very sensitive to direct operating costs of the air vehicles involved.

At the same time, the U. S. government was holding a competition for a new large military transport to be called the C-5A, and the final contenders were Boeing, Douglas, and Lockheed. In the summer of 1965, Lockheed won. Boeing took its assembled C-5A design team, added a substantial portion of people from its commercial programs, and asked them to see what they could do to meet the perceived requirements of the burgeoning commercial market.

Figure 34 shows, in gross terms, the manner in which the size of the 747 was established. Airplanes are designed to be a market "fit" about four years after their introduction and the 747 is shown in the situation which had been historically correct. Extrapolating conservative traffic growth curves and working back four

years, it could be seen that an airplane delivered in 1970 would have to have about 350 to 375 passengers.

In terms of direct operating cost, "bigger" has generally been "better," and a typical illustration of the effect is shown on Figure 35.

Juan Trippe, Chairman of Pan American World Airways and Boeing's Bill Allen saw the opportunity and its challenge and both wanted to "try for the big one"—and introduce an airplane combining higher technology with lower seat mile cost. Design-wise, the airplane had nothing to do with the C-5A except for the engine. Pratt & Whitney and General Electric had competed for the C-5A engine and Pratt & Whitney had lost. This left them free to develop a new engine for the 747. The C-5A engine had not been designed with community noise in mind, and G.E. was too busy to attempt to redesign it. A comparison of the two engines is shown in Figure 36. Pratt & Whitney was able to build on their C-5A development work, by substantially modifying the engine to meet commercial noise criteria. In addition, Pan American thought it would be a bonus if the

Airplane	Engine	Lbs thrust	Bypass ratio	Noise
C-5A	TF 39	41 100	8	Poor
747	JT9D-3	43 500	5	Good

Figure 36. Engine comparison.

165

Figure 37. Rollout of the 747.

airplane were fast, which of course required changes in sweep of the wing and bypass ratio of the engine. The 747 was aimed at a cruise Mach number of .88. However, now it is rarely flown at speeds that high, due to the effect of the 1973 fuel embargo and resultant fuel price increases.

But, for an airplane of this size there was no factory available, and Boeing had to start the airplane program and build a new factory at the same time. The airplane go-ahead was April 15, 1966, and first delivery was in December, 1969. Between those dates the airplane was designed, a new factory was built, and the two came together in the roll-out pictured on Figure 37 on schedule. It was, perhaps, one of the most ambitious, privately-funded ventures in world history. The plant alone was an enormous task, and is shown in Figure 38. Less than four years earlier one would have seen a dense forest in its location.

The most difficult decision on the 747 involved selection of the body cross-section. The most efficient passenger cross-section would have had two passenger decks and a "double

166

Figure 38. The Everett plant in 1969.

bubble" fuselage. However, the SST passenger potential appeared very real at that time. The airplane had to be designed as an efficient commercial freight carrier, since it was felt this would become its major job if the SSTs took over the passenger payloads.

In the first half of the 60s, maritime container growth using highway transportable containers was extremely rapid. As a result, it was perceived that applying the highway transportable container system to the airplane would be the way to go. But maritime containers were too heavy for air transportability, so the real question was what container cross-section should be used. The width was easy—it was the highway maximum of eight feet. The height was more difficult and could have been eight or eight and one-half feet. We finally settled on eight by eight and designed the airplane for two eight by eights abreast. This was the origin of the 747 "wide body." At the time, it had very little to do with "passenger appeal." Body cross-section comparisons are shown on Figure 39.

One of the more difficult tasks was to combine the speed requirement of .88 and the

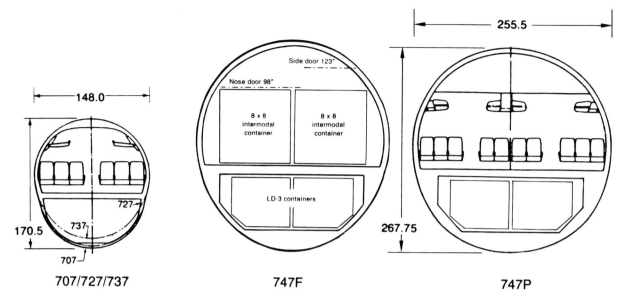

148.0

Side door 123"

Nose door 98"

8 x 8
intermodal
container

8 x 8
intermodal
container

727

737

170.5

707

LD-3 containers

255.5

267.75

707/727/737   **747F**   **747P**

Figure 39. Body cross section comparison.

freighter nose loading requirement involving a visor door. Time for aerodynamic refinement was also short, but the decisions were made, the cab was moved up over the freight compartment and the airplane was built to be sold in either passenger, freight or combination form. In fact, the first airplanes sold were all "P.I." airplanes which meant that they were passenger airplanes with insurance provisions for conversion into freighters if the SST took the passenger business away. Such, of course, never happened, and most of the provisions were removed before delivery. It was 1972 before the first new 747 freighter was delivered, but since then international freight progress has been rapid, as illustrated in Figure 40. Some 747 main deck freighters are side door conversions of older passenger models, but an increasing number are new and, in most cases, incorporate the visor nose door.

Three basic engines are used on the 747—the Pratt & Whitney JT-9 (the original engine), the General Electric CF6-50, and the Rolls Royce RB-211—plus variations. A further indication of program complexity is that the 747 production line contains wings of eight different strengths simultaneously destined for different model airplanes. This means eight different strength torque boxes, structural analyses, certification,

etc. As in all large commercial airplane programs, virtually every plane is customized, and one must face accurate control of hundreds of thousands of specially designed parts.

As noted earlier, the industry misjudged the effects of competitive frequencies and route system development in domestic operations. For instance, in the U. S. domestic market for certificated carriers, the number of scheduled jet service, non-stop city pairs tripled between 1966 and 1969. This adversely affected the "market fit" of all four "wide body" aircraft—the 747, DC-10, L-1011 and A-300, postponing that fit, particularly in U. S. and European domestic service. The 747 was less affected than most because it was principally targeted at the long range intercontinental market which is less frequency-sensitive. The domestic market situation, as noted earlier, resulted in massive sales of the improved 727. This proliferation of frequency and routes, and the potential seriousness of its impact, was not foreseen by any of the major manufacturers, so far as we know. Today, the 747 is being built at a rate of seven per month. Roughly one-third of these are main deck freight capable and are either freighters, convertibles or combination aircraft. They constitute a very large airlift with about 70% foreign-owned.

Up to this point we have been discussing airplane programs that have a large measure of

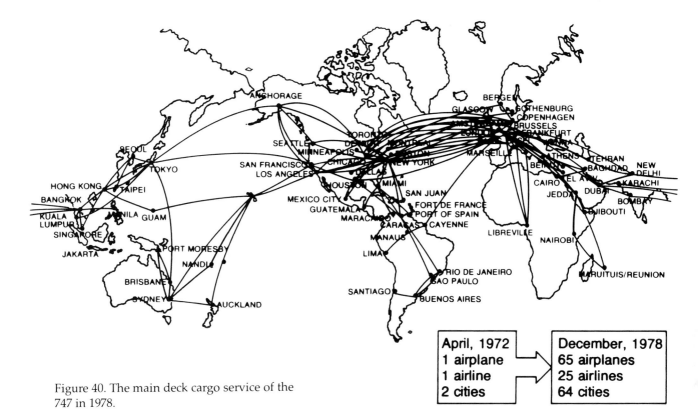

April, 1972	December, 1978
1 airplane	65 airplanes
1 airline	25 airlines
2 cities	64 cities

Figure 40. The main deck cargo service of the 747 in 1978.

success associated with each. Let us spend a couple of minutes now on an airplane, the SST, whose time has yet to come, but in our opinion, will. In late 1957, Boeing established its initial supersonic transport design study team. Early activities focused on understanding designs, cruise speed considerations, and sonic boom phenomena. We believed that the design cruise speed should be as high as the structural state-of-the-art would allow. Mach 2 represented the limit for the use of aluminum, and Mach 2.7 the limit of uncooled fuel. Steel or titanium limits are over 3.0. However, cruise efficiency varies in accordance with a number of factors, including cruise speed and wing design. After a great deal of analysis, we set our sights on a Mach 2.7 airplane as the best choice between engine and aerodynamic efficiency and structural and fuel limitations, and did considerable work on the development of efficient titanium structures. Configuration development is illustrated in Figure 41.

It should be noted that, in line with previous subsonic practice, Boeing had studied designs for a privately owned supersonic wind tunnel for several years. The Boeing supersonic tunnel was firmed up in 1954 and was operating in 1957. It has a four foot by four foot test section and operates, with a model, to Mach 4. Early SST research determined the fundamental relationship of sonic boom to lift (or aircraft weight) and brought to light the fact that supersonic flight would be limited principally to over-ocean or unpopulated land masses. In mid-1963, NASA selected Boeing and Lockheed to conduct a comparative study of four SST configurations —two with fixed wings and two with variable sweep. This was the so-called NASA SCAT program. In late 1963, the FAA started a series of requests for proposals covering the prototype development of a commercial SST. In late 1966, the final proposal was submitted, and in early 1967 Boeing was selected to carry the banner for the U. S. in the worldwide SST competition. A mockup of the final U. S. SST configuration is shown in Figure 42.

Although the cancellation of the SST program in 1971 represented a tremendous blow to the

Figure 41. The configuration evolution of the SST.

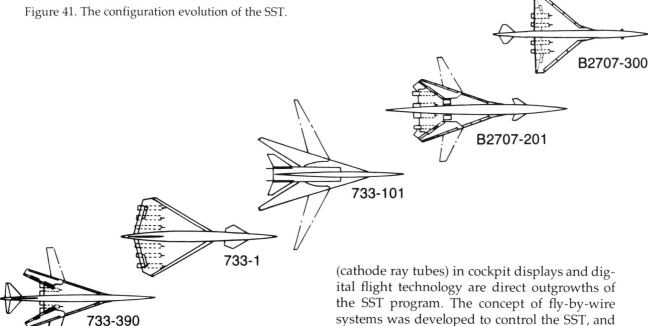

B2707-300

B2707-201

733-101

733-1

733-390

nation's aeronautical prestige and its ability to sustain technical leadership in commercial transports, with hindsight, the unforeseen fuel price escalation situation would have made it a less viable program. In any event, the SST program provided a valuable technology legacy not only to future supersonic programs, but to subsonic aircraft design as well, some of which is being applied in today's commercial transports. Some valuable elements of the SST's legacy are being applied in today's transports, as indicated in Figure 43. The application of CRTs

- Titanium Structures Technology

- Digital Flight Deck Technology

- Fly By Wire

- Composite Structures

- Metallic Sandwich Structures

- Certain Noise Technologies

- Propulsion Technology

Figure 43. The legacies of the U. S. SST program.

(cathode ray tubes) in cockpit displays and digital flight technology are direct outgrowths of the SST program. The concept of fly-by-wire systems was developed to control the SST, and represented the first implementation of the total fly-by-wire system. The SST's 4-channel stability augmentation system that provided pitch dampening and gave the airplane artificial and dynamic longitudinal stability over its entire flight envelope, was the forerunner of what we call active control technology today. The high state-of-the-art structural levels being pursued fostered the development of composite structures which are now finding their way into today's secondary structural items, such as spoilers, ailerons, elevators and rudders. In addition, a great deal was learned regarding the use of titanium which has led to an increasing use of this material for such things as the huge landing gear beams on the 747.

From a technical standpoint, the development and operation of the British-French Concorde unquestionably has resulted in substantial fallout benefitting both European aerospace and its supporting industries. This very large and long term achievement has not been given the credit in this country which it deserves. The Concorde accomplishment, we feel, is a substantial one. A relatively low level of SST research continues and its results are indeed encouraging. It is the view of the U. S. airplane industry that it is technically feasible to develop an economically viable, second generation supersonic transport.

Figure 42. The SST.

Such an aircraft would allow for ticket prices comparable to those of current subsonic airplanes, acceptable noise levels, trans-Pacific range capability, excellent over land subsonic performance, and good fuel efficiency and maintenance characteristics. With appropriate government and industry cooperation, the U. S. could produce an economically sound second generation SST and have it in operation by the end of the century.

Let us cover propulsion development first. Since the title of this discussion is "A Company Perspective," I will go back only to the J-47, the 5000 pound thrust engine which powered the XB-47. Progress in fuel efficiency in the 36 years since that engine first ran, is shown in Figure 44.

All of the engines on Figure 44 are axial flow. If one wished to plot an early production centrifugal compressor jet engine, its SFC would be approximately 1.4 and its year would be approximately 1942. Axial flow engines, of course, were longer and thinner, which made them potentially much easier to install from a diameter standpoint. However, the early axials such as the J-47 had a fattening ring of combustion cans around their middle which made installation somewhat more difficult. From an installation standpoint, then, the introduction of the annular combustion chamber in 1956 was a very significant accomplishment.

Figure 44 omits the TF-39 military engine, which was the forerunner of the CF-6 engine. Its SFC was at least as attractive, but its bypass ratio was not consistent with the commercial airplane balance between takeoff thrust and

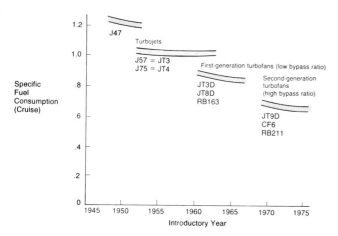

Figure 44. Progress in engine fuel efficiency.

cruise thrust. As noted, the J-57 military engine became the JT-3 commercial engine.

The word fan, or bypass, applies, of course, to engines having a split flow where the inner flow is hot, heavily compressed, and then fuel is burned in it. The outer flow is compressed much less and exits from the engine, without burning, into an annulus around the inner core. The first such engine extensively used was the Rolls Royce Conway RC02. However, its fuel efficiency was not significantly different than the JT-3 and JT-4. Fan engines are basically quieter than jet engines. The second generation turbofans were quieter than the first generation, and of higher bypass ratio. However, the development of quiet propulsive integrated power plants has included very extensive acoustic liner

development, both in the inlet and the fan exhaust. In the time period, these liners have gone through several generations of change. In this total process the appearance of the engine has greatly changed, as shown in Figure 45.

External noise reached its peak on engines like the military J-57 which incorporated high pressure ratio compressors and a very high exhaust velocity. In addition, such straight jet engines had less takeoff thrust in proportion to cruise thrust and takeoff climbout was flatter, exposing more land area to noise. When this was combined with certain heavily loaded military applications, an undesirable condition sometimes existed. The first suppression was the application of a set of tubes to the engine exhaust to entrain outside air and reduce exhaust velocity and air shear. Progress in noise suppression has been continuous and has involved improvement in both basic engines and their installations. Suppression trends are shown in Figure 46. The other fundamental is, of course, the wing and its progress over the period involved as shown in Figure 47. A long, thin wing is defined as a high aspect ratio wing. Increases in aspect ratio generally result in increased flight efficiency. However, high aspect ratio increases weight, elasticity and the difficulty of stowing fuel and high lift devices and, in the case of tricycle landing gear aircraft, the landing gear struts.

The highest aspect ratio wing ever used on a production jet airplane was that of the B-47 which, as you remember, first flew in 1947. Such an aspect ratio was required to obtain a high enough aerodynamic efficiency (L/D) to

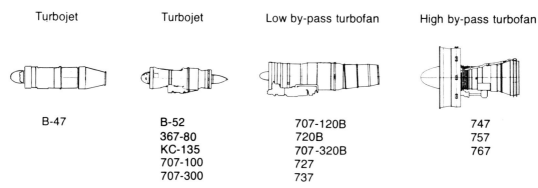

Figure 45. Engine evolution.

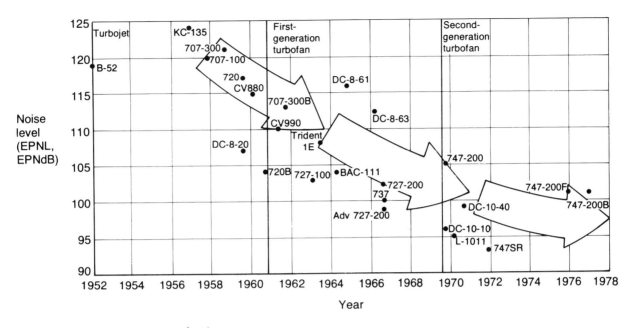

Figure 46. Progress in noise reduction.

balance the deterioration in propulsive efficiency as discussed earlier. However, the use of such an aspect ratio at a time prior to the discovery of inboard wing thickening is further evidence of the breakthrough represented by the B-47.

Over the time period, substantial changes were made in high lift systems. The B-47 and B-52 incorporated large Fowler flaps with a single slot between the flap and the wing. To accomplish the Fowler motion, the flap moved aft on tracks before it attained substantial deflection. Most of the deflection was at the far end of the travel. The 367-80 and the 707 gave up some of this Fowler action, but regained the lift involved by use of an additional slot. The slot, however, was built into the flap with a rigid structure, and the segments did not spread apart as the flap moved aft. Technical progress over the time period is shown in Figure 48.

As noted, the 727 represented a peak in high lift design. It incorporated three flap segments yielding three slots and the segments all spread with respect to each other as the flap traveled aft. It also incorporated a leading edge slat similar to that originally incorporated on the XB-47 but deleted on the B-47 production models. The

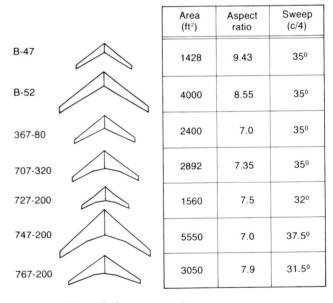

		Area (ft²)	Aspect ratio	Sweep (c/4)
B-47		1428	9.43	35⁰
B-52		4000	8.55	35⁰
367-80		2400	7.0	35⁰
707-320		2892	7.35	35⁰
727-200		1560	7.5	32⁰
747-200		5550	7.0	37.5⁰
767-200		3050	7.9	31.5⁰

Figure 47. Wing platform comparison.

simplification of the flap system in the years after the 727, and the lower lift coefficients attained, are in part a function of design for community noise reduction. The attainment of very high lift coefficients brings with it high drag, which means more engine power during approach, resulting in higher approach noise. This same effect, however, can be caused by an en-

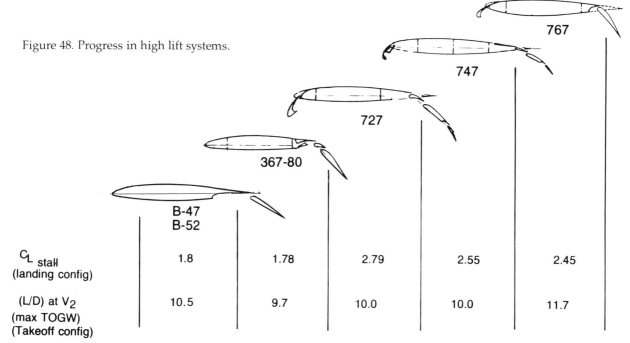

Figure 48. Progress in high lift systems.

	B-47 B-52	367-80	727	747	767
$C_{L\ stall}$ (landing config)	1.8	1.78	2.79	2.55	2.45
(L/D) at V_2 (max TOGW) (Takeoff config)	10.5	9.7	10.0	10.0	11.7

gine's acceleration characteristic which in some cases requires a relatively high approach thrust in order to be able to "spool up" for the "go around" case.

Over this period, of course, there was substantial airfoil development with an objective of "pushing out the corner" of the lift coefficient versus Mach number diagram. This is graphically shown in Figure 49. Such improvement can be used, of course, either for added speed or improved efficiency. Over the years, the structural

state-of-the-art has changed dramatically, both in terms of structural efficiency and in terms of structural durability. The structural efficiency part has been made up of improved aluminum alloys and, more recently, through the use of fibrous composites combining, for example, filaments of carbon fiber in a polymer matrix.

Just as complex a development has been the continuous improvement in structural durability. It has involved not only choice of materials, but more importantly, detail design, improved fasteners and better manufacturing machinery. In addition, over the period involved, we have made great advances in corrosion avoidance and protection. As a rather incomplete example of the above, Figure 50 shows more recent progress in structural durability.

Although we thought we were designing for durability in designs prior to 1950, our concentration was meager compared with what was to follow. Structural weight was all-important, and new alloys used to achieve higher strength (and lower weight) proved, in some cases, to have reduced durability. We had to reduce allowable design stresses, use more conservative alloys, and concentrate on detail design. Successive experience helped.

Coverage of technology development would not be complete without an illustration of the evolutionary and revolutionary developments

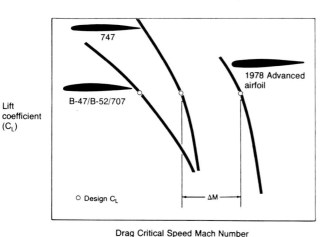

Figure 49. Airfoil technology.

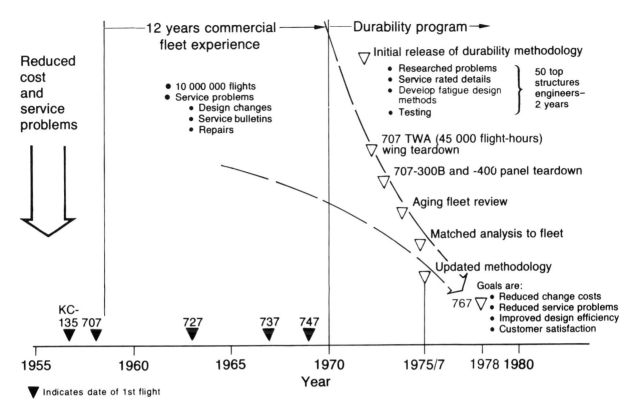

Figure 50. Structural durability.

in electronics and avionics. We started the period with the relatively crude electronics of World War II. We did not realize how crude they were at the time. We then got into greater and greater system complexity while maintaining vacuum tubes; progressed to solid state; and from there to the digital revolution. Today we can get infinitely more capacity and reliability at substantially less cost. I wish that there were more developments in which this phenomenon occurred. Figure 51 illustrates this situation.

The SST system illustrated depicts what would have been required had we built it based on analog technology. Our plan was to convert the whole system to digital so that the point shown probably never would have occurred. The noted technology advancements are illustrative. There are many other elements of aircraft design that have advanced during the period involved, including landing gear, flight control systems, cockpit displays, weight efficiency, crashworthiness, safety, and emissions, to name a few.

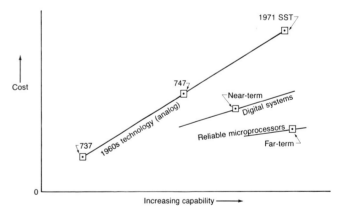

Figure 51. Avionics systems capability.

The fundamental reasons for today's new airplanes are fuel economy, noise reduction, the development of an extensive mid-size requirement, and the incorporation of new technology developed over the last 10 to 15 years for economic improvement purposes.

As the 1970s advanced, the U. S. domestic airline route structure developed in an unanticipated manner. In addition, the Civil Aeronautics Board initiated a trend allowing more competition on each route. This culminated in the passage of the Airline Deregulation Bill in December 1978, which, in all probability, will further increase route segment competition. This combination affects the size of vehicles required and would indicate that there will probably be large continuing purchases in the sizes smaller than the wide-body airplanes currently flying. At the same time that these developments evolved, the gradual gathering of a fund of technological improvements was made available beyond that of airplanes currently available in the intermediate-size category. A list of these improvements is shown on Figure 52.

- More efficient engines

- Lower noise

- Better aluminum alloys

- Advanced structure (e.g., composites)

- Superior avionics

- Superior displays

- More efficient wing design

Figure 52. Technology improvements

Our first major attempt to exploit the fund for a current product came in about 1972. It was to put high bypass ratio engines on the 727. However, this addressed only one of the technological improvements we have noted and also proved to be an extremely expensive undertaking. Although it came close to launch, it was never actually launched. Then, in late 1973, came the fuel boycott and a very rapid increase in fuel price had its effect on equipment new buy versus modification decisions. One of our problems was that modern engines do not vary much in price—at least not in any way proportional to thrust.

However, by 1975 we felt certain that there existed a requirement for a new airplane in the approximate category of 200 passengers and 2000 to 2500 nautical mile range. We called it the 7X7 and began a long preparatory period of test-

ing three engine designs, and subsequently both three and two engine designs that might be attractive. The airline industry was financially weak, however, and none of the airlines was willing to start a new program. The capital formation problem had plagued the industry for over half a decade. A sick customer results in a sick airplane manufacturing industry, whatever the cause may be.

The U. S. airlines, in general, became somewhat credible from a profit standpoint in 1976, but the scars of the previous years were deep indeed. Thus it was the middle of 1978 before we could start the all-new 767, and by that time it was apparent (as is indicated by the choice of 767) that there was apt to be a smaller airplane underneath it, for which we saved the model number 757. These airplanes are shown on the passenger versus range chart of Figure 53. It should be noted that the vertical scale of Figure 53 is a U. S. two-class configuration. The number of passengers for a given airplane varies widely with the interior arrangement. The 757 was provisionally launched late in 1978 and its go-ahead confirmed early in 1979. The two airplanes have totally different new wings. The 757 wing has a little less sweepback but they both have approximately the same aspect ratio which has been shown previously. The 757 wing has about 65% of the area of the 767 wing. The 757 has a standard six-abreast body, the same width as the 707, 727, and 737, while the 767 has a two-aisle, seven abreast body which approximates the smallest body that can economically be built around two aisles. The 757 has limited cargo and may perhaps "grow" smaller. The 767 may "grow" larger, with future derivatives, over the years.

The emergence of two designs, where we expected one, is a recognition of the precision with which airlines must now fit their equipment to their needs. The economics of the system have to be honed carefully and fuel consumption kept to a minimum consistent with the competitive realities of the routes involved.

Fuel burn characteristics of the 757 and 767 are shown in Figure 54. The bottom scale is total block fuel consumed for a particular trip. The trip is constant throughout the chart. The verti-

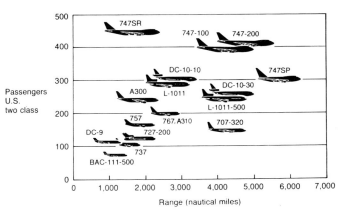

Figure 53. A passenger vs. range chart.

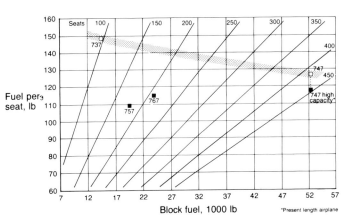

Figure 54. Fuel burn comparison.

cal scale is the fuel burned for that trip per seat for each airplane. Note that the zero is well below the bottom of the vertical scale. The shaded band is more or less the lows of previously available aircraft.

The two airplanes are powered by different engines, with the 767 engine being a derivative of the P&W 747 engine (the JT-9D) and the 757 engine being a derivative of the Rolls Royce RB-211. In both cases the "derivative" changes are very substantial with both engines incorporating technological improvements over their parent engines. Of course, other engines can, and no doubt will, be fitted. As noted earlier, community noise has become a major design criteria along with fuel burned.

Not all the changes in a new airplane contribute to reduced costs and each new model tends to be more complex than the previous one. In addition, the airlines expect even longer life, amortized over a longer time period, and demand service life policies that have now risen to around 12 years or more. Thus the superior economics of Figure 55, for the size aircraft involved, have been obtained in spite of the improvements which added significant cost.

Fuel, as we noted, has become much more important in the economic equation. A comparison of its impact in 1970 and today is shown on Figure 56.

The appearance of the two new airplanes is shown in Figure 57. The 767 will enter service

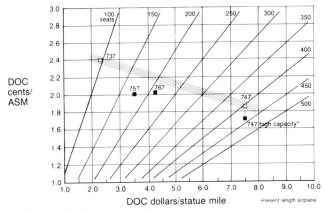

Figure 55. Direct operating cost.

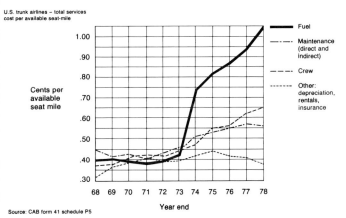

Figure 56. Influence of fuel price in direct operating cost.

177

Figure 57. The 757 and the 767.

in the third quarter of 1982, with the 757 entering service in the first quarter of 1983.

I should start by acknowledging that this discussion is of necessity confined to Boeing experience, which although continuous and extensive, has for the most part involved large subsonic airplanes. We have had some supersonic experience, but some other manufacturers have had more. In the application of jet power to airplanes in the 40 year period, one must also examine the experience of others and the development of supersonic fighters and supersonic bombers in great detail. While the B-52 remains the principal bomber of the United States, our Air Force has tried, on three different occasions, to successfully launch a production supersonic

manned bomber program. The problems have been partially technical. However, they have also involved government funding. The B-52 has been modified to fly close to the ground and avoid the enemy radar screen. There is a question as to whether a high altitude supersonic airplane would be significantly less vulnerable.

Thus, with an eye to the future, let us discuss briefly the commercial and then the military situation. The commercial situation is one of continued growth. While the rate of growth per year has varied, there has not been a negative RPM growth year in the last 40. Revenue passenger miles for the last 10 years and estimates for the next 10 are shown in Figure 58. As noted, we expect RPM's to double. However, this does not mean that the aircraft size will double. The impact of route proliferation, frequency, competition and deregulation cannot be fully as-

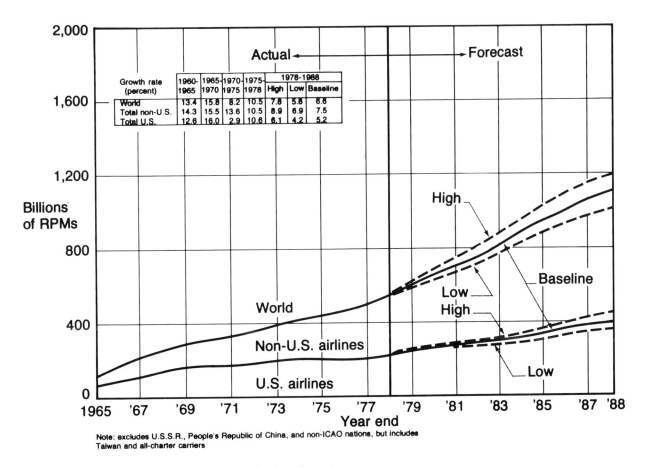

Figure 58. The world revenue passenger miles for all services.

sessed at this time, but will tend to keep domestic airplane size down.

To make the matter more complicated, bilateral treaties are being altered to permit more U. S. gateways and the same is generally true in foreign countries. This means that nonstop point-to-point service will increase on a global scale and what may be needed are smaller aircraft with longer ranges—a trend that presents a difficult design challenge.

The percentage of non-business travel in the total world system (excluding the U.S.S.R.) is now over 50%. The size of this segment of the air travel market is very sensitive to fare levels. This will no doubt result in a desire by the airlines for a stretched body version of the 747 and probably larger versions of some other airplanes as well.

The prediction, then, would be that in the next 10 years there will be a large market for airplanes of several sizes and ranges. While there is a tendency for the average airplane's size to grow with traffic, the tendency is a slow one, and is confused by the many other elements acting on the system. On the freight side, it now appears that international air freight has "taken off." We would expect a rapid increase from here on. Both international and domestic freight situations are included in Figure 59. The reason for the wide spread in the prediction of Figure 59 is at least partly due to the unpredictability of the domestic air freight systems in the United States, Europe and elsewhere. With the advent of the international standard LD-3 lower lobe container and its modified counterparts, a highly efficient domestic freight system was brought into being. A great deal of domestic air freight is now carried in this manner. However,

179

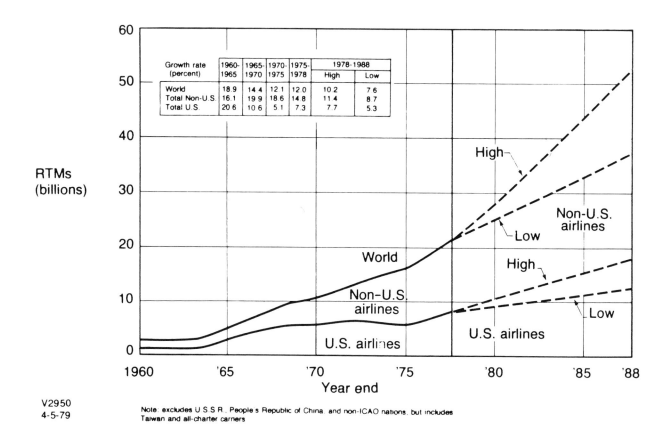

V2950
4-5-79

Note: excludes U.S.S.R., People's Republic of China, and non-ICAO nations, but includes Taiwan and all-charter carriers

Figure 59. The world revenue freight miles.

such a system tends to mix passenger and freight service and there currently exists no integrated United States air freight system. Major shippers, such as Sears-Roebuck, General Motors, etc., cannot contract with any central agency for true interline system management. This has tended to depress air freight growth in the past, and may continue to do so in the future. Air freight is now largely deregulated, and the future somewhat uncertain. Regardless of the above, the total air freight system will grow in the next ten years. It is only the rate of growth that is debatable.

These requirements when combined with the new airlift requirement generated by aircraft going out of service due to inadequate fuel efficiency, noise regulations, and non-competitive characteristics or wear-out, result in the ten year estimated market for civil aircraft shown in Fig-

ure 60. As indicated, this potential requirement is about $79 billion in constant 1978 dollars. It should support a major worldwide industry and this is the dimension in which we see the future competition.

To address this, a differing form of technology has emerged into Boeing discipline—much as aerodynamic testing did nearly four decades earlier. This is the discipline of efficient operations. A multiplicity of products is needed and production rates will vary widely and rapidly with changes in market conditions. Over this decade, we at Boeing have been rebuilding from the bottom up to marry planning, design and manufacturing elements into a common base of computerized efficiency. This brings with it the competitive potential of a capacity much more responsive to change with substantially greater productivity and lower costs. The capital investments have been enormous, and the technical challenges as demanding as any in our experience. In retrospect, our forty years that started

180

*Does not include $3 billion freighter market.
Total market through 1988 is $79 billion in 1978 dollars.

Note: Does not include U.S.S.R. -built jets

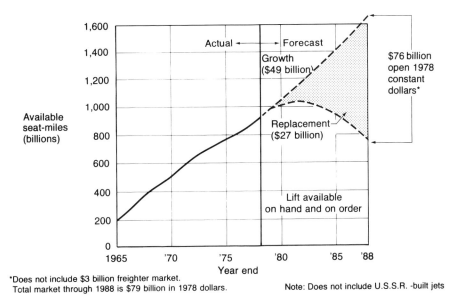

Figure 60. The world open airlift requirements, 1979-1988.

in the power plant and aerodynamics laboratory appear now to be focusing on the laboratory of operations and the shop.

A quiet, economical, and long range supersonic transport still remains a definite possibility. Major improvements have been made with both NASA funding and private funding. Supersonic range, and thus supersonic efficiency, has been improved by about 35%, and subsonic efficiency has, with the variable cycle engine, been increased dramatically, until subsonic range is no longer a limiting factor. I am reluctant to predict that an economically viable and environmentally acceptable supersonic transport will not emerge during the next decade or two. I believe that its deterrent may be more related to funding than it is to technology.

On the military side, we have the situation of the U.S.S.R. and Warsaw Pact nations producing weapons at over twice the rate of the U. S. and its allies. Its stable of aircraft includes fighters like ours plus a supersonic bomber not equalled on the U. S. side. In any military assessment one must consider the missile deterrent systems as well as the ground and air confrontation systems, and a reasonable analysis is far beyond the scope of this paper. A few of the significant trends are shown in Figure 61.

A difficult question involves the possible location of a confrontation site, and the ability of the U. S. and its allies to counter the perceived potential enemy forces at that site. We are heavily dependent upon Mideast oil, and the confrontation, if it occurs, is apt to be on the contiguous land mass occupied by the U.S.S.R. forces and not on the one occupied by the United States forces. If such is the case, we have a major military airlift problem to consider, since the critical time is measured in hours or a very few days, not weeks. We have chosen to solve part of our problem by prepositioning heavy armament. However, the prepositioned material may easily be in the wrong place, and its vulnerability is open to question.

It would thus appear that in addition to having a long range or strategic airlift problem, we have a shorter range or tactical airlift problem.

- Need for adequate intercontinental airlift
- Need for adequate intratheater airlift
- Relative single vehicle incompatibility of the two requirements
- Emergence of the cruise missile as a possible primary long range weapon system
- Seeking a solution to the "survivable and post attack operable" problem

Figure 61. Some U. S. military trends.

Figure 62. A recent Boeing STOL, a NASA prototype.

Boeing has been in the STOL business for many years and two Boeing built STOL prototypes are being operated by NASA. Figures 62 and 63 show the most recent of the NASA prototypes we have built, the QSRA (Quiet STOL Research Aircraft) and the two large STOL tactical airlift aircraft which we recently built for Air Force evaluation. However, no such production airplanes have been procured for either government or civil uses. The requirement, however, we feel is growing.

In conclusion, I would like to note the major decisions which I would list in a "Boeing perspective" of the last 40 years of jet aviation.

The first one was the decision to construct a large, powerful, accurate wind tunnel in 1941. While it was subsonic when built, it was upgraded in 1953 to a NASA developed slotted test section transonic tunnel with 58,000 horse-power. The value of this dedicated Boeing research facility in "breaking ground" with design and configuration solutions for the B-47 cannot be overstated. It gave us an early capability in swept-wing technology, a confidence in the future of jet powered aircraft, and perhaps most important of all, it instilled an aerodynamic testing discipline which has been integral to all the Boeing aircraft that followed.

The second major decision was, after two years of frustration, to "go it alone" on the 367-80 prototype. Betting nearly 25% of the Company's net worth on a program one has unsuccessfully tried to sell for two years is not the easiest kind of decision to make. However, despite the courage it took, and the risk entailed, it was this decision and its timing which proved to be most significant to Boeing's later role in commercial aviation.

The third major decision was to "stay in" on the 707 vs. DC-8 competition, even if it took virtually a new airplane to do it, and to combine

Figure 63. Two large STOL tactical airlift aircraft built for Air Force evaluation.

that determination with enough engineering development that a superior product emerged. In retrospect, this implied that our competitiveness was not based on a margin of technical superiority alone. We had to match that technical superiority to specific customer needs—and develop a number of aircraft to meet those needs. Thus, out of this decision was born the Boeing strategy of a family of jet aircraft and derivatives from which a new type or major derivative has been launched on an average of one every eleven months over the past quarter-century. We followed this strategy in decisions launching the 727 product line and also the 737. We established it early in planning for the 747, and most recently, in the 757 and 767.

Launching each of our new airplanes in themselves represented very major decisions and each in their own time—unbelievable risks. However, the three major decisions which I've just described formed the fabric of the others and I have no doubt, will continue to do so in the future years of jet powered flight.

The first decision (wind tunnel development) gave a discipline of technical superiority. The second (367-80 go-ahead) provided us with a very critical leading edge, and the third (stay with the 707)—which was as much a market de-

cision as our own—has served us well in making our technology truly competitive through the years.

I have no doubt that the rebuilding of our operations, which we noted earlier, will progress to rank among prevailing forces in the estimated $79 billion open market. In time, I believe we will recognize the decision to attain these enhancements as our fourth major decision.

A great many individuals have contributed to these decisions. Without meaning to slight the others, I believe I should name four. They would be William M. Allen, who was President and Chief Executive Officer, or Chairman, from 1945 to 1972; George S. Schairer, who left his technical mark on every Boeing airplane in the 40-year period; Edward C. Wells, who was the engineering and program leader over much of the period; and T. A. Wilson, our present Chairman and Chief Executive Officer. One started as a lawyer and three started as engineers, but all demonstrated courage and innovation that in retrospect has to be classed as almost incredible.

Forty Years of Jet Aviation: A Selective Bibliography and Research Guide

Dominick A. Pisano

Considering the magnitude of the published literature on jets and jet propulsion, the following bibliography is intended to be suggestive of titles which illuminate the historical origins and development of jet aviation during the past four decades. The majority of the works cited here relate specifically to the early development of jet propulsion in Germany, Great Britain and the United States, its subsequent use in World War II aircraft, and its applications, both military and commercial, up to the latter part of the 1970's.

These works will be found in alphabetical order by author in the section titled "General" in Part I, "Books Relating to Jet Aviation." Also listed in this section are books which relate to the development of supersonic flight and the beginnings of commercial jet transportation. Part I, "Engines, Fuels and Jet Technology," contains references to books which deal with the technical aspects of jet propulsion, jet fuels and associated technology. Part I, "Personal Narratives and Biography" includes titles which recount the personal experiences of jet aviation pioneers. Aside from these subdivi-

DOMINICK A. PISANO is the Reference Librarian at the National Air and Space Museum. He is a graduate of both the Pennsylvania State University and Catholic University of America where he received a degree in library science. He is the author of similar bibliographical and reference guides for *Charles Lindbergh: An American Life* (1977), *The Wright Brothers: Heirs of Prometheus* (1978), and *Apollo: Ten Years Since Tranquility Base* (1979), all published for the National Air and Space Museum by the Smithsonian Institution Press.

sions, which are also alphabetical in arrangement, no further attempt has been made to classify the titles listed.

Part II, "Bibliographic Note," presents in brief narrative form, a survey of some of the general reference sources available to the researcher who is interested in finding more specific information concerning particular jet aircraft and engines.

PART I: BOOKS RELATING TO JET AVIATION

GENERAL

Ahnstrom D. N. *The Complete Book of Jets and Rockets.* New York, 1970.

Allward, Maurice F. *Marvels of Jet Aircraft.* Glascow, Scotland, 1973.

Barfield, Norman. *Aerospatiale/BAC Concorde.* Windsor, Berkshire, England, 1973.

Berger, Carl, ed. *The United States Air Force in Southeast Asia, 1961-1973.* Washington, D. C., 1977.

Bergman, Jules. *Ninety Seconds to Space: The X-15 Story.* Garden City, N.Y., 1960.

Blackall, T. E. *Concorde: The Story, The Facts and the Figures.* Henley-on-Thames, England, 1969.

Bowers, Peter M. *Boeing Aircraft Since 1916.* Fallbrook, California, 1966.

Bright, Charles D. *The Jet Makers: The Aerospace*

Industry from 1945 to 1972. Lawrence, Kansas, 1978.

Brooks, Peter W. *The Modern Airliner, Its Origins and Development.* London, 1961.

Brooks, Peter W. *The World's Airliners.* London, 1963.

Broughton, Jack. *Thud Ridge.* Philadelphia, 1969.

Caidin, Martin. *Boeing 707.* New York, 1959.

Chatham, George N. *The Supersonic Transport: A Look at the Key Issues.* Washington, D. C., 1971.

Colby, Carroll B. *Jets of the World: New Fighters, Bombers, and Transports.* Rev ed. New York, 1966.

Cooke, David C. *Jet and Rocket Planes that Made History.* New York, 1961.

Cross, Roy. *Supersonic Aircraft.* London, 1955.

Davies, David P. *Handling the Big Jets: An Explanation of the Significant Differences in Flying Qualities Between Jet Transport Aeroplanes and Piston Engined Transport Aeroplanes.* 3rd ed. Redhill, 1971.

Davies, R. E. G. *Airlines of the United States Since 1914.* London, 1972.

Davies, R. E. G. *A History of the World's Airlines.* London, 1967.

Davis, John F. *The Concorde Affair, From Drawing Board to Actuality.* Chicago, 1970.

Dempster, Derek D. *The Tale of the Comet.* London, 1959.

Duke, Neville and Edward Lanchbery. *Sound Barrier: The Story of High-Speed Flight.* New York, 1955.

Emme, Eugene M. *Hitler's Blitzbomber: Historical Notes on High Command Decisions Influencing the Tardy Operational Use of the Me 262 in German Air Defense.* Maxwell Air Force Base, Alabama, 1951.

Frank, R., Jr. *Experimental Planes: Subsonic and Supersonic.* New York, 1955.

Futrell, Robert Frank. *The United States Air Force in Korea, 1950-1953.* New York, 1961.

Gantz, Kenneth F. *Nuclear Flight: The United States Air Force Programs for Atomic Jets, Missiles and Rockets.* New York, 1960.

Goldberg, Alfred, ed. *A History of the United States Air Force, 1907-1957.* Princeton, N.J., 1957.

Gray, George W. *Frontiers of Flight: The Story of NACA Research.* New York, 1948.

Gunston, Bill. *Early Supersonic Fighters of the West.* New York, 1976.

Hallion, Richard P., Jr. *Supersonic Flight: The Story of the Bell X-1 and Douglas D-558.* New York, 1972.

Hamlin, Benson. *Flight Testing, Conventional and Jet-Propelled Airplanes.* New York, 1946.

Hartman, Edwin P. *Adventures in Research: A History of Ames Research Center, 1940-1965.* NASA Center History Series. Washington, D. C., 1970.

Harvey, Derek. *Famous Airliners: The Comet.* London, 1958.

Harvey, Frank. *Air War—Vietnam.* New York, 1967.

Hensser, Henry. *Comet Highway.* London, 1953.

Herron, Edward A. *Cobra in the Sky: The Supersonic Transport.* New York, 1968.

Higham, Robin. *Air Power, A Concise History.* New York, 1972.

Hubler, Richard G. *Big Eight: The Biography of an Airplane.* New York, 1960.

Hubler, Richard G. *SAC: The Strategic Air Command.* New York, 1958.

Hudson, Kenneth. *Air Travel: A Social History.* Totowa, New Jersey, 1972.

Ingells, Douglas J. *L-1011 TriStar and the Lockheed Story.* Fallbrook, California, 1966.

Ingells, Douglas J. *747: Story of the Boeing Super Jet.* Fallbrook, California, 1970.

Jacobs, Lou. *Jumbo Jets*. Indianapolis, 1969.

Kane, Robert M. and Allan D. Vose. *Air Transportation*. 5th ed. Dubuque, Iowa, 1975.

Kuter, Laurence S. *The Great Gamble: The Boeing 747*. University, Alabama, 1973.

Mansfield, Harold. *Billion Dollar Battle: The Story Behind the ''Impossible'' 727 Project*. New York, 1965.

Mansfield, Harold. *Vision: The Story of Boeing*. New York, 1966.

Nalty, Bernard C. *Air Power and the Fight for Khe Sanh*. Washington, D. C., 1973.

Perry, Robert L. ''The Antecedents of the X-1.'' A Lecture Presented at the Second Annual Meeting of the American Institute of Aeronautics and Astronautics, July 26-29, 1965, San Francisco, California. [AIAA paper no. 65-453]

Rae, John B. *Climb to Greatness: The American Aircraft Industry, 1920-1960*. Cambridge, Mass., 1968.

Serling, Robert J. *The Electra Story*. Garden City, New York, 1963.

Shacklady, Edward. *The Gloster Meteor*. New York, 1963.

Stillwell, Wendell H. *X-15 Research Results*. Washington, D. C., 1965.

Stratford, Alan H. *Air Transport Economics in the Supersonic Era*. 2nd ed. New York, 1973.

Swanborough, Frederick Gordon. *Turbine-Engined Airliners of the World*. Los Angeles, 1963.

Tregaskis, Richard W. *X-15 Diary: The Story of America's First Space Ship*. New York, 1961.

Wagner, Ray. *The North American Sabre*. Garden City, New York, 1963.

ENGINES, FUELS AND JET TECHNOLOGY

Barker, Allan, T. R. F. Nonweiler and R. Smelt. *Jets and Rockets*. London, 1959.

Cassamassa, Jack V. and R. D. Bent. *Jet Aircraft Power Systems*. 3rd Ed. New York, 1965.

Chapel, Charles E. *Jet Aircraft Simplified*. Los Angeles, 1950.

Hage, Robert E. *Jet Propulsion in Commercial Air Transportation*. Princeton, New Jersey, 1948.

Hesse, Walter J. *Jet Propulsion*. New York, 1958.

Hosny, A. N. *Propulsion Systems,* Rev. ed. Columbia, South Carolina, 1974.

Katz, Israel. *Principles of Aircraft Propulsion Machinery*. New York, 1949.

Keenan, John G. *Elementary Theory of Gas Turbines and Jet Propulsion*. London, 1946.

Kerrebrock, Jack L. *Aircraft Engines and Gas Turbines*. Cambridge, Mass., 1977.

Miller, Ronald and David Sawers. *The Technical Development of Modern Aviation*. New York, 1970.

Neville, Leslie E. and Nathaniel F. Silsbee. *Jet Propulsion Progress: The Development of Aircraft Gas Turbines*. New York, 1948.

Schlaifer, Robert and S. D. Heron. *Development of Aircraft Engines and Fuels*. Cambridge, Massachusetts, 1950.

Treager, Irwin E. *Aircraft Gas Turbine Engine Technology*. New York, 1970.

Treager, Irwin E. *Jet Aircraft Engines: How They Work*. Modern Aircraft Series. New York, 1974.

Zucrow, Maurice J. *Principles of Jet Propulsion and Gas Turbines*. New York, 1948.

PERSONAL NARRATIVES AND BIOGRAPHY

Bainbridge, John. *Like A Homesick Angel*. Boston, 1964.

Bridgeman, William and Jacqueline Hazard. *The Lonely Sky*. New York, 1955.

Cochran, Jacqueline. *The Stars at Noon*. Boston, 1954.

Crossfield, A. Scott. *Always Another Dawn: The Story of A Rocket Test Pilot*. Cleveland, 1960.

de Havilland, Sir Geoffrey. *Sky Fever*. London, 1961.

Everest, Frank K. *The Fastest Man Alive*. New York, 1958.

Heiman, Grover. *Jet Pioneers*. New York, 1963.

Heinkel, Ernst. *Stormy Life*. New York, 1956.

LeMay, Curtis E. with MacKinlay Kantor. *Mission with LeMay: My Story*. Garden City, New York, 1965.

LeVier, Tony. *Pilot*. New York, 1954.

Lundgren, William R. *Across the High Frontier: The Story of a Test Pilot—Major Charles E. Yeager, USAF*. New York, 1955.

Reitsch, Hanna. *Flying Is My Life*. Translated by Lawrence Wilson. New York, 1954.

Whittle, Sir Frank. *Jet: The Story of a Pioneer*. London, 1953.

Xiegler, Mano. *Rocket Fighter*. Translated by Alexander Vanags. Garden City, New York, 1961.

PART II: BIBLIOGRAPHIC NOTE

While the references listed in the following paragraphs are by no means comprehensive, they represent a selection of some of the more accessible titles which will provide additional information concerning periodical articles, aircraft and aero engine yearbooks, photographs, motion pictures and miscellaneous sources which relate to jet aviation.

PERIODICAL LITERATURE

Researchers who are interested in finding periodical literature which relates to specific jet aircraft should familiarize themselves with August Hanniball's *Aircraft, Engines and Airmen: A Selective Review of the Periodical Literature, 1930-1969* (Metuchen, N.J., 1972). Hanniball's is a gold mine of information concerning aircraft of the jet era and provides references to articles which have appeared in aviation journals such as *American Aviation Historical Society Journal, Aviation Week and Space Technology,* and many others. Each citation is coded to reflect whether the article indexed pertains to the aircraft's history, design and development, construction and production, piloting or in-flight characteristics or testing and performance. In addition, there is also a code which designates the type of illustrative material accompanying the article. Hanniball's is also an invaluable source of information concerning periodical articles on jet engines. Indispensable for aviation research of any kind, Hanniball's is an authoritative source for historical aviation periodical literature.

Although not concerned with providing references to articles on individual aircraft, *Air University Library Index to Military Periodicals* (Maxwell Air Force Base, Alabama, 1949 to date) is an excellent source of information concerning aviation policy articles on military jets. In many instances, the *Index* also contains references to articles concerning jet engines. And, while it is not a periodical index *per se,* the Library of Congress's *Aeronautical and Space Publications: A World List* (Washington, D. C., 1962) contains brief descriptions of a number of periodicals published throughout the world which are devoted to aeronautical matters.

A comprehensive list of periodicals which include articles on jet aviation would be impossible to include. Frequently, many articles concerning military and commercial jet aviation and jet propulsion may be found in the following journals: *Aerophile* (San Antonio, Texas); *Aerospace Historian* (Washington, D. C.); *Aeroplane Monthly* (London); *Air Enthusiast* (Bromley, Kent); *Air Force Magazine* (Washington, D. C.); *Air International* (London); *Air Pictorial* (Windsor, Berks); *Airpower/Wings* (Granada Hills, California); *Aviation Week and Space Technology* (New York); *Business and Commercial Aviation* (New York); *Flight International* (London); *Interavia* (Geneva); *ICAO Bulletin* (Montreal); and *Naval Aviation* (Washington, D. C.).

AIRCRAFT AND AERO ENGINE YEARBOOKS

Published yearly since the early part of the century, *Jane's All the World's Aircraft* (London, 1909 to date) is still the first and foremost aircraft yearbook in continuous publication. Arranged alphabetically by country and manufacturer, *Jane's* contains up-to-date descriptions, specifications and illustrations of every major military, commercial and business aircraft since the inception of jet aeronautics. In addition to its yearly compilation, *Jane's* also publishes annual bi-monthly supplements to its aircraft section in *Air Force Magazine* (Washington, D. C.), beginning in February and continuing in alternate months through December. *Jane's* is also very useful because it provides comprehensive coverage of jet engines manufactured throughout the world.

Complementing *Jane's* in the area of jet engines is Paul H. Wilkinson's *Aircraft Engines of the World* (Washington, D. C., 1941-1970 irreg.) which also provides information and photographs pertaining to aero engines currently in world use.

And, although they are no longer published, *The Aircraft Year Book* (1914 to 1959) and its successor, *The Aerospace Year Book* (1960 to 1970), have reported significant developments in the history of jet propulsion. Beginning in 1944, this publication reported test flights of the Bell P-59A and continued to provide current information concerning subsequent developments in both military and civil jet aeronautics up to the time of its demise in 1970.

PHOTOGRAPHS

In the absence of a specialized published index to jet aviation photographs, researchers must rely on general photographic reference sources for information. An extensive listing of collections of photographs related to aircraft and aviation history appears in *Picture Sources 3: Collections of Prints and Photographs in the U. S. and Canada* (New York, 1975), edited by Ann Novotny and Rosemary Eakins. Among the collections represented are those of American Airlines, British Airways, Pan American World Airways, Trans World Airlines, General Dynamics Corporation, Lockheed Missiles and Space Company and Vought Aeronautics.

Picture Sources 3 also provides a brief sketch of the photographic collection of the National Air and Space Museum. The museum's collection, one of the largest of its kind in the U. S., contains photographs of virtually all of the jet aircraft and engines which have been manufactured throughout the world since the advent of jet flight. Additional information concerning the NASM collection may be obtained by writing to the National Air and Space Museum Library, Room 3100, National Air and Space Museum, Washington, D. C. 20560.

The National Air and Space Museum's counterpart for photographs of military jet aircraft are the United States Air Force's Still Photographic Depository, Aerospace Audiovisual Service, 1361st

Photo Squadron, 1221 South Fern Street, Arlington, Virginia 22202, and the U. S. Naval Photographic Center, Naval District, Washington, D. C. 20390. Photographs of naval jet aircraft in service prior to 1958 will be found in the collections of the National Archives and Records Service, Audiovisual Archives Division, Record Group 80, Washington, D. C. 20408. For descriptions of the Air Force, Navy and National Archives collections, see *Picture Sources 3,* referred to above.

MOTION PICTURES

As in the case of photographs, published information concerning the availability of motion pictures concerning jet aviation and propulsion is very limited. The U. S. Air Force Central Audiovisual Depository at Norton Air Force Base, California, receives millions of feet of motion picture film annually, much of it operational in nature, and available to qualified researchers by special request. Additional information concerning the services provided by the USAF Central Audiovisual Depository may be obtained by writing to the Director of Information Services, Office of the Secretary of the Air Force, Washington, D. C. 20330.

Motion picture footage of U. S. Navy jet aircraft and operations is available to qualified researchers at the Naval Photographic Center. Inquiries concerning the Navy film collection should be addressed to the Naval Photographic Center, Naval District, Washington, D. C. 20390.

MISCELLANEOUS REFERENCE WORKS

There are hundreds of books which either individually or collectively present information concerning jet aircraft of every country, type and vintage. Since a detailed listing of all of these books is impractical, the following selected titles should provide the jet aviation researcher with sources of quick and ready reference as well as basic facts at a glance. Titles of books on jet aviation which are currently in print will be found in the most recent edition of *Subject Guide to Books in Print* (New York) under the general term "Aeronautics" with cross-references to specific areas of interest.

Although it is now out-of-date and out-of-print, William Green and Roy Cross's *The Jet Aircraft of the World* (Garden City, N.Y., 1957) is still the best collection of information on jet aircraft ever assembled in one volume. Included in it are a simplified explanation of jet propulsion, a section devoted to jet engine development, data tables relating to the jet engines of the world up to 1957 and information pertaining to jet aircraft and helicopters, beginning with early German, British, Italian and American developments, and proceeding through the latter part of the 1950's.

Complementing and updating Green and Cross's book is Gordon Swanborough and Peter M. Bowers' *United States Military Aircraft Since 1908* (London, 1971), which includes descriptions, specifications, and photographic and line illustrations of jet aircraft through the early part of the 1970's. A brief world view of military jet aircraft is presented in John W. R. Taylor and Gordon Swanborough's *Military Aircraft of the World* (New York, 1971), which also includes photographs and silhouette drawings, and Norman Polmar's edition of *World Combat Aircraft Directory* (New York, 1976). Rounding out the selection of books on military jet aircraft is James C. Fahey's *U. S. Army Aircraft, 1908-1946* (Falls Church, Va., 1946) and *USAF Aircraft, 1947-1956* (Falls Church, Va., 1956). Fahey's not only provides information, such as simple dimensions and engine type, but also, changes in model designation and operational status. All in all, Fahey's is one of the most compact and versatile reference books of its type. No military aviation researcher should be without it.

The best source of reference information concerning naval jet aircraft is Gordon Swanborough and Peter M. Bowers' *U. S. Navy Aircraft Since 1911* (Annapolis, Md., 1976), which is identical to their *U. S. Military Aircraft* in format, and includes line drawings and photographs. Although not as thorough, Lloyd S. Jones' *U. S. Naval Fighters* (Fallbrook, California, 1977) may be used in tandem with the Swanborough and Bowers book for a quick look at the naval jet aircraft inventory. Also very useful is Norman Polmar's edition of *The Ships and Aircraft of the U. S. Fleet,* 11th ed. (Annapolis, Md., 1978) which continued the work begun by James C. Fahey and later, Samuel L. Morison and John S. Rowe.

Commercial jet aviation is well-represented by William Green and Gordon Swanborough's *The Observer's World Airlines and Airliners Directory* (New York, 1975), a rather up-to-date compilation of the various airlines of the world and the aircraft that comprise their fleets. Of particular interest is the second part of the book, which describes and illustrates each aircraft. Equally useful for the information it provides concerning contemporary jet liners is Kenneth Munson's colorfully illustrated *Airliners Since 1946* (New York, 1972).

For a brief look at the historical side of jet aviation, particularly in Germany, J. R. Smith and Antony L.

Kay's *German Aircraft of the Second World War* (London, 1972) should be the first step. *German Aircraft* contains a great deal of information concerning the earliest German jets, both actual and theoretical, including photographs and three-view illustrations of many designs which never went beyond the drawing board. Also useful, but not as comprehensive, is William Green's *The Warplanes of the Third Reich* (Garden City, New York, 1972).

Unfortunately, the earliest American and Italian jet aircraft such as the Bell XP-59A, Lockheed XP-80 and Caproni-Campini C.C.-2 are not well-documented either in profile or book-length studies. A good description of the development of both the Gloster E.28/39 and F.9/40 and subsequent "Meteors" will be found in Derek N. James' *Gloster Aircraft Since 1917* (London, 1971).

Finally, *Jane's All the World's Aircraft* is still the most useful and versatile aircraft reference book of its kind.